Lincolnshire
Within Living
Memory

Compiled by the Lincolnshire North,
Lincolnshire South and Humberside
Federations of Women's Institutes from notes
sent by Institutes in these Counties

Published jointly by
Countryside Books, Newbury
and
HFWI, Brigg
LNFWI, Louth
LSFWI, Sleaford

First Published 1995
© Lincolnshire and Humberside
Federations of Women's Institutes 1995

COUNTRYSIDE BOOKS
3 Catherine Road
Newbury, Berkshire

ISBN 1 85306 353 3

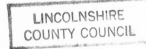

The cover photograph shows a steam thresher on a Lincolnshire
farm in 1938. (Courtesty of the Lincolnshire Echo)

Designed by Mon Mohan
Produced through MRM Associates Ltd, Reading
Printed by J.W. Arrowsmith Ltd, Bristol

Contents

Acknowledgements

Sincere thanks go out to all WIs across the three Federations who spent so much time in compiling and presenting their collection of memories for this book. We hope, like us, that you had a great deal of enjoyment reminiscing together whilst gathering material for *Lincolnshire Within Living Memory*.

Our thanks also go to Anne Mitchell of Sibsey WI for the combined map of Lincolnshire and south Humberside, Eva Harrison of Rauceby WI for the illustrations at the start of the chapters and the members of the North Wold Art Group — Marjorie Austin, Ann Brown, Margaret Fisher, Joy Hudson, Emily Parkes, Joan Perry and Hilda Young.

We are sure the publication of this book will give enjoyment to many who, like us, will have their memories stimulated about times that have passed.

Gwen Farrow MBE
Humberside Co-ordinator
Wendy Done
Lincolnshire North Co-ordinator
Pam Jackson
Lincolnshire South Co-ordinator

Foreword

Originally the County of Lincolnshire was divided into the three 'Parts' of Holland, Kesteven and Lindsey. In 1974, at the time of the local government reorganisation, these were abolished, with the northern part of Lindsey becoming part of the new county of Humberside.

Running through Lincolnshire is the Roman road of Ermine Street, which can still be followed for most of its route. Similarly part of the Fosse Way passes east to west through Lincoln.

The industrial areas have been developed mainly in the north along the Humber Bank – steel, chemicals and oil predominating. The docks in Boston have grown with the increasing import and export of consumer goods. Unfortunately, the fishing industry, both deep sea from Grimsby and inshore from Boston and other ports is declining. The county is still mainly agricultural with the rich grain lands and stock in the northern part and potatoes and horticulture further south. Indeed, the Fenlands are famous for their bulb-growing and reclamation of land from the sea. With the increasing use of high technology there has been a migration of families from the countryside to the towns. Many villages are within the commuter belt of the towns – some people even travelling to London.

This area is to many people a 'hidden' county. It is well worth visiting for its many spired churches and for its varied landscape, from the rolling hills of the Wolds to the wide horizons of the Fens.

Members of the WI have enjoyed looking back to life in the county before 1960. They have looked through their records, searched their minds, talked to their elders and recalled many long forgotten memories.

The co-operation between the Federations of Humberside, Lincolnshire North and Lincolnshire South has been greatly appreciated.

Hilary Mullineux
Chairman Humberside Federation
Wendy Oliver
Chairman Lincolnshire North Federation
Janet Turner
Chairman Lincolnshire South Federation

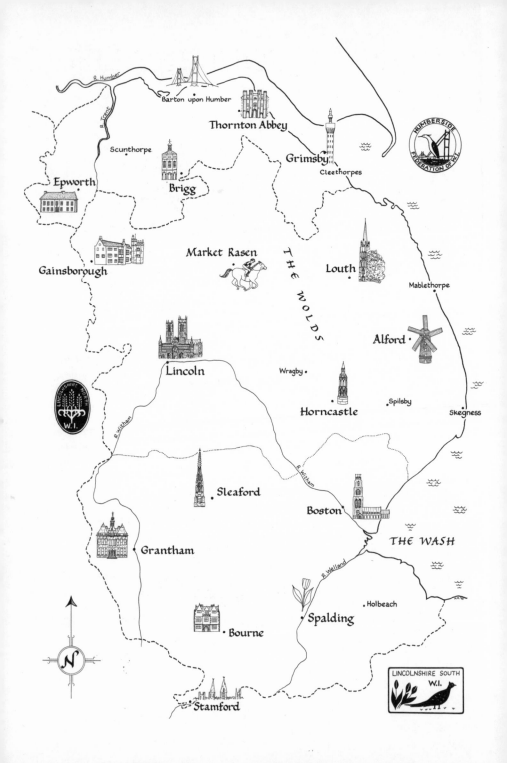

TOWN & COUNTRY LIFE

SOME TOWNS AND VILLAGES REMEMBERED

Life in Lincolnshire's towns and villages has changed almost beyond recognition over the past few decades. Within living memory the carrier's cart was the only contact some of us had with the outside world, the ring of the blacksmith's hammer was a regular sound and market days meant cattle in the streets and the world and his wife out to meet friends and do business.

NORTH SOMERCOTES

The marsh villages in the late 1920s consisted of a cluster of small farms and market gardens, the fields separated mainly by deep dykes and drains and a few hedges. In the summer the tall yellow irises and kingcups were a picture to see. Practically all the men worked on the land and lived in tied cottages. Most of them smoked Woodbine cigarettes, which were ten for fourpence, and dark, thick shag twist for their pipes – many of them clay pipes – was sevenpence an ounce. Wages were 32 shillings a week and out of this ninepence was stopped for insurance. Rent varied; men who had shepherding to do at weekends and who received no pay for this were charged one shilling, but three shillings and sixpence was the average rent.

It was about 1935 before wirelesses began to appear in the cottages at North Somercotes. They ran on accumulators and a Mr Good who had a small shop down Vickers Lane in Louth would deliver the recharged battery for the cost of sixpence, taking the old one back for recharging. The accumulator ran for a week, providing you didn't switch on too often!

There was a joiner in the village who was also the undertaker, making all the coffins required in the marsh area. When the church bell tolled everyone knew someone in the village had died. There was also a coal yard. Coal was delivered by lorry, loose at 36 shillings a ton. The majority of men bought a ton at a time, mostly after harvest when money was more plentiful. When the occasion arose, the lorry was swept clean and the deceased were carried to their resting place in the cemetery or churchyard, but farmers were carried to their resting place by horse and waggon.

In the late 1920s and early 1930s the first Wednesday in the New Year was known as the Poultry Stock Market, when farmers and farm

8

labourers went to purchase a new stock bird – some men buying a new stock bird every year. Four rows of cages were erected in the corn market at Louth, each holding a stock bird – cockerels, turkey cocks, drakes and ganders, and auctioning was very brisk. Some of the buyers had their birds transported home by carrier's cart, and later carrier's lorry, but the majority just popped the bird into a sack and travelled home by bus as usual. Strangely enough, the birds seemed to quieten down when imprisoned in their sack. A few men would "test" the eggs before setting them under a broody hen. A sewing needle was threaded with cotton and the cotton then held tightly between the fingers with the needle suspended over the egg. If the needle swung from side to side it foretold a cockerel, if in a circular movement a pullet. The men swore good results by this method!

Several of the men kept ferrets for rabbiting and quite a few men had a gun, but snaring and ferreting made a cleaner job. Rabbits were plentiful, especially in the sand dunes, and there was always a ready market for them in Louth.

North Somercotes had its own road sweeper employed by the county council. In the winter some of his time was spent tidying up the grass verges, staking a length out first with sticks and cord. The cord was made from thick string soaked in Stockholm tar and creosote and this lasted for several years. In the summer time he was kept busy with brush and shovel and scythe, mowing the grass verges. Some of the small farmers who had a few cows would let their cows graze the road sides, but this was mainly done in the evenings.'

SKATING ON THE WASH

'I have such happy memories of skating on Cowbit Wash. Even my home town of Spalding became a different place. The ironmongers hung up skates outside their shops at the first signs of frost. These were not the fancy skate-attached-to-the-boot variety, but simply wooden "soles" with metal blades underneath that turned up saucily at the front. We bought our boots separately and, with a bradawl and a lot of hard work, managed to screw the skates on through the heels of the boots.

As children, we were always warned never to go on the New River, but to stick to the flooded land which had comparatively shallow water. A fall through the ice on the New River was a fall into deep water and the threat of drifting right along under the ice and drowning.

We young ones learned that bandaging our ankles helped stop them bending at alarming angles as we skated, and made us feel like racehorses as we cycled off to the Wash. As soon as we reached the ice, we dumped our cycles and the first thing you had to do was to look around for some kindly soul to provide a chair and some help to get the boots really tightly laced. The fainthearted could borrow one of these chairs to get themselves on to the ice and as a support until they found their feet, so to speak.

There was certainly something unnerving about this vast expanse of ice, with nothing in sight to hang on to. This was no ice-rink ice; frozen weeds and grasses stuck out here and there over most of the surface, so you had to keep your eyes open all the time.

For every day there was ice, we would skate and skate until our poor ankles finally gave out. We could never risk having our "racehorse" bandages tied too tight as that was how you got chilblains, if you were unlucky as I once was.

There was a wonderful sense of urgency about these skating days, because no one knew exactly when the water would freeze over, nor for how long it would last. If you wanted to skate, you had to go *now*! My father, always so meticulous about attending his shop, was up, off and away when the ice came. I loved skating with him with crossed hands and feeling so absolutely safe on the ice. He was as steady as a rock and quietly encouraging. The high spot for him was being timekeeper for the Racing Mile, skated by the really fast skaters (many of them from a single family, I seem to recall), in special Fen runner skates. I still have his blue rosette badge with "Timekeeper" stamped on it.

It was not just a battle against time on the ice, but against the elements too. There was the year when, arriving home, I was amazed to find the hall radiator festooned with ten shilling notes and Mother bustling about with towels and dry clothes. It turned out that the crowd watching the Racing Mile had rushed to the finishing line and the ice had given way, plunging my father and several others into the freezing waters. By some lucky stroke, a cousin of mine from Kirton was over to watch the event and was able to bring my father home. Father hadn't taken the car, much preferring his "velocipede", as he called his bicycle.

Because the frost was such a short-lived and unpredictable event, it gave Cowbit Wash a special, magical quality. My grandfather, father and I in turn owned a piece of land on the Wash which was rented out for grazing in the summer and also for the sale of hay, which I believe is called "eddish". As a child, it seemed that at one minute we could be standing watching the cattle peacefully grazing on this land and then, just a few months later, the floods would suddenly come and these same fields and cattle would have completely disappeared as though they had never existed at all.

The floods were naturally a worry for those living near the bank of

Cowbit Wash. I remember motoring along there one night when the water was lapping right up to the top of the bank and to complete the eerie picture, a full moon was shining down on to the black waters.

Now, due to modern drainage methods, the Wash does not flood any more. The land looks just like any other piece of south Lincolnshire land. The seasons are no longer marked in quite the same way with those hot summers of grazing cattle followed by the floods and then, hopefully, by the ice and that wonderful chance to experience the pleasures of skating, movement and freedom.'

MAREHAM LE FEN

'I was born in 1909 in Mareham le Fen, a village with a population of about 600. My first recollection is of my schooldays. I was fortunate in living near to the school, as it meant that I could go home to dinner. Some children had to walk two or three miles bringing their dinner in a satchel over their shoulder.

The only means of transport in those days was a bicycle or a horse and cart. A carrier's cart went into the nearest town once or twice a week.

There were four public houses, two baker's shops and a small sweet shop where an old lady lived. She was nearly blind and wore a white lace cap. I can see her now feeling the money between her fingers. The post office was at the main grocer's shop where my father was a van driver. He did a daily round to local villages with groceries and paraffin, carried at the back of the van in a five gallon drum and measured out at the door, the only lighting in country districts being a single or double burner lamp or candles.

The mail was brought daily in a horse-drawn mail van. I often watched the mail bags loaded in and taken to Boston, collecting at other post offices on the way, a distance of 15 miles. The driver lived in the village and left every night at five o'clock, sitting up on a seat outside the cab, as it was security locked. I didn't envy him in the dark or in the winter time when it was snowing. He stayed the night at Boston, returning next morning about six o'clock.

In the village there was a barber's shop, and a smithy which was kept busy mending carts and farm implements and shoeing horses. It was always fascinating to see the furnace blowing up to such a fierce red glow. There were two butcher's shops and some of the milk was brought into the village by milk float. The milk was carried in large cans and it was measured out at the door. One or two farmers sold their milk at the door and I always fetched ours in a pint can before I went to school.

There was a church, a Primitive chapel and a Wesleyan chapel. We were Wesleyans and went to chapel every Sunday morning and night and to Sunday school in the afternoon. Every June it was the Sunday school Anniversary which was a great treat. On the Sunday we had a large platform erected for all the children and adults, and we sang and recited. On the Monday the village brass band led us round the village followed by two leaders of the Sunday school carrying our banner and singing as we went along. We came back to a lovely tea of bread and butter, seed cake and plum bread, I can almost taste it now.'

SPALDING

'Come with me back to the Spalding of the 1920s, where children in the Westlode Street council school are playing with whips and tops, and skipping. A peculiar smell comes from the factory further on, where hay is cooked and made into cattle cakes. Across the road is the Prince's Cinema, where children pay two pennies (three for a plush seat) on Saturdays, to watch a black and white silent film. A lady plays suitable music to accompany the film, on the piano.

Into New Road, where the cattle are weighed and stand in temporary pens, made by inserting poles in the road and putting planks across on brackets. Occasionally a beast runs away down the road; one bullock fell into the river Welland and had to be rescued. Later in the day the drovers drive the unsold cattle along the roads, back to the farms. Around the corner squealing pigs and bleating sheep are in the sheep market pens, while people are busy in the poultry market opposite. An auctioneer is selling second-hand goods on the cobbled stones in Hall Place. A tall, ornate drinking fountain stands in the centre.

In the market place, the stall-holders shout to the women, offering their home-grown fruit and vegetables at bargain prices. Other stalls are filled with clothes, pottery, linens, fish, and many other goods. Here, the farmers gather in groups, discussing the sale of their stock, then go into the Red Lion or White Hart hotels to compare notes on crops and equipment over a pint of cool ale, and relax with their pipes of "baccy". The women hustle and bustle among the stalls and shops, stopping for a chat with a neighbour or friends.

The smell of fresh baked bread and cakes, and the delicious home-made pork pies, haslets and succulent local hams, wafts over the town, mingling with the perfume of the fresh cut-flowers, standing in galvanised buckets of water on the cobble-stones, while the clock on the Corn Exchange chimes musically every 15 minutes. Inside the hall are stands packed with small sacks of corn, where the buyers are checking the contents for the quality. The Corn Exchange is used for furniture auction sales, demonstrations, dances, concerts and other activities. Outside is a passageway along the side of the building. At the rear end, and going partly underneath the building, is the cool Butter Market, where fresh butter, cream cheese, chicken and duck eggs are being sold.

Another narrower road leads from the market place to the lovely old stone bridge built in 1838. This is Bridge Street, with more shops on each side. Over the bridge spanning the river Welland stands an ironmonger's warehouse on the bank side. Across the road is a seed merchant's, and the beautiful White Horse Inn, with its thatched roof. The road ahead, Church Street, leads to the parish church and cemetery.

To the right, in Cowbit Road, the magnificent Ayscoughfee Hall can be seen, with its beautiful gardens, goldfish and lilies lake, with the war memorial in the background. The public relax on the many seats, or walk in the rose garden under the rose arches, or under the avenue of trees. On the lawn the children play, running up and down, and round the rustic wooden bandstand where the Spalding Silver Prize Band entertains the people on Sundays and special festivals.

Some folk prefer to walk on the riverside path, chatting to the residents of the cottages and the workmen on the wharf, who are lifting heavy sacks from the carts by crane and swinging them into the warehouses. Across the river a barge is being unloaded of the sacks of grain, linseed cake, cattle cake, beans and meal, which the horses take across the road to the granaries in High Street. The workmen carry the 18 to 20-stone sacks on their backs and stack them in the storehouse, while the corn is taken to be milled.

To turn the barges, the barge-men swing them across the river into the "swinger", which enables them to turn around more easily without hitting the banks. A "swinger" is a portion of the banks cut away. These silt up sometimes with the flow of the tides, and men have to shovel it away, until it is clear for the barges to manoeuvre round. Before making the return journey to Fosdyke the boat-men have to wait for the turn of the tide. As the tide rushes into the river, it creates a wave of built-up water called the eagre, or bore. At times, the sound of a seal is heard, and people lean on their tidal walls, built to withstand flooding, looking for its bobbing grey head, and hoping the outgoing tide will take the creature back to sea again.

As soon as the tide is high enough the barges go on their way, past the houses and the public houses, the beer storage warehouse and the coal-merchant's yard where his cart is kept and the beautiful chestnut shire horse, with a white blaze on his forehead and four white feet, is stabled, and the mineral water factory.

On reaching the footbridge from Albion Street to Commercial Road, the harbourmaster comes to turn a large handle which swings the Albert Bridge from the Albion Street bank, across to Commercial

Road. This bridge is still called the "Chain Bridge" by the locals, because it originally had two central sections pulled upwards by chains to allow the barges to pass through. After much damage to the masts it was dismantled and the Albert Bridge was built, a swing-bridge.

A cheery word is exchanged with the harbourmaster, as the boat-men pass by. He is the blacksmith and farrier, and many children and adults have watched him in his workshop on the river bank, taking hot metal from the red embers and hammering it on his anvil into horseshoes. After cooling them in cold water, he takes the horse's hoof between his knees, removing any stones which are embedded in the foot, then nails the new shoe onto the hoof, filing around the edge to smooth it. The fascinated onlookers ask for an old shoe, and many cottages have horseshoes hanging on their gates or doors. They are considered to be an omen of good luck, as long as they are hung open-end up. Otherwise the luck is said to "run out". When the farrier is not busy with horses, or the barges, he makes and repairs implements for the farms.

Further down the river are more cottages, and the gas factory wharf with coal trucks running on rails, as the coal barges fill them. Horses and carts then take the coal across the road into the gas factory, where it is burnt to produce gas, and coke for the coke stoves in the town.

The slipway into the river is seen next, used by the boat builders who shout and wave as they work in the yard, repairing boats and making the huge sluice gates for the river. Ahead now is the large bridge from the end of Albion Street across to Commercial Road, which opens upwards to allow the barges through, while pedestrians, horses and carts, cyclists and an occasional car or lorry, wait behind large chains strung across the bridge ends.

The barge continues, passing the sugar beet factory, where sugar beet is brought from the land in the autumn and is processed into sugar and stored. The beet pulp that is left is used by the farmers for animal feed.

Now the barge sails onward into open country with wide panoramic views over the flat fens, and the vast expanse of sky, dominated occasionally by the towering spires of churches and a windmill, with its great sails turning in the wind.

The barge is almost at the end of its journey, and the barge-man skilfully manoeuvres it under the Fosdyke Bridge, where the big ships are waiting for it to draw alongside and pick up their cargo. When the tide is right, the barges make their journey back to the granaries at Spalding. The *Violet Birch* tug tows the *Sarah*, *Nelson* and *Harold*, as they do not have engines and rely on the tides carrying them along. The *Pride Of The Welland* has an engine, and the *Agriculture* is a sailing barge with a tall mast.

Once a year the town is a-buzz with excited children carrying buckets and spades, on their way to the railway station in Winsover Road. This is their big day, the Sunday school trip to the seaside at Skegness or Mablethorpe. On their return home they happily tell the old people sitting outside their doors about the sea, and the donkeys, and the sand-castles they built. As dusk approaches, the lamplighters with their long poles light the gas lamps in the streets. When the house lights go out, the reassuring footsteps of the policeman can be heard as he makes his rounds, shining his lamp, checking business premises to see that all doors and windows are secure, and house doors are shut. As he walks away, peace descends on the sleepy market town of Spalding.'

BURGH LE MARSH

'Our little market town stands just on the edge of the marsh. By the time of my childhood in the 1930s no market stalls were ever seen in the ancient market square but there was a thriving cattle market held every Thursday. A considerable space near to the centre of the town and on the main road through it, was taken up by permanent wooden cattle pens and metal pens for sheep and pigs. But it was the cattle which predominated because the good pasture of the marsh was used extensively to fatten cattle up through the summer months. In the autumn they were either sold or returned to the safety and shelter of inland farms and their crew-yards.

Very early on market days groups of cattle would be driven on foot through the streets to the market pens. It was a time of much noise and excitement as the nervous animals escaped the attentions of their drovers and ran off up the many side streets and by-ways en route. It was the delight of small schoolboys to arm themselves with sticks from the hedgerow and whack the poor creatures on the backside.

Eventually the ringing of a loud bell could be heard over the town – before the days of noisy, perpetual road traffic – which signalled to us all that the auctioneer was about to start his work of selling off the various animals driven into the ring. As lots were sold, then began the task of driving the cattle back to their new owners' farms. Many went up to Burgh station to be loaded into cattle trucks and taken to the meat markets of some of our big cities. So many cattle went by rail that there was a separate siding for the cattle trucks, safely away from the busy main Grimsby–Kings Cross line.

Market day was the occasion for all the farmers and their wives from the surrounding villages to drive in by pony and trap to buy and sell or to do other business. Local traders were ready for an

15

influx of customers, meals were provided by the local butcher's wife and the local inns, three of the principal banks opened offices in the town just for that day each week and it was a great time for meeting and greeting friends and family. The cattle have gone from the marsh, the market has gone and the banks have all gone, but Thursday continues to be a day for coming into the town to meet and shop and do business.'

LINCOLN PAST

'We were brought up in Lincoln near the South Common in the years following the First World War. We were lucky, our house had a back boiler which supplied water for a bathroom and a kitchen, although we had an outside water closet. We had gas lighting downstairs and in the big bedroom and bathroom, otherwise candles were used.

We played games in the street, collected tadpoles from the river and picnicked on the common. We spent our penny pocket money at the local shops – it took all day to choose between Spanish strips, halfpenny dabs and kali suckers. Fish and chips was twopence for the fish and a penny for the chips. There were hot ducklings once a week, meat and gravy – take your own jug. The milkman came with horse and cart and ladled the milk into your own basin, and all groceries, bread and meat were delivered. An electric tram service took us into Lincoln itself.

We were not allowed to play outside on Sundays. Most children went to Sunday school (there was nothing else to do), no shops were open and people had Sunday clothes, not worn on any other day. In strict Methodist homes, all preparation for Sundays was done on Saturday, even the cleaning of shoes. All you did on Sunday was go for a walk with your parents, though sometimes there were band concerts in the parks. There were big processions on Whit Monday, when the religious organisations decorated waggons and paraded, with all the children following.

Hiring Day on 6th April was held in Lincoln when the farmers hired their workers for another year. Very few people had cars and most got about on foot or bicycle. The trains had day trips to Skegness and Mablethorpe which were very popular and there were often evening trips to the coast.

There was a local bus service by the 1930s and a lot of people managed a week's holiday, but unemployment was very bad until the late 1930s so many people had no holiday at all. Before wages were paid during the holiday period, they just could not afford to go away. Working hours were long and in Lincoln most men worked in the heavy engineering industry and cycled to work and came home for the midday meal. In the early 1900s they went to work at 6 am

16

and had half an hour for breakfast, which a member of the family, often one of the children, took to the foundry. Most men had to work overtime to earn a living wage.'

'I was born in 1936 into a very different Lincoln to today's city. I remember going to the races with my parents, when the excitement was almost too much to bear. I had a new dress and shoes for the occasion, but I think the excitement was really for after the racing, when we children searched for and found all the dropped coins in the grass!

I was in the isolation hospital at St George's with scarlet fever during the war. There were only a few of us in the ward. War had just started and the sirens would sound at night but I was really too young to be frightened. My memories of the war years are of the siren's weird howling and having to sit under the stairs. My father was an ARP warden and one night when I went to the Theatre Royal with my parents, we heard a bang and he went outside to investigate. A bomb had dropped on Battles the chemist by the Stonebow, but the show went on. When we went home policemen and wardens were everywhere, directing people away from the incendiary devices that had fallen.

There were plenty of cinemas in Lincoln and I went nearly every night as I grew older, or to the local dances. There was the Astoria Ballroom over Bainbridge's next to Mawer & Collingham's, the Co-op Ballroom in Free School Lane, the Drill Hall and Rustons Club, and the Montana Ballroom by the theatre. Before going we would all congregate at the Spotted Cow Milk Bar by the Savoy in Saltergate, and spent many a happy hour there thinking about the night ahead bopping and jiving.'

STURTON BY STOW

'My family came to Sturton by Stow in 1911, when I was two years old. We worked hard, even as children. We delivered milk in tins on the way to school – we left it at the doors, then collected the empty tins on the way home. There was always plenty to do, like cutting turnips for the cows to eat, bringing milk into the dairy to separate, or helping with the haymaking – everyone would help with this. Saturday morning we picked up bits of broken pots or china and broke these up finely with a hammer. It made grit for the chicks.

We all wore stout boots – I got my first pair of shoes when I was confirmed. I can remember Mr Middleton, the shoemaker, making what was his idea of a pair of baby's shoes – they were all studs and leather tops!

There were more shops and industry in the village in those days.

Mr Wardell, joiner/painter – his sign is still to be seen on one of the houses – was next door to the smithy. What is now the post office used to be a butcher's shop, with a slaughterhouse behind. Then came the White Hart, an alehouse, now a dwelling. The small space between this pub and the Red Lion next door, was a paper shop run by a Mr Charity. He lived at Stow, in the thatched cottage in the centre of the village. Next to the Red Lion was the Plough – there was a fish and chip shop in what is now the pub's car park. Over the road, in one of the cottages opposite, was a sweet shop – the doctor used to order "expensive" chocolates to hand out to the children. When the doctor died, I can remember that Mary Ellen, who owned the shop at the time, was worried because she still had a stock of these chocolates which she didn't think she would be able to sell. Then came Lucas's, the main village store.

Round the corner, into High Street, was the post office and at the little shop on the corner of Twitchell/High Street was Smalley the tailor – he used to sit crosslegged to do his work. He was good at telling what the weather would be. There were two butcher's shops in Fleets Road, and Bradshaws, the transport people, in the High Street. Gelders made milk tins etc, and Mr W. Adams ran a fish shop – as a child I thought he was a Mr W. A. Dams. Marshall Drury made agricultural things. Mr Drury bred Black Minorka hens – they had large red wattles which he oiled with olive oil to make them shiny.

I can remember taking chickens to Mrs Knipe on a Thursday, she lived in the cottage next door; she killed and plucked them, I collected them in the evening and Mr W. Andrew took them to Lincoln market on Friday. The shoemaker, Mr Middleton, lived further along the High Street, and there was a Mr Picksley – he ran a collection for the Hospital Association; I was one of the collectors. Couples and the over-18s paid sixpence each every month – this entitled them to free treatment at the County Hospital. Children had free treatment anyway. The "Institute" (the village hall) and Stan Wiles' cycle shop came further along the High Street. Bricks were made at "Brickyards", on the edge of the village.'

SLEAFORD

'Sleaford market place on May Monday was once full of would-be employees come in from the surrounding villages looking for work. Mostly agricultural workers, farmers and others were there to select whom they wanted. When the event took place in the late 1920s girls at the High School were given a day's holiday because the Head considered it would be dangerous for them to walk through the town.

Monday has always been market day in Sleaford. The livestock market was in Northgate and the animals were driven on foot

Sturton by Stow before the village pond made way for a new road.

through the town, some escaping down side streets and having to be retrieved with the help of bystanders. The Corn Exchange was a large building in Eastgate, no longer in existence but now identified by a carved sheaf of corn over the shop front. Later it was held in the yard of the Bristol Hotel, now the Bristol arcade. Pubs were open until 4 pm and the farmers adjourned there after the market to discuss the day's prices. Their wives went to the produce market and then met their friends at local cafes.

There was quite a lot of entertainment here for young and old between the wars. A Miss Aram held a dancing academy in her house in Northgate. This was for the younger ones. Mrs Brown held classes for older pupils. Both put on displays to demonstrate the talents of their pupils. Mr Norman Snow, a local solicitor, organised a thriving Gilbert and Sullivan Society and he conducted the orchestra. Once a year an opera would be put on for a week in the Corn Exchange and it was very much an occasion, evening dress being worn. There was an annual pantomime and dancing displays. Some of the town's businessmen showed an unexpected aptitude for acrobatic and tap dancing.

The Corn Exchange was the usual venue for such entertainments. It was a large building with a good stage and the auditorium could be used for holding balls. During the Second World War it became a NAAFI. Tea dances were held in the Barn Cafe in the Market Place, now the headquarters of the Sleaford Football Club.'

WALESBY

'I was born and brought up in the small village of Walesby at the foot of the Lincolnshire Wolds. It was a very agricultural area. I attended the village school from the age of four; it had two rooms, one for the infants which had a large stove in the middle, the other for the remainder of the children. We were taught by the headmistress in every subject from religion to drill. I was one of the first pupils to move to the new secondary modern school at Market Rasen.

April 6th was known as Flitting Day, when the farm labourer who was changing his job made the move from one farm to another. As children we watched waggons piled high with furniture and household goods moving through the village street, pulled by large shire horses. We looked forward to meeting the new children who would attend the village school.

The blacksmith's forge which was at the centre of the village was always a hive of activity, with horses waiting to be shod and farm implements to be mended. The smell was sometimes indescribable. None of the cottages had water laid on, it had to be carried from the two taps in the village. There were always one or two water tubs outside the cottages and this was used for washday on a Monday and hair washing on a Friday night, as well as for watering the gardens.

In spring and summer children had to fetch the cows in for milking from the outlying fields. If your father was a farmer it was a labour of love, if not we were paid a penny. Milk was collected from the farmhouse in cans and was straight from the cows. As children we worked in the fields on a Saturday morning during the growing season to single sugar beet, for which we were paid sixpence, and for two weeks in October we had the potato picking holiday.'

THE GREAT FLOODS

'March and April 1947 will never be forgotten by the people that lived in the fens. It was the year of the great floods. I was only a schoolgirl but I remember all able-bodied men and women working all day and night to fill sandbags to form a barrier along the banks of the Wash, trying to prevent the water from flooding Crowland. Eventually the water won, a hole of about 180 feet wide was torn in the bank and beyond it the torrent scoured out a great hole in the fen. I remember the great bell of Crowland Abbey tolling to warn everyone that a breach had occurred. The village of Crowland was almost totally cut off. Hundreds of soldiers were drafted in and billeted in the Foresters Hall opposite our home. Amphibious ducks were brought in and the soldiers would take us children with them in the ducks across the floods to deliver food to the farms on the High Bank on the opposite side of the river. To the children it was all terribly exciting.'

'I was 14 at the time of the 1953 floods and lived in Mablethorpe. On Saturday evening I went to the cinema with my sister and my parents. We had gone to the first showing which started at 5.30 pm. Around 7.15 pm water started to come into the cinema. The manager announced that the sea was coming in. We were not too worried at first as the sea often came over the sea-wall on a high tide and flowed into the High Street.

This particular night though, the sea had breached the sea defences and the water kept getting higher and higher. We all left our seats and stood on the stage and some people went upstairs. We had to stay there for two and a half hours. The water was lapping up at the stage. I had on a new pair of fur-lined shoes which my Dad had bought me with a small win he had just had on the football pools. They were a special treat as I suffered with chilblains. My Mum kept saying, "Mind those new shoes. Don't get them wet!" I kept stepping back away from the water to the back of the stage.

Then at last at 10.30 pm help arrived. Some local men came and carried us out fireman-lift style. By the time my turn came the man was getting tired and he nearly dropped me. We were put on a lorry and taken to a hall in Maltby le Marsh where we had to spend the night. All the younger children went to sleep but to us teenagers it was a great adventure and we sat up playing cards.

The following morning another lorry came and took us to Alford grammar school where we were given porridge and a cup of tea. As you can imagine we were all ready for a drink after spending the night in a hall.

After breakfast my sister and I went in a taxi with two others to Louth to stay with my grandma. We ended up staying there for a whole month while my Mum and Dad cleaned and dried the bungalow out. The water had come up to three feet high and left deposits of sand everywhere.'

THE RAN TAN

'Many years ago in Stickney, in the 1920s, a man and his wife took in a single girl as a housekeeper. The villagers thought the man was taking more interest in the girl than he should, so they met and decided to "Ran Tan" him to show their disapproval. He was expected home on this particular night off the train at Stickney station. Villagers gathered there with sticks and tins to bang and jeer and shout at him. They were well worked up to fever pitch as the train drew in, but luckily for him he did not arrive on it so the whole episode fell rather flat.'

FREISTON

'Freiston is a typical agricultural village bordering on the Wash, but in the late 1880s the Plummers Hotel and the Marine Hotel were included in the "London season" and society people arrived by charabanc to spend a week enjoying balls and banquets in the hotels and horse racing along the marsh. Sadly the Marine Hotel is now a ruin; the Plummers became a pub but is also now closed and the ballroom and reception areas have been converted to houses. Due to land reclamation both buildings are now some quarter of a mile from the marsh. Before the reclamation Freiston shore was the venue for many children's outings from Boston. One resident remembers coming out from Boston on a horse-drawn farm cart with the Sunday school outing. There was also a tea shop in the area, but that is now a residential property.

Very few people had cars in the years between the wars, and the bus service ran twice a week, Saturday and Wednesday, for the market in Boston. Many traders visited the village on a regular basis. "Tinny" Smith had pots and pans and general hardware, a baker called once a week (as long as the weather was good), and a man came round occasionally selling pegs, clothes lines and an assortment of household linen and goods. Gypsies also visited quite regularly, and set up camp on the main road to Skegness.

All villages had a roadman. His job was to keep the roads clear of mud and horse manure, to fill in ruts on unmade roads and to trim the grass verges. He could also make sure that farmers using public roads did not drop straw or anything on the road that could make it dangerous. He was employed by the parish council.

Occasionally a fair or circus would be in the area. One local man remembers leading a horse from his father's farm, to be met by an elephant being led along the road. The horse would not pass the elephant, so it was led into the farm entrance while Fred got the horse past. The elephant left a huge pile of manure in the gateway, which was put to good use on the farm!'

LIFE ON THE ESTATE

'Allington was an estate village, owned for many years by the Welby family, until it was sold in 1947. Almost everyone in the village worked directly or indirectly for the Welby family.

The last member of the family to live in the Hall was Sir George Welby. He remained a bachelor all his life though the feminine influence was maintained by the frequent visits of his two married

The wheelwright's yard at Oasby in 1903. Wheelwright John Longland stands on the right and seated is the village postman, William Mears.

sisters. Created Mayor of Grantham twice, he was well thought of in the community and generally considered to be a good employer though he was strict about the civilities. Men and women, boys and girls were expected to doff their caps or bob a curtsey to Sir George and his sisters should they meet. He was also a staunch Tory and churchgoer. The *Daily Herald* was a banned newspaper and anyone expressing left-wing views found themselves out of a job and a house. Church attendance was compulsory and absence from Sunday service was followed by a Monday morning visit to discover the reason. There used to be a Methodist chapel in the village but Sir George so strongly disapproved of Nonconformism that it was pulled down.

If you toed the political and religious line then life in Allington under Sir George Welby was as good as anywhere, and better than many places.'

'When we went to live at Revesby in the 1940s, it was my first experience of a great estate. This was a time when the old feudal system was rapidly dying out.

Revesby Abbey, still occupied by Lady Beryl Groves, was a house of considerable grandeur, built for the Stanhopes by William Burn a century before I saw it. It was once kept smoothly running by a small army of servants. By the time we arrived on the scene, there was just a cook-housekeeper and casual domestic help. It seemed that vast distances separated the domestic quarters from the principal rooms. It was an immensely inconvenient house, and except in summer it was cold and draughty.

During the Second World War a succession of army units was billeted at the Abbey, so that soldiers became a familiar part of the local scene. The late Dr Dorothy Taylor, president and a founder-member of the WI, used to recall how the ladies ran a canteen at the village hall for the troops. The most popular delicacies, she said, were their special fried-egg sandwiches!

The whole village was very much influenced by the estate, for it had been entirely owned by the squires for 400 years. The estate office was a room at the rear of the Home Farm house. The resident agent was a kindly, old-fashioned man named Hugh Walker. I don't think I ever saw him attired in anything different from his habitual dark suit, butterfly collar and trilby hat.

The village shop, by the great tranquil green, was one of those amazing storehouses of almost everything that a village community needed for day to day subsistence. It was combined with a post office, and run by the Johnson family. It was housed in the oldest surviving dwelling in the village centre. The other buildings were mostly of the standard estate style, with latticed windows and ornamental barge-boards, dating from the middle of the 19th century. The vicarage, too, was of a similar style. The vicar, John Holden, had a grand piano in his drawing room, and it was a great treat when I would be invited to play it after Sunday evening services. Along the west side of the green, next to the school with its bell turret, was a row of dark and pokey almshouses provided in 1729 for "ten decayed agriculturists".

The church, at least the third on the site, is an expensive and impressive building put up by the Stanhopes in 1892. By the time we moved to Revesby, churchgoing was no longer considered obligatory, and congregations were not large although the place could seat 192 worshippers. Other boys and I would ring the tubular bells, then go to the top of the tower to see who was coming to church. Well into this century the church was still the private chapel of the squires. The parsons were their chaplains, engaged and paid by them.

Fred Jux was carrying on the blacksmith's craft in the traditional way. The ringing of the anvil and the stamping of horses could be heard there any day except Sunday. Those were the days when people not only respected the fourth commandment; they also considered their neighbours and kept noise to an absolute minimum. Nearby was Ellis's garage, highly regarded for the quality of their care for local cars. The business was run then by Horace Ellis from a cottage near the church. An example of his immense kindness was when he took my mother to visit my father in hospital at Lincoln, despite the ice and packed snow on the roads.

The deer herd – probably the descendants of the abbot's animals – roamed the park, as they still do. The Abbey had splendid formal gardens, once kept immaculate by a sizeable staff of gardeners. By the 1940s, Charles Tye was looking after them single handed. He was keen on playing the church organ. When he asked me if I would blow it for him, I said I would do so on condition that he let me have a turn at playing while he blew. There was a wood-yard near his cottage, where a steam engine was at work quite regularly, its wide leather belt clicking over the pulleys, sawing up timber from the estate's great tracts of woodland.

The drinks cart used to come round and we would buy real ginger beer and real dandelion and burdock. Groceries were brought to our door by Twelvetrees' van from New Bolingbroke, driven by the quiet and ever-obliging Jim Bradshaw. He always gave me a little paper cone of coconut mushrooms or liquorice allsorts as he handed me my eagerly awaited *Mickey Mouse Weekly* or *Beano*. Our milk came from Carrington, brought by Mr King in his motor car. We would have to fetch it from a house near the green.'

BOURNE

'My childhood memories are of Bourne. In the late 1950s it was my pleasure, on Thursday mornings during the summer holidays, to visit the "pig market", actually the cattle market where all manner of livestock was auctioned. With one or more siblings it was a great thrill to wander about the empty pens and gangways, then get in the way as cattle or pigs were driven towards us so that we had to flee. Our shrieks increased the din of the squeals, bellows and clatter of the poor animals. Being the leader of the gang I must have been a great nuisance, but with only the odd "Mind out the way, duck", drovers and farmers alike were very forbearing.

Except for "Snitch". His real name was Harry and he was a crusty old chap who swilled out the cattle wagons and pig trailers, and we used to aggravate him until he snarled and turned the hose on us. He was something of a character, and years later he was to become, by marriage, my great-uncle. He drove a horse and cart and owned a smallholding where he stored all the clutter he somehow mustered. His house was built alongside a disputed right of way to the "Klondyke" piggery belonging to T. W. Mays & Sons, and he regularly barricaded the road so that lorries could not pass. My husband, who worked for Mays, was sent to negotiate with his great-uncle; to no avail!

Although he lived in ramshackle conditions old Uncle Harry was actually a man of means. Not like another town character from that era. Ray "Mich" was a dear old soul who made a bit of pocket money by trundling a handcart around the streets calling, "Want any logs or kindling, Missus?" He wore a tattered overcoat tied up with string, was muffled up with scarves and always had a drip on the end of his nose, for which a wipe with his sleeve sufficed!

Selling at the door was common after the war and Mrs Foster, of Romany stock, was a regular visitor, winter and summer alike. She had no teeth, wore a pinny, headscarf, slippers, or some other dilapidated footwear, sometimes an old mac, and carried a basket over her arm. This was filled with all manner of delights for a child – buttons, lace, bits of elastic, pretty cottons, brushes and combs, bottles of scents and hair lotions. Outside she had a pram (at one time it was one of our cast-offs) and in this she carried the hardware – baking tins and yard brushes, and all her bartered goods. She would always be invited in to our house for a sit down and a cup of tea. This particularly caused us children amusement because she always poured her tea into the saucer and slurped it!

All personalities of a past age who stir the memories and we are the poorer without them.'

WORLABY

'I would like to tell you a few things about Worlaby as I remember it when I was ten years old at the beginning of this century. Now I am living in a new council bungalow, so different from the old house I left which has recently been demolished. Near here was the old "pinfold", a square brick yard with just a gate. If anyone found a horse, cow, sheep, or pig, they were to lock them up there and whoever claimed them had to pay a fine to get them out again. Quite near also was the horse pond, filled with water which came down a dyke from the drain (halfway down Carr Lane) when it was full. There was a wall around the pond with an outlet, covered by what the old folk called a "spud", something the same shape as a spade which was put over the outlet.

Farmers used to fetch water from the pond in water carts for their cattle and bring their horses to drink there. I remember one winter it was frozen over and when children were sliding on it, one of them pulled up the spud and let all the water out. Then when the ice gave way with so many children on it, you can guess what sort of a pickle they were in, because the bottom of the pond was thick mud.

The house in the village which is now called Hill Foot Farm, was then called Sparrow Hall and my great grandma used to live in it. She used to declare that all the sparrows in Worlaby came to nest there.

The man who was the sexton and grave-digger was club footed, a cobbler by trade and he lived opposite the school. We used to go watch him work through the window, and one day he hit his thumb with his hammer, and of course we all laughed. He threw his hammer through the window at us and then chased us – could he run! We had to look sharp.

There is some land up the hill called the hollows. Gypsies used to camp there. One morning they found one of the gypsy women dead and she was taken to Brigg where it was diagnosed that she had died of pneumonia. Her caravan was taken to the carpenter's shop and rotted down, as they say that gypsies will not live in a caravan in which one of them has died. The funeral was a great affair. They brought her back to the village and placed her on a set of trestles and anyone could go and look at her. Everything was of the very best; oak coffin, bricked grave, and the tea on long tables. What a spread! Everyone was invited to the tea and I went. Before going to the church everyone had biscuits and wine. For the tea itself there was a whole ham (home fed), a stone of beef, home-baked bread, plum and seed bread, all cooked by the local people. There was a beautiful linen tablecloth, china cups and saucers, cut glass dishes and real silver teaspoons, and all the cutlery of the very best. I have never seen anything like it before or since.'

CHURCH AND CHAPEL

Sunday was a special day, when most children attended Sunday school and many families went to church or chapel once or even twice. When holidays and outings were few and far between, the Sunday school treat and Anniversary were eagerly awaited and are remembered with great affection and delight.

A DAY SET APART

'Sunday was a day set apart, a day for the family. Our lovely chapel at Bardney, the one I was married in but which sadly stands no more, was visited for worship three times a day. Sunday school in the afternoon was a much needed respite for parents and a happy time for children.

Sunday school events were quite something. The once a year Anniversary was a day-long celebration with the majority of children in new frocks and with a recitation or song to perform in front of a packed chapel. The Sunday school outing to the seaside was for most the only outing of the year. There was great excitement and anticipation when approaching the chosen resort, with cries of "I can see the sea".

During Sundays playing games was frowned upon. My mother would neither sew nor knit. The only work undertaken during the day was to cook and wash up after meals, the Sunday lunch being a traditional family affair. The evening saw the whole family going for a walk, with all the wonderful sounds and sights of nature.'

SPECIAL DAYS

'The children at Hykeham Moor attended Sunday school in the afternoon. We went until we were about 15 years old, often under protest, and by then we were helping with the smaller children.

My favourite Sunday in the 1940s, when I was about five years old, was Flowering Sunday in July. We all dressed up in our best frocks and straw sunhats trimmed with flowers and we took a bunch of fresh garden flowers to church as well as a little basket of banty eggs. These were later distributed to people in the village. The Harvest Festival was also a grand affair. We took a basket of Father's finest vegetables and eggs to church, as well as fruit and flowers. Sheaves of corn, huge pumpkins and marrows also adorned the church and every pillar and windowsill looked beautiful. The produce was later sent to the children's home or the local hospital.

The Sunday school had an annual outing to Skegness. The excitement at seeing the water tower and knowing we were nearly there was almost too much, as the six majestic buses made their way down to the sea.'

THE ANNIVERSARY AND THE TREAT

'In the 1920s we were sent to chapel in the morning and Sunday school in the afternoon. As I was born in the last of a row of cottages in Chapel Street and was christened in the Wesleyan chapel, I was sent to the Wesleyan Sunday school in Maltby le Marsh.

Of all the events that took place, the Anniversary was the most important. Each child had to take part, either saying a poem or singing a solo or duet. This took many weeks of practice both on Sundays and weekdays. New dresses were to be made, so there was a visit to the draper's to buy the material. Mother's sewing machine whirled away and at last the new dress was hanging in the wardrobe waiting for the special day.

28

Sloothby Methodist Sunday school outing to Skegness in 1922, a great treat for the children.

The great day has arrived. I can see it now. The chapel has been decorated with flowers, the platform erected and the forms and chairs set out. The sun is shining and we are told to walk to chapel and not to run. Who would want to run in a new dress, new black patent shoes, white socks and white gloves? The boys have new suits and boots. Hair is brushed until there is not a hair out of place. We walk primly off to chapel. We are met by the teachers who tell us where to sit. The organ plays and the special preacher sits in the pulpit. We file on to the platform, the big girls and boys at the back and the smaller ones at the front. The preacher announces the first hymn, *Summer suns are glowing*. After the morning service we hurry home for dinner.

The afternoon is very special. As we hurry back to chapel we are getting more and more excited. Mums, Dads, aunts, uncles, older brothers and sisters fill the chapel. Once again we file on to the platform. The preacher says how pleased he is to see so many people there. After a prayer he says, "The children will now entertain us." We stand up and sing *Angel voices ever singing*. Our great moment has come. The poems are recited, the songs sung. The little ones sing *Jesus bids us shine with a pure clear light*. The preacher tells us a story. He says because we have been so good the Treat will be on Thursday. The Anniversary is over and all the family come home for tea. How we got into our small cottage I don't know. There would be two sittings. We would have stuffed chine, trifle and cakes. What a lovely day!

The following week we had the Treat. We had a whole day off school, and were told to meet at the chapel at ten o'clock. We were there a long time before that. The sun was always shining and there would be much laughter and talking. "Hurrah, the charabancs are coming!"

The boys go in one and the girls in the other. We are on our way, past the school where the other children are at play. How we shout and wave. No school for us today! After a lovely ride through the country we come to South Thoresby. We pile out at the village pub yard. We sit on forms or the grass and eat our sandwiches. With the teachers leading the way we go to the valley to run races and play games. But wait, we come to the village shop with bottles of aniseed, spearmint dabs, barley sugar, lemonade powder, gob stoppers and other delights. On we go over the brook. Off come our plimsolls for a paddle. We run in the long grass in all kinds of races. We scramble for sweets.

Tea is in the long room over the pub bar, set out on trestle tables. They are piled high with potted meat sandwiches, plum bread, seed cake and fancy cakes with pink and white icing. Grace is sung and the tables are soon empty!

The charabancs are waiting. After three cheers for the teachers we are on our way home, bunches of wilting wild flowers in warm, sticky hands. A wonderful day is over for another year!'

HOW I ENVIED THEM

'Brought up an Anglican in the 1930s, with church service in the morning and Sunday school in the afternoon, how I envied my Methodist school friends who I thought had a much better time. On their Sunday school Anniversary in the summer they all had posh new dresses, hats and shoes, and sat on the platform of the chapel to do their pieces of recitation and songs. The following night was even better, when they would be driven round Halton le Moor singing their Anniversary hymns. They were seated on forms in horse-drawn vehicles, or in later years a lorry. Finally they would stop in some farmer's field for games and races. Nothing like that for us.'

EXCITING EVENTS

'The Sunday school outing at North Somercotes was a most exciting event. Every year the children and some of their mothers travelled to Mablethorpe, a distance of about twelve miles by horse and waggon, leaving at 8 am for the day. The waggons were loaned by local farmers and were gaily decorated with flags and strips of coloured crepe paper entwined in and out of the wheels. Sandwiches were eaten on the way amidst great hilarity. Waggons were open to the elements of course, but then, it never seemed to rain. The waggons arrived around midday. Everyone had a little money to spend as this was the only outing in the year for many of the children. Tea was provided by one of the Methodist chapels in the resort, and the team of waggons – as many as eight of them – left for home at around 5 to 6 pm.

The harvest festival was another grand occasion when once more the chapel was full to overflowing. Rosehips were gathered and threaded on to cotton and draped around the windows. There were masses of home-grown fruit and vegetables along with pickles and jams. All this was auctioned at the close of the Monday evening service – proceeds for chapel funds. Auctioning went on until after 10 pm, which was considered to be very late.

A rabbit pie supper was held in March in the Sunday school room. The ladies of the chapel made the pies at home and these were then baked in a nearby bakery. There was great rivalry between the women as to whose pie tasted the best – the pastry coming in for much criticism. Vegetables were cooked by ladies in adjoining cottages. Cold apple pie and custard completed the meal – all for the cost of one shilling and sixpence.'

WE WENT ON STRIKE

'During the war years I attended Scampton Church of England school. Our family always went to the chapel Sunday school, until they started one at the church and then we began to go there instead. When it came time for the annual chapel Anniversary, with recitations, new bonnets, teas and going "round on the waggon", we were not part of it anymore. The "waggon" was usually a farm horse and cart, gaily decorated, with chapel seats on and people would go round several villages singing. This had always meant a day off school, but now we had to go to school, with a few other children and some from neighbouring villages.

My brother didn't think this was fair and we agreed that we would go on strike. Our parents sent us off to school but we decided to hide in the wooden hut which served as a washhouse. It had wooden benches with holes where enamel bowls fitted, and we all squashed in and crouched under these benches. The teacher, who came from Lincoln on the bus, went into the school and then started looking round the grounds. We hardly dared breathe and we had to keep the little ones quiet. The teacher looked in the window but couldn't see anything so went on to look in the toilets and air-raid shelter. Not being able to find us she made her way back to the bus stop and we crept out, stiff and aching from being cooped up. Unluckily for us, the lady from the shop saw us and ran after the teacher, who then returned to school. If only we had waited a few more minutes.

We were punished by sitting all day with our hands on our heads, listening to a lecture about our conduct. This was quite tiring but we proved our point because the vicar said from then on everyone would have a day off when it was the chapel Anniversary.

I am a great one for justice and things being fair so perhaps it all began when we played truant all those years ago.'

ALWAYS BRIGHT AND BEAUTIFUL

'The day of the Sunday school outing from Fulstow was always bright and beautiful. We eagerly gathered outside the chapel Sunday school dressed in our second best. We travelled to the seaside town of Cleethorpes, riding on farm carts, seated on forms out of the Sunday school. The day before had been spent decorating the carts with flowers and streamers, how lovely they looked. The farm horses had been groomed by the waggoners until their coats shone, their hooves were polished and the horse brasses sparkled in the sunshine.

We must have started the journey very early, singing and laughing all the way, shouting greetings to people as we passed by. On arriving at the seaside we all made for the sands to paddle. The boys rolled up their trouser legs – which in those days were down to their knees – the girls held up their dresses or tucked them into their knicker legs, with shouts of delight to see who could go out the farthest, and perhaps we would get a ride on a motor boat.

We had dinner in a cafe, with sandwiches and cakes supplied by the ladies from the chapel. The tea poured from big white jugs into mugs was sweet and hot. After dinner a walk along the promenade to the amusements – down the helter skelter, a ride on a roundabout and a donkey, and for the very brave, the galloping horses. A few goes on the halfpenny slot machines hoping to win. Ice cream would be a must and a bag of chips for a halfpenny. Our carefully saved two shillings had to go a long way. We bought a trinket for our mother if she wasn't with us, and a stick of pink peppermint rock with "Cleethorpes" right through the middle.

On Friskney Sunday school feast day decorated horse-drawn drays paraded round the village.

We had tea at the same cafe, perhaps another look at the sea and sands, and then made our way to the picking up place for the long ride home. What a wonderful day it had been, to be treasured and discussed until next year.'

PROCESSIONS AND PRAWNS

'At Friskney chapel Feast Days have been a tradition for 150 years, always on the second Sunday and Monday in June, when the school would close for the day. A procession of horse-drawn drays filled with children would travel around the village. The drays were decorated with fern fronds and I can remember the smell of the ferns very vividly; at one time there were 14 drays. Men who worked with horses also took the time off and were in charge of the waggons.

A village collection was made at the same time, all proceeds going to the chapel Sunday school funds. On the Sunday there were three chapel services and at each one the congregation overflowed the building; wooden forms had to be added in the outside aisles. Children took their own packed sandwiches on the waggon trip for their midday meal but tea was provided. Grandad got up early, caught the tide and brown shrimps were added to the bread and butter and seed cake provided by the village baker, gratefully received by all.'

WE LOVED IT ALL

'We had church and chapel at Burgh le Marsh. Both were well attended, usually by a lot of the same people. We went to both, though we were Church of England. Church Sunday school was in the afternoons, and a youth club called the "King's Messengers" was held in the vicarage kitchen, the leader of which was the vicar's maid! Chapel Anniversaries were always a great occasion followed by a tea and sports on the Monday night. No rivalry here – we loved it, all of us. The church Sunday school treat was another highlight, with lunch on the beach at Skegness, tea at the Violet Cafe under the pier followed by the circus at the Winter Gardens and often a visit to the cinema too. Always a lively day, and the "chapel" children often came too. The bus was always full.'

SEND SOME RAIN ON MY 'TATIES

'My mother in law was brought up in a strict Methodist tradition and had to attend chapel every Sunday, sometimes twice in one day. One year at the turn of the century it had been very dry with hardly any rain for some time, and the preacher this Sunday was a local smallholder with, amongst other crops, only one field of potatoes, which were obviously wilting through lack of rain. When the service came to the point for prayers, the preacher prayed: "O Lord, send some rain on my 'taties, and if Thou doesn't know the field, it 'es a thorn bush in the middle."'

NEVER THE SAME AGAIN

'Sundays were a special day in the villages, and both churches and chapels had good Sunday congregations. Each village had a resident vicar or rector, while the chapels had a circuit minister and a large number of local preachers, some of whom cycled several miles to their appointments. By the late 1930s in our village, the Sunday school had 15 children but sadly, not one parent attended chapel. The coming of radio was blamed for this, then television. Then more people bought motor cars and village life was never the same again.'

GETTING ABOUT

**At one time it was either the horse and trap or Shanks's pony that
we relied on – we walked! Bicycles brought us greater freedom, and
then came the early cars, though not for many families. The buses
and the steam trains were our usual modes of transport, or perhaps
the local ferry.**

FROM HORSES TO CARS

'In the early 1900s the main transport was horse-drawn, bicycles
with solid tyres were also used and people walked to surrounding
villages. The roads were very rough and many were no more than
cart tracks. Some of the farmers at Scartho would send their goods
to markets at either Grimsby or Louth and this could be done with
their own transport or by the carters who travelled to and fro and
would also take people to the towns or villages on their route.

In the 1920s many families owned motor bikes and side cars and
Father would have to make more than one journey, depending on
the number of children, to take the family for a picnic. Private bus
companies were now operating; one firm was called Ada and ran
every hour on their way to other villages. The early buses had
solid tyres and threw up clouds of dust. In 1930 the Grimsby
Council decided to alter the layout of the roads in Scartho and
with compulsory orders purchased two cottages and the smithy,
which were pulled down, and most of the land at the side of the
chapel. Gate House lost a large piece of its land and some barns.
The road had previously run in front of the house, turned left at the
end of their land and then right towards Louth. The new road ran
at the back of the house, cutting out the bends but resulting in the
house having roads on all sides and so the Kirman family renamed
it Island House.

The Corporation buses began a regular service, the early ones
having open tops. Cars were becoming another form of transport,
also lorries and vans, although horses were still being used until
after the Second World War. Bicycles were a very popular form
of transport, especially for children travelling to and from school.
During the war with the shortage of petrol and the blackout, not to
forget the removal of all signposts, many people immobilised their
cars and jacked them up in the garage until the war was over.

Waiting patiently to go to Louth market, 1914, when the main form of transport was still horse-drawn.

By the 1950s many more roads had been built and the main roads were very busy, particularly Scartho Road.'

BY CARRIER'S CART

'At Colsterworth we had a carrier's cart once a week to take goods to Grantham and to buy things in town for people instead of them having to go into town themselves. Goods would be delivered all the way home. The first bus was run by Cecil Blankley who charged ninepence return to Grantham.'

'Mr Lorne of Aisby went to the livestock market in Grantham with his horse Taffy and float, carrying chickens, potatoes etc to market and perhaps bringing piglets back. His dog Floss would sit on the side of the "top road" to listen for the horse's hooves coming from Welby, then hop on the float for the last quarter of a mile ride home. Mr Longland of Oasby brought bulky goods from town in the carrier's cart, retiring at the end of the war.'

THE FIRST BUS

'The first bus in Navenby started a service on 2nd December 1919, owned by Joseph Hodson, a local farmer. It was a Model-T Ford and had 14 seats and solid tyres. He operated a service from Navenby to Lincoln on Fridays and Sleaford on a Monday (market days). This service was very popular with the locals who took their produce to sell in the market.'

THE VILLAGE BUS

'During the 1930s the village bus was the vehicle that enabled us to escape from our hard-working country life to catch a taste of the world outside our insular village. This heyday of the bus also coincided with the heyday of the cinema – "the pictures".

"Loweth" (Louth) and Grimsby were the Sodom and Gomorrah of our times. Before the Second World War Louth offered two cinemas and no less than 52 public houses. I can't say much about Grimsby as it was too far away, 20 miles, to make visiting (even at two shillings and threepence return fare) possible very often. The bus fare to Louth, at one shilling and sixpence return for eleven miles, was just within reach. Dad's wages amounted to 28 shillings weekly, with four of us to be provided for.

On a Saturday night (the great night out) the bus left Louth after the second house of the pictures, often this would be nearly 11 pm. Sometimes as many as 60 to 70 people would be aboard this last bus home (a 36 seater). It must have been an odiferous affair, even allowing for Friday being tin-bath night. Many of the lads would have managed a few pints either before or after the pictures and fish and chips, of course! For one shilling a huge parcel of fish, chips and peas was on offer. Some were consumed on the bus on the way home.

A girl had not much choice about whose knees she sat upon on this journey. Much was the jostling for position as the bus boarded, many the romance that bloomed or was doomed in the next eleven miles. The shouting, the laughter, the singing, made it impossible for requests for stops to be heard by the driver. These had to be passed from person to person up the bus and it was not unusual for the passenger to be dropped a quarter of a mile or so beyond his lane end. Was it accidental that those who wanted to get off the bus en route always seemed to be squeezed in towards the back of the bus, which meant a mass exodus of those who were standing in the aisle and a long stop, with often revised jostling for position before we were off again?

On more than one occasion the driver had to negotiate the steep banks of a dyke to get a can full of water to cool down his boiling radiator. We were often very late arriving back in the village and many folks had still long walks to make to their marshland homes. Some had left their bikes at the village pub, but even if alone the nights held no terrors then, with no street lights, only the brilliant beauty of the stars. I often have a little smile to myself when I read the old saying that "It is better to travel hopefully than to arrive", remembering the days of the village bus.'

CHANGING TIMES

'In 1903 the Axholme Joint Light Railway was opened and provided rail transport for goods and farm produce between Goole and Haxey. There was also a passenger service and this provided a good connection at Goole for Hull, so a day out at Hull was quite an event. The passenger service came to an end about 1933 but the goods service continued until after the Second World War. Finally this also ended and the line became defunct in the early 1960s. The service from Crowle's other station was on the Doncaster line through to Scunthorpe and Cleethorpes. During the summer months special excursion trains to Cleethorpes were a feature and cheap evening excursions to Cleethorpes became very popular, particularly with the younger generation. In the fishing season special trains were run to bring hundreds of fishermen for fishing in the canal, which runs parallel to the railway. Important fishing competitions were often held, and still are today. Nowadays the fishermen come in cars and coaches.

The proprietor of the White Hart Hotel, in Crowle, owned a horse-drawn bus, seating about ten people and he used to go the mile and a half to Crowle Central station to meet each passenger train and this saved people the long walk. Eventually he bought a small 20-seater motor bus to replace the horse-bus. The fare was twopence for adults and a penny for children. This valuable service finally came to an end in the early 1930s.

Until 1916 the only way over the river Trent at Keadby was by the old rail bridge. The only road bridge over the Trent was at Gainsbro', so Scunthorpe was not very accessible from Crowle, except by rail. There were several little ferries across the Trent, by row boat, but I think that would be rather a risky journey. In 1916 the new Keadby road and rail bridge was opened and this opened up the way to Scunthorpe for people on the west bank of the Trent. Soon a regular bus service was established from Scunthorpe to Crowle and other villages. As the Scunthorpe steel works expanded many local men found work there. In the early days most of them cycled the ten miles to and from work. Eventually "shift" buses were run but as

The Women's Meeting of the Portland Street Methodist church off on their annual day trip to the sea, by charabanc.

people became more affluent and were able to afford cars these "shift" buses eventually stopped. The way to Cleethorpes by bus was now possible and I remember in particular our Sunday school annual summer trip. This was a great event.'

STIXWOULD FERRY

'Stixwould ferry was an important factor in the lives of the farm people who lived in Blankney Fen in the 1920s. It was the link between isolation and civilisation, conveying people and goods to Stixwould railway station and children who walked two miles to Stixwould school. Part of the inventory of Ferry Farm, it was operated by a member of the farm foreman's family or a worker.

Built of wooden planks, it was rectangular in shape, a shallow boat with sloping ends, covered by a wooden top. Railings were on the long sides, on one of which was the operating gear. On the short sides were hinged flaps which were pulled up and chained in place when vehicles or animals were cargo. A chain secured at the ends on each side of the river, passed through the hand-operated winding gear wheel. A pump was built in to remove the bilge from under the deck. Fares were displayed on a board – on foot twopence, bicycle threepence, etc. Scholars travelled free of charge. On each side of the river was a landing stage, secured by a chain to a post. They were moved to suit access and departure from the ferry according to the water level in the river Witham.

In order to put less strain on the horses pulling loads of grain, hay, straw or sugar beet, the approach to the ferry was started about 50 yards away up the pullover, a diagonal path to the top of the Witham Bank and down the other side, in like manner, on to the boat, and then to the station. Once, accidentally, horses and a load of straw bales missed their mark and went into the Witham. A quick thinking waggoner cut the horses' traces and they swam to the bank. The waggon was retrieved later. Another time an excited steer jumped off into the water. It was captured and went with the rest of the herd in a cattle waggon by rail to Lincoln market.

One day, when children were crossing, the boat chain broke and the craft started to drift downstream. Wilfred Davidson, the station porter, happened to see this and quickly ran to grab the broken end of chain, which he fastened to a fence. By this time the school train, on which some pupils travelled, had arrived. The engine driver saw the situation and he and the signalman held up the train until the scholars were persuaded to jump on to the bank, without a landing stage, and then go on with their journey.

The river in spate was alarming, as the water level was high and the crossing took longer because the chain was slackened to avoid too much strain on it. On one such occasion, the bilge water had not been pumped out and the boat sank overnight. Mr "Dubby" North, an old fenman, was called into service and he rowed passengers across in his little eel boat. We sat very still, petrified by the turgid water lapping so near.

Mr North and his wife lived in a houseboat, man-propelled on Metheringham Delph. In summer they dwelt in a willow booth in a field corner, where they grew vegetables and cooked on a portable range. Each night "Dubby" set his eel hives in the Witham. He also caught eels with a stang, a three-pronged fork. His wife took a basket full of live eels on Fridays, when she went by train to Lincoln market. He was a "catch hand", that is he would take on various farm jobs for anyone who would employ him.

By the 1930s cars were becoming more common and a road was made to link Blankney Fen to Martin Fen. After the war, the number of train passengers declined and the Lincoln to Boston line closed, so the ferry boat was no longer needed. What was its fate?

Some years ago I approached the former river crossing from the Kesteven side. Rails, cattle pen and station buildings had vanished and across in Kesteven there was a void where the farmhouse once stood. Nothing moved but the river, it seemed a desolate and inhospitable place. Stixwould ferry was just a memory.'

HOUSE & HOME

THE WAY WE LIVED THEN

Candles and oil lamps our only lighting, the fire our only heating, the old range our only oven – the old cottages looked picturesque but it was a hard life before 'mod cons'. Still we look back with nostalgia, and perhaps those old places did have a warmth and a personality lacking today?

THE HAPPIEST PLACE I KNEW

'My home at Bardney was the happiest place I knew. The farmhouse kitchen with its scrubbed, red brick floor had a pegged rug, usually made from cut snips of old clothing, in front of the kitchen fire. A boiler on one side, the oven on the other, and didn't it bake some substantial meals?

What a welcome home from school, to see a roaring fire and sometimes the bread put to rise under its snow-white cloth; on a cold day, slippers on the bright steel fender and best of all, a mother to greet us with a smile. There was an easy chair each side of the fireplace for Mum and Dad, and more chairs, often stuffed with horsehair, for the family. Lots of knick-knacks on the mantleshelf, a pair of brass candlesticks, the friendly tick of a grandfather clock, and to adorn the place, "the biggest aspidistra in the world".

Sunday was the highlight of the week, when it was customary to have a fire in the drawing room. As little work as possible was done and there was no "gallivanting" on the Sabbath Day. Dressed in their Sunday best, complete with gloves and hat, most people attended a place of worship at least once, and often went walking during the afternoon. Newspapers were put away excepting the *Sunday Companion* or the *Christian Herald*, and of course everyone had a Bible. If there was a piano, family and friends gathered round and sang hymns. Most households had a joint of meat on Sunday, often roast beef and Yorkshire pud. The snow-white cloth, linen serviettes and a jug of clear water adorned the table. In many homes the youngest child said grace before and after a meal. Little chatter was allowed at meal times, and table manners were taught. This sounds rather strict, but it proved excellent for discipline.'

BOUGHT WHEN THEY MARRIED

'Dad worked on a farm as stockman. Mother worked on the land – catchwork, ie part-time to help eke out the small wage. For this work the women wore an "harden" apron to protect their dresses. Mother, as did most women in the 1920s who lived in the villages, wore a wool cap when pegging out clothes.

Most of the furniture was bought when they got married in 1906 from Bells of Brigg. The basic items, including a table and a bed, cost twelve shillings and sixpence the lot, including an oil lamp with blue glass vessel. Over the years as we moved round on "flitting day" things didn't always fit. Some furniture had to be sold cheaply or swapped. Mother has been known to make extra shelving with a plank of wood and some bricks to put things on in the kitchen or pantry.

Snip rugs were made from bits of material from coats, trousers, dresses, etc. A special wooden peg was used to push the "snips" through the hessian sacking. They lasted a long time but were very heavy to take up and shake. Most of the floor would be red bricks or tiles downstairs while upstairs wooden floors were covered in lino and a mat each side of the bed. The bed would have sheets, blankets, an alhambra quilt and an eiderdown. Pillows were stuffed with chicken feathers. The mattress was either filled with feathers or flock. The latter one was useful to put over the metal slats which criss-crossed the bed frame. These feather mattresses had to be shaken and turned frequently, else they got lumpy.'

MUD AND STUD

'Near the old bed of the river Witham stood several thatched, mud and stud cottages, now all gone. They were sited on "islands" a little higher than the rest of Wildmore Fen. Country lore has it that if anyone could build a fireplace and have the chimney smoking in the morning, they could claim right of habitation, if they did not already own the land.

There was no solid foundation to these dwellings, the floors were bricks laid on the soil. When the Cades moved to such a home, the grandfather clock was too tall, so a hole was dug in the floor to accommodate it, which rotted parts of the plinth. Holes were dug in the soil, in which was placed a chunk of Ancaster stone, on which stood the oak king posts. The roof tree was a roughly snedded Scots pine trunk. Clay was dug from the river, mixed with reeds or straw and plastered on the framework. To conserve heat the fireplace was in the centre of the house. Reeds, which grew in abundance were used for thatch, secured with home-made thatch pegs. A wooden step-ladder was used to reach the upper chambers.

Firegrates were small, with hobs on either side. Kettles and cooking pots were suspended from a "reckin hook", a vertical bar of iron secured in the chimney. Pittlebeck Booth's cottage was surrounded by a brick "causey" (path) which led to the backhouse, constructed of old railway sleepers and a pantiled roof. In it was an iron wash boiler, a firegrate for summer use and a brick oven, this last was a bread oven. "Kids" (bundles of twigs or hedge trimmings) were burnt in the oven to heat it. The ashes were swept out, then bread and pies etc were placed inside with a long-handled peel, similar to a spade. There may have been a pottery nearby, as I have picked up blue earthenware trivets for salt pans and fragments of yellow and brown pottery in an adjoining field.'

PAINTED WITH TAR

'My father was a ganger-platelayer on the Legbourne length of the LNER track of the Grimsby to London railway, now no longer in existence. When I was born in 1930 our home was a semi-detached cottage just inside Little Cawthorpe parish boundary. It was painted with black tar year after year and this formed a thick, smooth skin which was waterproof. These cottages were demolished in the 1950s.

Our cottage had a main room which had a door to the outside; in winter we had a thick curtain in place to keep out the draughts and thanks to an ingenious device the curtain lifted when we opened the door. A door also led to a winding staircase, another to a long narrow pantry, and one to the kitchen which was down three steps. All of the doors were of a different shape and design, and all had snecks. Over the kitchen was a loft reached by a wooden ladder where apples and hams were stored. The ceilings upstairs were low and sloping, to look out of the window you had to kneel on my parents' bedroom floor. There were no wardrobes so clothes were stored in drawers and chests or hung in the chimney alcove behind a curtain.

We had brass bedsteads and feather mattresses. Lino and scatter mats covered the floor, and it was fashionable to have a mat at the entrance of each room. The floors downstairs were rough and uneven and covered with either lino or coco matting; we had snip rugs made from worn out clothes or odd pieces of material. The ceiling in the main room was varnished and treated with linseed oil. We had candles except in the main room where we had a paraffin lamp, which gave a very good light.'

THE FIRE

'Until probably after the Second World War, a typical terraced house would have no central heating. The kitchen/living room had a Yorkshire/Lancashire range incorporating a side oven. The fire, lit every day, winter and summer, provided domestic heating and the sole means of cooking. Lit between six and seven o'clock, its first use was to boil a kettle and cook breakfast. Everything was cooked on the open fire, except when the oven was used, so the fire had to be solid enough to hold cooking pots, saucepans and frying pans, sometimes unattended.

The fire was the most important feature of housekeeping. Without a good fire, cleanly burning, life would have been very difficult. When I first took in such matters, coal was 15 shillings a ton.

Breakfast was always cooked – fried bacon, black pudding, lentil cakes, fried bread, eggs occasionally, especially round Easter when they were always cheap.

The main meal was at midday, when everybody came home from work or school. When I began work at Scunthorpe in 1929, I walked home for the first three weeks, the best part of two miles, for my midday meal, and back in 75 minutes. After three weeks I was put on shift work and took sandwiches. So accustomed were we to the midday meal it had not occurred to anybody that I could have taken sandwiches from the start. This may have been because cooking for six was little more expensive than cooking for five, but something special would have had to be bought for sandwich filling. In those days, pennies counted.

The midday meal was our main one: soup made from bones and thick with vegetables; stews; meat pies, including rabbit pie; rice puddings; apple pie and custard. The Sunday roast was often sirloin, a leg of lamb, a piece of pork.

Tea was generally bread and butter, sometimes jam, sometimes a bun or a piece of apple pie or jam tart. The older and adult members had supper, sometimes fish and chips ("a tuppenny and one" – a generous piece of cod was twopence, a piece of haddock threepence, chips one penny or twopence).

My mother made her own bread, making up a stone of flour at a time. I fetched a stone of flour often enough from the Co-operative Stores near Crosby school. The other ingredients made the dough up to nearly 24 lbs, mixed in a pancheon by hand, formed into eight two-pound loaves and a great cluster of bread cakes.

Before the dough was mixed the oven had to be cleaned out. The oven was on the left side of the fire, and a flue went from the fire sideways under and around the oven and back to the chimney. The draught was controlled by a damper. With the damper in, the products of the fire's combustion went directly up the chimney; with the damper out the fire was drawn under the oven. A good deal of soot formed. By removing two small metal caps, the soot could be removed with the use of a specially designed scraper, and the effect of removal was dramatic. Soot removal was done at least twice a week, and always before the baking or cooking of something special.

There were small fireplaces in two of the bedrooms, and one in the front room. This latter room was the least used in the house, and a fire there would be lit only on rare occasions, always on Christmas Day, sometimes on Sundays in winter, and very occasionally if we had visitors. To come home from school on a winter afternoon and find a fire in "the room" was as great a treat as I can remember.

Occasionally, when someone was ill, there might be a fire in one of the bedrooms.'

THE CHIMNEY SWEEP

'The chimney sweep would walk from Owsten Ferry to Haxey Carr (five miles) to clean a chimney for sixpence and a cup of tea.'

MOVING HOUSE

'House moves in the country were made by horse and waggon. The last job before leaving a house was to clean the ashes from the fireplace and whitewash inside the part where the ash collected.'

OUR BEDWARMERS

'When I was a child in the early 1930s we had an old fashioned blackleaded grate, with a boiler on the left of the fire for hot water, which we filled with water using a bucket. In very cold weather we wrapped the oven shelves in brown paper and used them as bedwarmers. I imagine the shelves were made of iron, they were certainly solid and very heavy. We also had to be careful they were not too hot!'

A NEW RUG FOR CHRISTMAS

'We had a new pegged rug every year at Christmas time. These were made using old clothing such as coats cut up into pieces about an inch by two inches, prodded into hessian with a pegging tool.'

'Floors were covered by lino, with a few mats around. The hearth rug was pegged with strips about one inch by four inches cut from old clothes. The base was a good sack opened up. "There must always be a few bits of red in it," the old folks would say. Bedroom mats were made from old lisle stockings dyed and cut into strips and looped through sacking.'

CANDLES AND BEETLES

'We lived in an old stone cottage at Hykeham Moor. We had gas lights on the walls with fragile mantles which shattered at the least vibration and we always had to keep a spare one handy. Upstairs we only had candles to light us to bed. They cast frightening shadows on the walls when nearly burnt down, so it was wise to go to sleep before this happened.

Another hazard of the night was the large black beetles that came out from behind the fire as soon as the lights went out. If you went downstairs in the night there were beetles all over the floor, in spite of putting beetle powder down. When my cousin came to stay she put on her wellingtons in the morning and crunched on a beetle – I knew better than not to check inside the boots first!

Eventually, in about 1949, we became the proud tenants of a new council house. It was like being in heaven.'

THE FIRST VACUUM CLEANERS

'Carpets were swept with dustpan and brush after being "damped down" with used tea leaves. Later a Daisy vacuum cleaner was used. It was operated by one person standing on a platform working the bellows with a long handle, while someone else used the nozzle at the end of a hosepipe. The Star cleaner had a hand-operated bellows on the handle of a cylinder.'

SEEING THE LIGHT

'I was born at a lodge farm, that is a farm standing alone outside a village. The year was 1920, the lighting was oil lamps in the living rooms and a candle to light you to bed. The heating was by coal fire. The cooking was all done on a coal-fired range; this had to be blackleaded every day and the ashes cleaned out. Once a week the flues were cleaned out, a very dirty job but if this was not done the oven would not get hot. The chimney had to be swept at least twice a year.

A primus stove was another thing we had to deal with. This was filled with paraffin, then to get it going a metal channel which ran round the middle was filled with methylated spirits. When lighted it heated some pipes that held paraffin. When the pipes were hot you pumped the paraffin. If you had misjudged it, and the paraffin was not hot enough the flames shot in the air and you had to turn it out and start all over again.

When I got married in 1949 I had an Aladdin lamp which had a white net mantle. This had to be treated with great care. On going out of the room, if the door was banged the lamp went "up". Flames shot through the mantle and blacked the glass chimney. Then it had to be turned low to burn the soot off the mantle.

Several years after I was married the electricity arrived. What a joy! I was on the bus to Grantham at the first opportunity and returned loaded with an electric iron, a kettle, and an electric fire. How easy everything became!'

WATER AND WASHDAY

Water was precious when we had to bring every drop into the house by pail or by pump and fetching the water could take some time every day. Washday used gallons, and was a full day of toil for the housewife.

THROUGH CHARCOAL

'As I sat in my home at Belchford sipping a hastily brewed cup of tea, my mind slipped back to the days of my childhood, in the late 1920s, when I and my mother's family (six of us in all) lived in a two-up and two-down cottage on the bank of Hob Hole Drain, New Leake. Apart from what was caught in the rain butt, all the water had to be carried from the drain (some 40 to 50 yards from the house) and, to make it palatable, it had to be filtered; this was achieved by passing the water into an earthenware container where it ran through a layer of charcoal and was caught in a bucket underneath.

The toilet was an earth closet in the garden. This consisted of a wooden structure with a large hole for grown ups and a small hole for the children, housed in a small shed. In those days there was no need to dispose of newspapers – they had a use here, cut into squares, with a hole through, threaded together and suitably located! Ashes from the fire were also deposited in the toilet, and when the time was right and the garden was lying fallow, the toilet contents would be removed from behind with a shovel/scoop and buried in the garden; an excellent fertiliser.'

WITH THE MILK!

'I grew up in a small mud and stud cottage on high ground at Scamblesby. There was no water supply and we had to fetch water up the hill from the pump at the bottom of Church Lane – later on the milkman was kind enough to deliver three churns of water each day when he delivered the milk!

The houses on Rowgate Hill had to make do with collecting water from the opposite hill; the drips of water appearing were marked by a stone slate and a bucket was always kept under the drips, as water took so long to collect. Not all dwellings in the village were lucky enough to have wells, and a lot of sharing and saving of rainwater went on. Some of the bigger houses had a well in the cellar, and a system of hand-pumping water up to the "bathroom" for use in the hip or tin bath. Mains water did not arrive in the village until 1958, and it cost £5 to be connected. It was after 1960 that the first bathrooms, as we understand them, began to be installed.'

A BETTER CUP OF TEA

'Some houses in Allington had their own well, but for those who didn't there was a pump on the village green, though most folks preferred to walk down to the Salt Well as the water made a better

49

cup of tea. The Salt Well is a freshwater spring, so called because the water has iron salts dissolved in it. It has never been known to dry up though it has never flowed at more than a trickle. All the farmers used to bring their horses and cattle down to drink at the well in the summer. People would come with horses and carts from Foston and Sedgebrook to fill up barrels of water. In a dry summer you had to be there early or you would have to wait up to four hours for it to fill up enough for the pump to work. Piped water was eventually brought to the village in 1948.'

500 PUMPS A DAY

'There was no mains water in Crowle until about 1936 so there were no bathrooms except in a few of the larger houses. Here the rainwater collected in a tank and was "force-pumped" up to another tank in the roof so it could circulate through the bathroom taps and down to the kitchen sink. I remember my grandfather used to give 500 pumps daily to keep the tank in the roof full of water. Drinking water was mainly from underground springs and there was usually a pump in the back yard for this purpose. Rain water was also collected in tubs for general use.'

ONLY ONCE A WEEK

'Bath night was once a week when I was a child at Hykeham Moor. There was no hot running water so every drop had to be heated in a big zinc bucket on top of our gas stove. The bath was a large tin bath which was kept hanging on a nail in the outside shed. It took quite a lot of buckets to get it reasonably full, and in cold weather was usually placed in front of the living room fire. It was quite a performance to manage without splashing all over the living room rug. I had the bath all to myself but in large families they had to share the bath water, topping it up occasionally.

As I got older it was quite embarrassing as bath night always seemed to coincide with the insurance man calling or one of my uncles visiting. Very often I had to jump out quickly at a knock on the door, wrap myself in a towel and rush upstairs. I have been rather averse to baths ever since.

The other ritual connected with bath night was the dreaded dose of syrup of figs. I made the most awful fuss about this and was often chased around the table by my mother brandishing a spoon. Meanwhile Granny was trying to listen to her serial on the wireless, usually *Dick Barton, Special Agent*, and it was fading fast as the accumulator (battery) was running out. This was changed every so often by a man who came in a mobile van. Granny would get very annoyed at the noise I was making. Thank goodness it was only once a week.

In the backyard we kept a water butt to catch the rainwater. This was also boiled up on the gas stove and used to wash our hair – it was supposed to make it shine. The water often contained tiny wriggling red worms but I seemed to come to no harm and I had lovely shiny hair.

Our toilet was sited next to the pig sty down the yard, which was about 30 yards away from the house but to me as a small child it seemed miles. It was actually called the "lav" and was a small stone building whitewashed inside. There was a high wooden bench seat with two holes in it; one was bigger in circumference than the other and I was always afraid of falling in. There was no light inside and it was terrifying to have to go there in the dark with only a torch or matches to light the candle on the shelf. I lived in permanent fear of the green caterpillars which climbed the walls every summer from the garden nearby and threatened to drop on me. The door had a big gap at the top and the bottom for ventilation – I always expected a mouse to come in!'

THE BODY AT THE DOOR

'After living in a town until the 1940s, we moved to the country, where I was married in 1945, living "in rooms" with my parents until my son was born in 1947. My husband and I then found a country cottage (two rooms up and two down) about two miles' walk from the nearest village. There was no electricity – we cooked in a "tin" oven which stood on top of a primus stove. Our "lav" was about 30 yards down the garden path with one high seat and one low one (presumably for mother and child) and our water supply was a well. To get the water a bucket was tied on a long length of rope, then turned upside down and thrown into the well. You had to avoid letting go of the rope – which I once did to the great consternation of my neighbour, who opened her back door to find my husband lying full length on the ground at the side of the well with hands and head dangling into the gaping hole in the ground. He had a long-handled pole with a hook at the end and was "fishing" for the bucket, but she was shocked to find what she thought was a body outside her door. Needless to say it took a very long time for me to live that episode down!'

FIRE!

'Living in the town we had a flush lavatory. However, we spent many holidays with relatives in the Wrangle/Old Leake area of the county and I remember vividly an incident which occurred when I was eight or nine years old. Along with Mum and Dad I was staying for a week with Great Aunt and Great Uncle Wilson, strict Primitive Methodists. They lived on their smallholding, with of course the privy nearby, indeed a two-seater – one for adults, one for children. There was a strict no smoking rule.

An uncle who had travelled from Lincoln with us for his Trip Week holiday was in the habit of going to the outside toilet for a cigarette. One morning Great Uncle Wilson saw a wisp of smoke coming through the aperture which served as a window in the small brick building. He ran across the yard to where three buckets of water stood, grabbed one of the buckets, flung open the door of the toilet shouting "The privy's on fire!" and whoosh, a bucket full of water landed on a bewildered Uncle Bert. I feel sure in my own mind to this day that Great Uncle was well aware that Uncle Bert was sitting there.'

WATER FROM THE RIVER

'Water for home use was taken from a rainwater well, drawn up by a bucket on a rope with hand over hand method. Great skill was needed and the children soon learned that if you dropped the bucket fast enough it would immediately fill with water. During droughts, my father would take a barrel on a cart to Salem bridge at Wainfleet and draw water from the river with the aid of the pump situated there, then transport it back to Friskney.'

THE VILLAGE POND

'All the houses at Cranwell had a well in the garden. My father had to pull up two pails of water before going to work at 6.30 am and that had to last my mother all day till he came home at 5 pm. Piped water did not come to the village until 1949.

There was a village well and pond in the centre of the village. In the early years of the century the pond was very important for the watering of cattle and each year the parish council appointed a Pump Warden to be responsible for its management. The water in the pond was not very deep except by the well. By the 1930s it was stagnant, covered in weed and the receptacle of village litter. In hot weather it smelt! However, it was a mecca to us children who loved to catch the newts and brought jars and jars of frogspawn home to sit in the kitchen window where it duly hatched into tadpoles. Somehow, it always seemed to disappear before the emergent frogs could jump out! In very wet weather the pond would overflow and it was not uncommon to find newts and frogs in the road. Most of us fell into

Ingoldsby villagers queuing at the pump during a very dry summer. The pump was only unlocked each evening at 6 pm.

the pond at least once and received a good hiding when we went home wet and crying.

Following a polio epidemic, the pond was filled in as part of the village coronation celebrations in 1952/3 and became the present village green.'

QUEUING AT THE PUMP

'A memory of summer evenings at Ingoldsby in the 1930s when there was a drought is of the evening procession of people queuing up at the village pump for their ration of two buckets of drinking water. Promptly at 5 pm Mr Simpson, the Parish Clerk, came down the street and unlocked the padlock on the chain around the pump handle. After everyone had been "served" he would lock it up again. Water had to be used sparingly, but of course all the houses had a soft water butt for their own washing etc.'

THAT SPOILT IT!

'We were many years without mains water at Denton, and this meant earth lavatories for most cottages. These had to be visited by candlelight after dark – terrifying! For some reason the so-called "ash pits" were always emptied on Good Friday, though it was hard

Doing the washing was a hard day's work in 1921, when this picture was taken at Laceby.

to see the connection.

There were no refuse collectors and almost all household rubbish was consumed by the copper fire. The soapy water often boiled over with the heat of the fire and came out of the washhouse to meet us. At the end of washday the copper would be refilled and the zinc bath brought on to the kitchen hearth. The reflection of the warm fire on one's wet skin was lovely, but after the bath the two teaspoonfuls of that awful stuff, syrup of figs, spoilt it all.'

A MARATHON FOR MOTHER

'In the 1930s life for a housewife was much harder than today. In Legbourne there was no electricity until 1938 and no piped water or mains sewerage until the late 1950s. There were no labour saving machines in my home in the 1930s.

It took all day on Mondays to do the washing. We had water to pump in the garden about ten yards from the house door and 15 yards from the washhouse. It was even further to the coalhouse where the copper was. The pump had a wooden frame regularly

54

painted green. The wooden handle was shiny with use as this pump, which gave sweet drinking water, was also for the use of two other houses; our neighbours had to carry their water even further than my mother.

My mother washed in a large corrugated shed called the wash-house. Three yards from the house, it was also used for salting the pig, storing potatoes and cycles, and bathing in the warm weather.

The copper was a large, round cast-iron bowl set in a brick framework with a coal fire underneath. The first thing to do on washday was to fill the copper with water, add the white washing and the soap and light the fire. When the washing had boiled it was transferred to the washhouse. My mother did not have a dolly tub but a special washer she had won in a raffle. It was like a half cylinder laid on its side about three feet long and two feet wide. The zinc cylinder was lined from end to end with rounded strips of wood. A frame shaped like the cylinder fitted inside the base, made of strips of wood. Using the handle pulled it forwards and backwards in front of her, and the clothes were rubbed between the strips on the frame and the strips of wood on the cylinder. The cylinder was on legs and had a bung to let the water out. I never saw another one like it.

After rinsing in a large zinc bath using a blue bag, the washing was put through the mangle before being hung out to dry. The wash baskets were made of cane. Many clothes were starched with Robin's starch powder. By midday all the clothes lines were full and the hedges utilised as well. The clothes took a long time to dry as they were mostly thick cotton or linen and the sheets unbleached twill.

On rainy days it was misery as the washing was dried in the main room before an open fire, the room was full of steam and the fire out of sight. Lunch was called dinner in those days and was easily prepared – cold meat from Sunday and fried potatoes were a must on washdays.

When the washing was dry it had to be folded and the starched items dampened by sprinkling them with water from a basin and left to settle. Mother usually ironed after tea, on the table, using four flat irons and an iron holder of cloth or a knitted one to hold the handle.

Normally no more washing would be done until the following Monday and never on a Sunday.'

ON THE DEWY GRASS

'The left over soapy water after washday was thrown over the rose bushes to kill off greenfly.

Mother laid out washed handkerchiefs and tea towels on dewy grass – to whiten them.'

SHOPPING AND CALLERS TO THE DOOR

Every village had its local shops, providing everyday needs and making trips into town a rarity for some. Tradesmen also delivered direct to your door, becoming a part of our lives as the same men called every week. Buying clothing was a more complicated business then too, we seemed to wear so many layers!

THE VILLAGE SHOPS

'Hollands of Swineshead ran a general store, where they employed a milliner, Miss Fryer, a draper, Miss Holmes, a cashier, Miss Cullen (my mother), a roundsman and domestic staff. Each morning, jars containing boiled sweets were well shaken to prevent the contents sticking together. The brass scales were polished ready for trade. Butter and eggs were brought in from farms as the roundsmen delivered orders. In the evening, cashier and roundsman counted the cash takings and went through the order books and neither was allowed to leave the shop until every farthing was accounted for.

Sugar was delivered in hessian sacks from the wholesaler; granulated sugar was weighed in pounds and put into blue paper bags. Brown sugar went into rose pink bags and washing soda in brown ones. All were tied with fine white string. Weekly newspapers were folded in a special way, tied with string and posted on Fridays. Mrs Willows kept pages of old seed catalogues suspended near the sweet counter; she made pokes from them in which to put the sweets. All purchases of clothes and household goods were wrapped in a brown paper parcel and tied with string.

The Misses Wells (Mary, Sarah and Ethel) of Billinghay gave trading stamps to customers before the First World War. Our paraffin lamp which hung from the ceiling, the striking wall clock and Frister and Rossman sewing machine were all acquired from savings stamps. If a customer's bill amounted to a farthing less than a round sum, the Misses Wells would give a sheet of pins instead of a coin for change.

Mr Tomlinson, the chemist, wrapped graduated glass bottles of medicine in white paper (apothecary's wrap) and sealed with red sealing wax. 'Carotene' butter colouring and poisons were always in blue glass bottles.

Pastel-coloured lucky packets were a big draw at Everards of North Kyme. They contained a motto, a few cachous and a small ring, miniature top etc. On the counter was a grommet which, when the neck of an aerated drink bottle was pressed against it would release the drink by pushing the marble into the bottle. A mini-guillotine was used to cut up pipe-sized pieces of thick twist tobacco for customers.'

DAILY VILLAGE LIFE

'In the 1930s life in a small village such as Stickford, in retrospect, was pleasurable and satisfying. There was a true community spirit – everyone knew everyone else within the village bounds, and very often beyond. Certain people in the village such as the squire, the parson, the policeman and the headmaster were held in great respect by the parishioners and their help was often sought when problems arose and difficult forms had to be filled in.

The daily needs of the villagers were catered for by tradesmen living and working in the community. The milk lady (my husband's aunt) cycled round to the households on her "sit up and beg" bicycle with heavily loaded, lidded, milk pails after having milked the cows earlier in the day – the milk couldn't have been fresher! One particular village milkman used to come round delivering the milk on days which were misty with the greeting, "It's a bit houry, missus", or when the sun tried to shine through the mist, "It's a bit gleamy, missus"!

The butcher from the next village – Stickney – prided himself on delivering meat which the previous week had been grazing in the farmer's field opposite; the baker delivered freshly baked bread several times a week, with a sideline of fish and chips on certain evenings when the local girls and boys of the village would congregate to exchange chatter.

The travelling grocer was another feature of village life; my uncle had several vans all packed with anything from pins to prunes or even a gallon of paraffin. Goods were bartered with local farmers' wives and at least one lady in the village exchanged eggs and butter for light blue bags of sugar and chunks of cheese to be used for her husband's "thumb bits" during the day. If you needed a new jacket or a pair of boots these were ordered and bought by the grocer when he went to Boston market on a Wednesday, and they were then delivered the next week to the customer. The grocer's shop was a veritable Aladdin's cave – grocery on one side and drapery on the other. In the grocery side there were two highly polished gleaming brass weighing scales with shining brass weights, rows of large sweet jars filled with liquorice laces, gobstoppers, sherbet

Mr Derek Hipkin delivering at the Plough Inn, Stickford in 1920. Hipkin & Sons would bring drapery, groceries and hardware to the door.

suckers, peppermints and barley sugar twists; there was also a cabinet with pills and potions from gripe water to syrup of figs and Angiers Emulsion. In the drapery side there were yards of material, drawers full of buttons and cottons, thick striped flannelette shirts, corsets under the counter, table-cloths and sheets, in fact almost anything that one might need. Across the yard, where the garages held the grocer's vans, there was a large granary up some steps. Here there were white basins and yellow bowls, enamel potties and refined china chamberpots, tea services and cooking pots, dolly pegs and zinc baths of various sizes.

The greengrocer visited on Saturday night with his basket full of goodies that one did not grow in the garden – oranges, bananas, nuts, dates, figs and tangerines at Christmas time looking especially attractive wrapped in silver paper in the lace-edged fancy boxes. Every Sunday morning a little packet of Sun Pat chocolate coated raisins appeared as if by magic, obviously purchased the previous night and used as a ruse to keep young children in bed a little later on Sunday mornings.

Another person of great importance and necessity was the man who walked the village street very early on a Saturday morning, well before the villagers were astir. The school had separate boys' and girls' toilets which were across the school yard. Each toilet had its own bucket, which were emptied every week through little doors in an outbuilding backing on to the toilets or a door in the front part of the toilet seat by the man with the "dilly cart". It was not until after the Second World War that flush toilets appeared in the village.'

WE DEPENDED ON TRADESMEN

'In the years preceding the Second World War, Gunthorpe, a small village in Owston Ferry parish, had no shops. One resident sold cigarettes, matches, tobacco and sweets from the back door of his house. People depended on visiting tradesmen. There was only one bus a week, on Tuesday to Gainsborough on market day.

The grocers would come round on bicycles collecting orders and deliver next day by horse and dray. One grocer came from Owston Ferry every week and one from Gainsborough every fortnight. There were three bakers who came through although many women made their own bread. The bakers would sell bread, yeast, buns, teacakes and a few special items at the weekend. Each had a horse-drawn van with a hood. On Fridays, usually called "market day" in the village, the greengrocer and butcher would come. The butcher would walk through the village with his trap, the meat covered with a net curtain. Hanging inside the back of the trap would be sausages, polony and other small items on dishes, all neatly covered. The fishman also came once a week, this attracted the cats when they smelled the fish.

Two or three times a year Mr Inskip came from Gainsborough with his horse-drawn cart piled high with pots, pans, jugs, basins, hardware etc. This was quite an event when word spread that "Inskip's here". He was a jovial man with a ready wit, telling jokes and tales when he got an audience round. He would juggle with plates, knock glasses together and then start his sales talk, starting at a high price, coming down to a few pence for mugs, cups etc. His finale was always "guzzunders", which caused much amusement. Mr Staff was another character. He rode a bicycle from Gainsborough every fortnight with a large basket on the front and a carrier on the back piled up with cases, bags and parcels. He could hardly be seen for his baggage. He sold socks, stockings, underwear, towels, remnants, buttons, cottons and always sweets for the children. He was a small cheerful man and always wore a trilby hat, tied on with string on windy days. He had several houses where he stopped for a cup of tea or a meal.

Dave Aldam came once a week selling paraffin, candles, lamp wicks, soap, donkey stones etc. He would call out "Any oil in today". His van had its own distinctive smell. Jack and Harry were the coalmen who delivered once a week with black hands and faces. A dirty ten shilling note was always called a "Jack and Harry note". People soon got a nickname in our village. One man who came on a bicycle selling things was named "Sharp Drink", no one knew his real name. He always asked for a "sharp drink" not tea. One of the bakers was nicknamed "Bundust" as he always had flour on his khaki overall.

Not many people got a daily paper but weeklies were delivered on Saturdays, *Epworth Bells, Sunday Companion, Family Journal* and comics for the children. Another friendly man came round with various goods but could not add up very well, he trusted people to pay him. The horses that pulled the drays would often walk on, eating hedges and plants while the owners talked. The ice cream cart came on Saturday, selling halfpenny and penny cornets and twopenny wafers.'

THE MILK DELIVERY

'Early every morning of the week, as regular as clockwork, down our road and into the village at Market Deeping came the milk float. This was always clean and shining and was painted yellow with dark red trims. It was drawn for years by a knowing piebald pony called Dolly. The milkman stood behind the two large churns which held the fresh sweet milk straight from the farm. They had been scoured inside and polished on the outside until the copper plates denoting their capacity and the owner's initials gleamed.

One flick of the reins brought the horse to a halt and the milkman descended to deliver. He came to our back door with his usual "Let's be havin' yer". He lifted the lid of the large oval-shaped bucket which contained a gallon or two and from the measure that hung inside he poured a pint of foaming milk into a large basin. This was placed on the top of the safe in the cool dark pantry and covered with muslin held down by a fringe of large blue and yellow beads. When the milk in the basin had settled the cream was skimmed off for a treat. In the very hot weather, which we did get sometimes, it was feared the milk would turn sour and so it was boiled.'

Mr Bateman going out on his bicycle to sell his home-made ice cream, at Spalding in the 1930s.

MY DAD'S ICE CREAM

'In the 1930s my parents had a small general shop on the outskirts of Spalding and my Dad made ice cream and then went out on his cycle to sell it.

Each early evening, the teenager who helped in the shop and in the house, cycled to the farm about a mile away, arriving just after the completion of the evening's milking and returned with four gallons of fresh milk – two gallons in each can balanced either side of her handlebars.

By the time she arrived back, my mother had the fire going under the galvanised copper in the corner of the kitchen. There was plenty of wood available for this, as many things came to the shop in wooden boxes.

Then the milk was put in a four-gallon pail and hung into the water suspended from a stick across the top of the copper. When the milk was boiling, a thick custard was made with ice cream powder and sugar added to taste.

The next morning this cold custard was put in a tall metal cylinder which, in turn, was in a wooden tub and ice was packed in the space between the cylinder and the tub. The ice was delivered twice a week, great blocks of it which were kept in a small wooden shed and covered with hessian sacks. My father broke it into small pieces with an ice pick to make it fit into the available space in the tub.

Then a handle was fixed through a hole in the tub and with the aid of various cogs, Dad turned the handle and the cylinder turned inside the tub. Salt was added to the ice to melt it and to enable more ice to be added so the custard was frozen.

This process was carried out in the backyard, or in a shed on the rare occasions it rained. After an hour or so, and after a continuous replenishment of ice and salt, the custard thickened into the consistency of cottage cheese, but drier, and it was sold as ice cream in halfpenny and penny cornets.

It was available in the shop all day but children did not have money as they do today, so the main amount was sold in the evenings when my Dad went out round the housing estate close by, ringing his handbell, and he stayed until he had sold out. Even the Sundays when we had an outing to the coast, the milk had to be fetched and boiled ready for the next morning.

It was the best ice cream I have ever tasted, and a lovely yellowy colour, and many people of my generation still remember it. Unfortunately the Second World War ended the operation.'

IT WAS AMAZING WHAT THEY BROUGHT

'I was born at Barrowby and can remember one man who travelled round the villages. It was amazing what he could pack in his trunk – needles, cotton, elastic and mending wools, towels, tea towels and dishcloths side by side with ladies' and children's underwear, stockings and socks. He had a bicycle with a wheel on the side of a small rack for his trunk, which had a wide strap attached for when he carried it on his back.

An elderly lady came round with an old pram with cottons, tapes etc, and she also collected rabbit skins.'

'The rag and bone man came round on an old cart drawn by an old nag. He gave the children a balloon or a goldfish in exchange for rags, but we seldom had anything to swap because old coats and other clothes were usually cut up to make peg rugs.'

'I remember the muffin man calling three times a week. He also sold crumpets, which we knew as pikelets.'

FOOD AND DRINK

Perhaps we have more choice today, but our food was plain and wholesome in the past, often home produced and certainly home cooked. Most of us grew our own fruit and vegetables and many kept hens in the garden, making us self sufficient in so many ways.

PUDDING FIRST

'When I was quite small we always ate pudding first and the meat and vegetables second. A sizeable steamed pudding was very filling and considerably cheaper than the meat. When I was eleven and had passed the scholarship, as I was eating my packed lunch and watching the girls who could afford school dinners, I learned that the correct procedure was meat first, sweet second. Eventually this became the way at home although my father always had Yorkshire pudding first on Roast Days.

Talking of Yorkshire pudding, I remember my grandmother supervising my first efforts at mixing a Yorkshire and she told me to be careful not to put too much milk in or I would put the miller's eye out. I wonder if anyone else has heard that expression?'

'In many households at Osgodby butcher's meat was considered a luxury, so to cut down the demand for meat the pudding was served first. Puddings were either milk puddings or good filling steamed suet puddings.

There would be a joint to roast for Sunday dinner. The remains were eaten cold on Monday, stewed up for Tuesday and, if anything was left, it was minced up for Wednesday. By Thursday there was a rabbit or hen from the stackyard and on Friday and Saturday the home-cured ham came in handy – or if the Saturday butcher came in time for dinner, chops or liver were chosen for that day.'

SELF SUFFICIENCY

'Chickens and geese were a source of food for the family. They were fed on boiled potatoes (cooked in a copper similar to the one used for boiling clothes) and meal. They were kept for several years for their egg-laying and then used for the pot. At Christmas time villagers at Bardney would take their geese and turkeys to the local bakehouse where they were cooked overnight in the large ovens. A special paste was made out of flour and water to coat the birds and removed the next morning. The birds were then collected during Christmas morning ready for the meal.'

'At Colsterworth most people shopped in the village, sometimes on credit and paying so much a week when money was scarce. Most folk had a few hens. When harvesting we had the occasional rabbit – stewed, roasted or in a pie. Pies were baked in Arthur Branston's baking ovens. He sold ready mixed dough, which helped during the war. Farmers' wives churned their own butter in their kitchens and sold it at market, either at Grantham or Melton. People did lots of preserving and jam and wine making, and also made their own pickles, usually using ingredients from their own gardens or from the hedgerows.'

'Food such as stews and rice puddings was often eaten because it used the heat from the fire to give long slow cooking. We went out collecting wood with a pram (with or without the baby!) as this helped eke out the coal. Bread was delivered from Lincoln to Heighington by the "Midnight Bakers", so called because they delivered late in the evening. At harvest time extra bread was baked at home because the men had to be provided with enough food to last them all day, from early morning until late in the evening.

We kept a pig and a few chickens. These were fed on scraps and also on feed from the mill where we got our flour. At harvest time we gleaned to get straw and corn for the pig and chickens. We could also buy "separated milk" very cheaply from the farm and used this for milk puddings.'

'With a family of six to feed, food was plain but nourishing. The budget was stretched by wild rabbit in pies and stews, and in the spring by crow and pigeon pies. Tripe and onions was just one of the tasty dishes not so popular today. Meat not used straight away was salted down for use later, giving those wonderful flavours that can never again be attained.'

'My mother made a lot of wine. The two I remember best were her cowslip and damson. In the late 1930s we had an old Singer car with celluloid windows and a canvas top, and we would fill all the back seat with cowslips for wine-making. It took three of us to pick enough.'

'At Ropsley in the 1940s almost all shopping was done in the village. During the period of rationing, we saved the cream off the top of the milk for a day or two to put into a good screw-top jar and shake for a long time until it became butter. The whey or buttermilk was used to help feed the pig that most people kept. All peelings were cooked in an old saucepan on the fire to help supplement the pig's diet. Most people kept a few hens and cocks for eggs and extra meat and on summer evenings these were tented on bits of grass (not lawns) to keep it down and provide them with green.'

'We kept bantams in a long, flat-roofed chicken run at the bottom of the garden. I loved the little eggs they laid, but looking back it's a miracle the poor little things ever laid at all, as we were always using the chicken house roof as a stage for our regularly held concerts. Our tap dancing routines must have given the bantams a severe headache.'

OAT PUDDING

'Baking was done in a kitchen range with upper and lower ovens. I remember oat pudding, a sweet pudding made with oats, milk and sugar and cooked slowly in the lower oven. This was given as an alternative on Christmas Day to those who did not like Christmas pudding.'

HARVEST AND HEDGEHOGS

'At harvest and haymaking at Allington there used to be a barrel of beer out in the fields but later on that got too expensive and we had to have cold tea. Everyone set off for work in the morning with a bottle of cold tea and the farmer's wife would send a lunch out to the field.

I remember when I was about 17, at the end of harvest the boss's wife gave us all a big dinner. We had roast beef and Yorkshire pudding with lots of gravy and vegetables – it was smashing. Then she came in with a great big rice pudding with a Spanish onion cooked in the middle of it. Everybody else helped themselves to a big spoonful with a slice of the onion and seemed to enjoy it. I couldn't fancy it so I didn't have any and couldn't tell you whether it was good or not.

One morning I was taking the cows up the lane to turn them out in the field and there were some gypsies camped up there. They had a fire going and called out to me and asked if I was hungry. I was only a lad at the time and was always hungry so I said yes. They fished something out of the fire, broke it open and gave me a piece. It was hedgehog; and it was delicious. I've never eaten it before or since but I enjoyed it that morning.'

THE COW CLUB

'Stickney Cow Club was founded in 1851, for cottagers and small farmers who owned a house cow to keep them supplied with milk and butter. Members had to live within a radius of four miles from the church. Quarterly meetings were held at The Rose and Crown on the second Monday of February, May, August and November. Members paid a fee to join and it acted like insurance, so that if your house cow died the Cow Club helped to pay for a replacement, which might otherwise not have been possible for many households. Just before Christmas they had a share-out from the remaining money.'

KILLING THE PIG

A surprising number of people kept a pig at the bottom of the garden in the quite recent past, and pig-killing day came to be an accepted part of life for many of us. Every part of the pig was used, so it was said, except the squeal!

PUTTING THE PIG AWAY

'The suppressed excitement of us children – someone at Frampton was killing a pig. The grown-ups were always trying to keep us out of the way until the dreadful deed was done. The pigs squealed and squealed, perhaps they sensed their imminent demise. Eventually we got to see the dead pig, usually when it was being washed with hot water and scraped to remove the bristles. It was lying on the cratch, which was a large, short-legged wooden table with extended handles at each corner.

After scraping, the pig carcase was hoisted onto a tripod with chains and a block and tackle. The butcher then cut open the pig and the "innards" were cut out and the older girls and women started to sort and clean them. We children stood in awe at the steaming, colourful mass of liver, lungs, heart, kidneys, bowels and most important to us, the bladder. Were the grown-ups going to use it for storing lard, or could we have it as a plaything? If we could have it, it was duly washed and blown up, tied and allowed to dry. What games we had using the bladder as a ball or tied to a short stick for lightly hitting people, in much the same way as medieval jesters used their pig's bladder tied to a beribboned stick.

Once the work of dealing with all the pig meat was under way we children lost all interest. That is, until the first sausage rolls and mince pies were out of the oven and then we almost burned our fingers and mouths in our greediness to "taste the pig".

We were usually given one other chore and that was to take the "pig cheer" to friends and neighbours. The pig cheer might be sausages and spare ribs, a pork pie or more usually a "fry" consisting of small amounts of pork, kidney, liver, heart and sweetbreads. The fry was laid on a china plate and covered with veiling (a piece of caul of fat that lined the pig's stomach). When the fry was delivered it was always carefully placed on another plate and the bloodied plate returned unwashed. This was supposedly to bring good luck to both the giver's and the receiver's families. With the dirty plate carefully held in one hand and a few coppers for delivering the fry in the other, we would race home for our taste of fry or perhaps the first sausages and some spare ribs.

How different, for girls, a few years later when one was considered old enough to help "get the pig out of the way". This usually happened at about nine or ten years of age. The endless hours of work dealing with the meat, fat and offal before it could go "off", in the days before it could be packed into the freezer.

There were mammoth baking sessions producing seemingly scores of sausage rolls, mince pies, pork pies, haslets and ducks and quantities of grey gelatinous brawn. Every pan, pancheon, basin, colander, chopping board, knife, spoon and baking tin and tray in the house seemed to be in continuous use. Every available surface held trays of meat or fat awaiting treatment. There were piles of greasy pots needing washing and the fire always had a large pan either simmering or boiling and the oven always appeared to be in use.

The fire had to burn evenly so the oven at the side kept to the right temperature. During pig killing a fire was always kept burning day and night under the built-in washing copper in the scullery. This was to provide the supply of hot water needed for washing up – no turning on the hot tap into the sink! Sometimes there was no sink and even washing up was done in the large bowl on the table. The water was drawn in buckets from the pump in the yard and woe betide anyone who used the last bucket of water without replacing it.

The butcher who killed the pig usually jointed the carcase into hams, shoulders, flitches, loins, chine and head. The hams, shoulders and flitches were cured to make rashers and joints for the family. They were cured with dry salt or wet-soaked in brine. The salt was bought in large blocks and had to be scraped with a knife to make loose salt. The meat to be salted was cooled and drained of blood overnight, then saltpetre was rubbed into the meat nearest the bone to dry any remaining blood and any cavities were filled with brown sugar. The swathe or skin was well pricked with a stainless steel fork and salt rubbed in. The joints were then turned and salted on the meat side. More salt was added over the next 12 to 14 days for a small pig or two to three weeks for a large pig. The meat was then washed, drained and dried and covered in absorbent paper (ie newspaper) and then sealed into cloth bags, often made from the backs of old shirts, and hung to cure from hooks in the kitchen ceiling. The bacon could be used one month later, as "green" wet bacon, but was better two to three months later as "dry cure" bacon. The cured meat kept for a year as long as it was kept fly free. How long it kept also depended on how hungry the family were.

Pigs were killed in the autumn or winter and usually in a waxing, not a waning moon, because it was thought that the meat kept better. A menstruating woman was not allowed to touch the salting meat in case the cure "didn't take" and the meat went rotten.

The meat was trimmed and sorted – some for sausages, some for pork pies, some for fries or chops, the chine for stuffing and the loin for a "joint of pork". The head, trotters, swathe, ears and any oddments of meat and bone were boiled together. This was then strained, the meat shredded and placed back in the stock and boiled up again to make brawn. The brawn was set in small basins and sealed with pork fat. The cooked tongue was boiled and eaten cold with "scraps". These scraps were the residue of the fat that had been cut up, minced and heated to render the lard. The hot liquid lard was poured into large basins and lidded enamel buckets to set and then stored for future use. Sometimes a pig's ear was scalded and well cleaned and set to cook with a fry. Onto the ear was placed the pig's brain and this was either eaten with the fry or sliced on hot toast. The "pluck" or lungs were cooked and minced and used to make mincemeat with dried fruit, sugar and alcohol. Some rendered "scraps" were minced and added in place of suet.

Lean pork and fat were minced to various degrees of coarseness to make sausages, haslet and pork pies. Each family had its own closely guarded secret recipe for sausage with varying additions of salt, pepper, breadcrumbs and herbs; it was not unknown for sausages to be hung like game, until they had green whiskers growing on them, then they were considered fit to eat. Many families tell the tale of Mother, or some helper, losing their wedding ring while kneading sausage meat, which meant that each bowlful had to be carefully searched until the ring was found. We worked in shifts, turning the handle of the mincing machine screwed to the table. It was very tiring, especially when the meat was put through for the first time. Anyone, including casual callers, who lingered too long in the busy kitchen would find themselves turning the mincer handle for a while. It really was "all hands on deck" during pig killing. While the meat was minced the intestines were prepared to make skins. All the contents were squeezed out into a bucket and the skins rinsed. They were then soaked in brine or carefully scraped with the back of a knife, on a wooden board, rinsed, turned inside out, scraped again, rinsed and then placed in clean brine until needed. The sausages were then made and linked and hung in the pantry.

When everything but the squeak and the bristles had been eaten, cooked, salted or stored in some form or other, there came the mammoth task of clearing away all the utensils and cleaning the kitchen and scullery. Every surface seemed to be greasy. Before starting on "putting the pig away" the kitchen and scullery rugs would be beaten, rolled and put away and the floors covered with newspapers. The papers saved some grease getting onto the quarry tiled floors and were safer to walk on than greasy floors. The greasy newspapers were screwed up and made excellent fire lights. All the paintwork was washed and windows cleaned and furniture wiped or scrubbed. Finally the floors would be scrubbed and when dry the rugs would be replaced. When the kitchen and scullery were clean then the rest of the house would be cleaned because no housework was done during the three or four days of pig killing.

Eventually the house would be clean, the pantry full to overflowing with pig cheer and everyone very tired but satisfied, that they had successfully "put the pig away". They could rest on their laurels and eat well until the whole process was repeated in a few months time, because most farming families killed two pigs a year.'

'To test if the hams were properly cured, a red hot steel knitting needle was pierced through the ham near the bone. If it smelled like good cooked ham the curing was a success.'

'We kept a pig at Oasby and in early December, when the pig was killed, one of my uncles from London, a main-line train driver, would hitch a lift on the footplate of another train, get off at Grantham station, catch the one o'clock bus to Oasby and return on the three o'clock bus with three packs of "pig cheer" to be shared with other members of the family in London.'

THE PIG CLUB

'The majority of working men at Heckington kept a pig which had been bought as a "weaner", ie at eight or nine weeks old. The animal was housed in a sty in the back garden and fed until it weighed about 25 to 30 stones, sometimes more. To insure against disaster, the men belonged to a Pig Club. The committee met monthly at The Red Cow to receive subscriptions of threepence a week for each pig. In addition to the usual officers, the Pig Club had a marker – insured pigs had an ear pierced as a means of identification – and a valuer. Should an insured pig die, the committee would estimate its value at the time of death and in most cases would replace the loss with another pig, rather than give money.'

GRANDAD'S PIGS

'My father was born in 1910 in a small yard in Barrowby known then as Cabbage Court, later renamed Welby Terrace. Grandad kept pigs and chickens and the pigs lived in a sty just outside the toilets down the yard; I never knew which smelled worse, the pigs or the toilets. When the pigs were fattened up, the time came for them to be slaughtered. Grandad would walk them down to the local butcher, Tom Griffen, at the bottom of Main Street.

The dead pig was then brought back to Grandma's small kitchen where the family were all ready to help cut it up and make pork pies, haslet, sausages etc. The pig was salted and cured and hung up on the wall in the main room of the cottage (it was only a two up, two down). When anyone wanted a piece of bacon or ham it was just cut off, leaving an odd shape where that joint had been. Grandad used to eat fat bacon with no lean on at all, just spread with mustard and a chunk of bread to help it down. I never could fancy this but it seemed to do him no harm at all. When he was at work on the ironstone works he walked to Harston every day.'

STUFFED CHINE

'As Heckington Feast Sunday approached, stuffed chine had to be prepared. The pig's chine is the joint between the neck and the shoulders. After being cured in the usual way with the rest of the bacon, the chine was soaked and then cut through with a sharp knife at intervals of about one quarter of an inch. A large bowlful of parsley had to be stripped of the stalks and "picking the parsley", as it was known, called for all hands on deck! A small quantity of thyme, sage and marjoram was sometimes added to the parsley and then this mixture of herbs was finely chopped with a knife. The crevices of the chine were stuffed with the herbs and the chine tied parcel-wise in a cloth. The next step was to fill the wash-copper with water and boil the chine for three to four hours according to size.

Stuffed chine is eaten with mustard and vinegar and very good it is too! However, a certain town dweller celebrating Heckington Feast for the first time described the dish as "that meat stuffed with grass".'

OLD FRED'S PIG

'Old Fred, our neighbour at Aby, looked so sad as he leaned over the pig sty wall. "The old boy doesn't seem rate," he said to my father. "I shall stay up all night with him tonight." The next morning the pig died, so my father helped Old Fred bury him. A little while later one of the old chaps out of the village called to see Fred and was told the sad news of the pig.

"Why, it wud ha' been all rate if yah ha' killed it, it would only ha' been a bit of a code." No more was said. Fred got a spade and with help from my father, the pig was dug up again. They stuck it to bleed it, scraped it clean and hung it up until the following day, when it was cut up into various joints and shared out with the neighbours. No one was any the worse for it.'

FROM THE CRADLE TO THE GRAVE

We were more likely to be born, to suffer our illnesses (and even undergo minor operations) and to die in our own homes in the past. Before the NHS, calling the doctor was expensive and home cures were often relied on, though the district nurse came to be a respected and trusted figure in the neighbourhood.

ARRIVING IN THE WORLD

'My mother was born two months prematurely, weighing in at three and a half pounds. Her parents feared she would not live and wrapped her in cotton wool soaked in olive oil and placed her in a drawer. She was fed only on brandy, not bathed for ten days and christened in the bedroom. She is now a healthy 76 year old!'

'I was terrified the day my mother gave birth to her sixth child. I was ten years old at the time, but we weren't told anything in those days and I had no idea another baby was on the way. I arrived home at midday to find a strange lady getting the meal ready and no sign of my mother. When I asked where she was I was told, "Upstairs, but you can't see her because the doctor and nurse are there." I remember going to the outside loo and crying my eyes out, thinking my mother must be dying. The strange lady found me there and I was eventually allowed to go upstairs and there was this new baby asleep in the bottom drawer of a chest of drawers. These bottom drawers were often used as cots in those days, especially if the births came thick and fast.'

'They were very good to the village, the Longs (the vicar's family at Swinderby). On Christmas Eve they used to go to the folks with children and leave a parcel and there was always a little present in for each of the children. And when anyone was having a baby, if they hadn't got any clothes and that, there was a "bag" as they called it, and you could fetch that bag and it had in it all that a baby wanted and you could keep if for a bit and then take it back. All the babies were born at home. Mothers would act as midwives and Dr Smith used to come.'

'My grandmother was the midwife at Heighington. A clothes prop

72

was left outside to be used to knock on the window if she was needed during the night.

I had twelve children, all born at home. The midwife then used to come by bike and had her terrier dog in a basket at the front. One of my children was born with the cord around his neck and she said to my husband, "You had better get the doctor, he's a black baby." The other children were home for lunch and went back to school to report they had a new brother and he was black! He was a bad colour from lack of oxygen but recovered and people were very funny with me for quite a while until someone demanded to see the baby. They were very relieved to find he was the same as his brothers and sisters.'

'After the war when I had my children everyone wore smocks when expecting. This was supposed to hide the bump, but was a real give-away to nosy neighbours.

Being "churched" was a custom which nowadays has gone out of fashion. After a woman had been safely delivered of a baby she had to go to church or chapel and say a prayer of thanks and the parson would bless her. It was supposed to be unlucky to have the mother in your house if she had not been through this ritual.

Mothers were kept in bed ten days after giving birth at home. A relation or friend would come in and take charge of the household, till the mother was strong enough. The baby was breast fed, at least for a while, much more hygienic than bottles but often inconvenient. I fed my babies "on demand" but the modern way was every four hours. This was supposed to be a routine to train the infant to wake up like clockwork, be fed, then go to sleep again thus enabling mother to get on with chores and even get a rest now and again. Being a farmer's wife with three children under five it never seemed to work for me. A carrycot was used when the baby was small and later a wooden cot with rails, and some were painted white and had pictures painted on a panel at the head end.

Nappies made of terry towelling were the order of the day. All had to be rinsed, washed and boiled to keep them a good colour. About three dozen were required, one lot for the wearing of for 24 hours, another pile being washed and the rest being aired. I had a clothes rack hoisted up on the ceiling and this would often be full of nappies, ready at all times. It was a day of rejoicing when the toddler was pronounced "dry".'

'MISS MILLIE'

'Let me introduce you to my Great Aunt Millicent Mary, to give her full name, known throughout her life as Aunt Millie to the family and Miss Millie to the villagers. Though married at the age of 20 and widowed at 42, she was still referred to as Miss Millie.

The villagers held Great Aunt Millie in almost awed respect for as soon as a crisis hit the village, whether childbirth, death, measles, mumps or some other ailment, someone would be knocking on the door. She had of course no medical training in the accepted sense but many people had faith in her treatment. Miss Millie's remedies worked, they said. The origin of those remedies she collected throughout her long life is obscure, some undoubtedly handed down, some so spartan that the very thought of undergoing treatment might have produced an instantaneous cure.

Her "dispensary" as she called it was a large Georgian press which stood in the alcove one side of the chimney piece in the parlour. Its contents might not have won a vote of confidence from any Medical Association but were undoubtedly comprehensive. These, according to a list recorded by a relative, were the medicines and appurtenances essential in every home: three thermometers, Condy's Fluid, lint, flannel, bandages, mustard, spatula, castor oil, quinine, sal volatile, Elliman's Embrocation, and feeding cups.

Great Aunt Millie was convinced that flies, bugs and such "varmints" had much to do with the spread of sickness and had her own drastic measures for dealing with them. "For an Ant Trap sprinkle a damp sponge with sugar and lay on a plate by the Ants' haunts: as soon as it was full plunge into boiling water." Wood ashes thrown into drains and on rubbish heaps were known to destroy flies' eggs; and fried camomile flowers scattered about got rid of fleas.

Mustard played a useful part in the home in those days as indeed it can now – not only for its edibility but as an efficient emetic; it can be particularly effective for drunkenness, narcotic and other poisoning. Mustard, along with linseed, bread, bran and charcoal was also used for poultices but these were heavy and messy.

Millie had varied and colourful first aid remedies. For bleeding a handful of flour on the cut and bind. Bruises, sprains, contusions and local inflammation were treated by diluted vinegar. Nettle rash was rubbed with parsley but nettle stings were rubbed with the juice of nettles.'

SELF HELP THE NORM

'The doctor was based in the next village three miles away. The district nurse was in the next but one village, a further three miles away. There used to be a letter box at Hibaldstow, sited next to the shop on the main road, for you to leave a message if you wanted the nurse to call. If she considered it was serious enough she would arrange for the doctor to call.

Self-administered remedies were therefore the norm. These included Indian Brandy for settling stomach ailments. Syrup of figs was taken every Friday night as an opening medicine and brimstone and treacle had a similar effect. A warm onion was tied to the ear to cure earache. Brown paper and a warm iron were applied to the neck for stiff necks, bread poultice was the cure for boils. Boils could also be removed by the bottle treatment; a bottle was immersed in very hot water then placed over the top of the boil. As it cooled it caused a vacuum and sucked out the pus. Styes were rubbed with a gold wedding ring. Sore throats were treated at bedtime when you had Father's sweaty sock fastened round your neck. Goose grease poultice and nutmeg was a cure for chest complaints.

Infectious diseases were rife. Whole families could be affected and children had to stay off school until infection was clear of the family. Scarlet fever, whooping cough, measles and mumps were all common. School records show that the school had to be closed in January 1903 because of scarlet fever. The classrooms were disinfected in the March and permission given by the Medical Officer for school to reassemble. Care had to be taken that no families still infected were present at school. Closures meant that holidays had to be reduced. In one year the children were only allowed the Boxing Day off at Christmas time because there had been closures prior to Christmas due to illness. In 1916 epidemics were rife and the school was closed for most of the year. Scarlet fever would keep a child out of school for six weeks and if another member of the family contracted it, another six weeks' isolation was necessary.'

'The doctor was not called at Osgodby until all home remedies had failed. For a cold, we were rubbed with camphorated oil and put to bed with a brick warmed in the oven and wrapped in a blanket. For upset tummies a dose of castor oil was the usual remedy. One family I knew had a regular Saturday morning dosing of brimstone and treacle, guaranteed to clear the blood!'

'Ropsley had its own doctor, who also served the four or five smaller surrounding villages too. He arrived about 1910, straight from Guy's Hospital, and practised until about 1960 when we were absorbed into much larger practices. People did not call the doctor for minor ailments. Remedies included goose grease or camphorated oil rubbed on bad chests, an onion hung on the bedpost to collect poisons from a fever, a swede cut up and covered with honey for coughs and sore throats, Friar's Balsam on a spoonful of sugar (ugh!), and senna pods soaked overnight and the juice drunk for constipation.'

'The healing qualities of salt were widely recognised for gargles, wounds and grazes, and even for cleaning our teeth. My mother filled small flannel bags with salt which were then warmed and used in the treatment of mumps.'

BEFORE THE NHS

'Illness in the 1920s could be most traumatic and very often fatal. Doctors were seldom called until the patient was in dire trouble because very often the household was unable to pay the fee. Most relied on home treatments, some of which were horribly crude or downright dangerous. The recipes for some of the potions were closely guarded family secrets. It was usual for the doctor at Burgh le Marsh to travel by pony and trap, with a groom in attendance, or simply on horseback. Doctors were some of the first people to obtain cars, which caused both curiosity and wonder amongst the villagers.'

'I can remember two of my aunts attending mothers-to-be and working alongside the district nurse at confinements. My grandfather and mother were connected with the Heydour Friendly Society and attended society meetings at Skegness. They collected subscriptions and a small sum would be paid out to sick members. In 1930 Meliora, the eldest daughter of General and Mrs Adlercorn who lived at Culverthorpe Hall, was killed in a car crash at Colsterworth. She was only 18. Her parents created a trust fund to build a nursing home for the benefit of the locality. After some two decades and with the introduction of the National Health Service, this home was leased as a private dwelling, but in 1978 it was sold by the Charities Commission, the Meliora Trust Fund created and the sick and elderly of the parish still benefit from the interest accrued.'

'One of my earliest memories is being taken to a village concert in aid of the Red Cross during the First World War. Kirkby-cum-Osgodby had such a good reputation for supporting good causes; I don't know if people were more generous or more prosperous then. One cause was Lincoln County Hospital. Built on 13½ acres of land, it was surrounded on three sides by public roads and on the fourth by a footpath. It was maintained by public subscription.

Hospital Associations were formed for the purpose of raising money. In 1930 it was found that the hospital needed to be urgently enlarged and improved, and by 1936 about half of the improvements had been done and £55,000 spent of which only £38,000 had been raised. The whole scheme was expected to cost over £100,000, as not only the building work had to be completed but day to day running

LINCOLN COUNTY HOSPITAL

Contributory Scheme

ASSOCIATION

CONTRIBUTOR:

Mrs Spurr Tilly Dale

COLLECTOR:

Mrs Schofield.

In the 1930s many families paid into contributory schemes which entitled them to the services of a nurse or to a referral to hospital. Medical treatment could be expensive.

costs paid for as well, hence the enormous fund raising campaign that was launched.

Funds also had to be raised to keep the district nurse on her rounds, although some of the cost was covered by subscribers. The doctor also charged for his professional services and medicines, but I suspect this was on a sliding scale according to what you could afford.

Home cures were the thing! To cure chilblains it was recommended to run in the snow. For boils a salve of soft soap and sugar, or buttermilk drunk three times a day while fasting. Whooping cough could be cured by garlic in the socks while sleeping. Or what about eyebright eye lotion, or a potato in the pocket for rheumatism?'

'In some villages there was a medical club, and people would pay a subscription each month from which the doctor's bill was paid. There was a sick and dividing club at many of the country inns; members would receive a weekly payment if they weren't able to work as there was nothing to live on when ill, no sick pay from the employer. I remember the appointment of the first district nurse for Eagle and several of the surrounding villages. In the early days she travelled round on a bicycle. My friend and I volunteered to collect the quarterly subscriptions for our district as we thought it was such a good thing to have a trained nurse. We organised functions to help with equipment for our nurse, and in 1948 when the NHS was formed we bought a wheelchair for the use of the village with the money left in the fund.

I well remember in 1918 the school health visitor came to see my mother to say I was to have my tonsils out. I was at home and heard the news. We had the operation at the blacksmith's house as they had a spare unfurnished room. The scrubbed kitchen table had been put in the room and four children were done that morning. I got very anxious the night before and was sick but when the time came my mother and I walked to the house. The doctor asked me to climb on to the table, a kind of mask with a pipe attached was put over my mouth, then the doctor touched my face and told me to wake up. We sat down for a little while and then doctor had a look at us and said we could go home. We walked home. My mother had put a pillow onto the couch and covered me with a blanket, and I went to sleep. When Dad came in from work at tea time he looked at me, my nose had been bleeding a bit. He went outside again and cycled to the shop for some bananas for me.'

'In the Stickney Parish Almanac for 1926 details are given of the Coltman Lodge of Oddfellows who met in the school on the first Thursday of the month at 7.30 pm. This was like an insurance group. When you paid to become a member, if you were off sick, the Oddfellows paid you one shilling and sixpence a week until you were well again.'

'Both the Nag's Head and the Wagon and Horses public houses in Kirton Holme had Sick and Dividing Clubs in the 1930s. Members paid into the club and when ill they had a little money coming in to help feed the family. Rules were strict and members had to be indoors by 8 pm or benefits ceased.'

WARTIME NURSING

'It was war time and January. I met the outgoing district nurse and was given the car keys. I had had eight driving lessons at two shillings and sixpence each. In one I learned to change a puncture, in another about spark plugs. The car's headlights were hooded for the blackout and many by-lanes I had to travel were blocked off and used for ammunition dumps. The terrain was so isolated it was difficult for us to get around. Only doctors and nurses had the petrol to drive around and the consumption of it was strictly monitored. My district comprised 23 villages and later included twelve more.

I was accountable to a council who set out the area's needs. A private nursing service, everyone over 14 years old paid sixpence a month and deliveries cost seven shillings. This was for 14 days' aftercare, then daily visits for the next ten days. Mothers to be were visited monthly until the eighth month then fortnightly until the ninth month, then weekly until the birth. As some cottages had a ladder up to the bedroom it was preferable to have the bed downstairs, since water for the birth was heated in a copper in an outhouse. The St John Ambulance would gladly get the bed down as most able-bodied men were away at war. Breast feeding was absolutely essential as there was no baby milk about, although midwives had their own formula for feeding when absolutely necessary. Our main disinfectant was Dettol and we had no penicillin. On booking a nurse for the delivery a list for the layette was given to the mum-to-be as items were often difficult to come by. The villagers always rallied round. Doctors worked very closely with the nurses and stayed on call until the delivery was safely over.

Most minor surgery was performed on the kitchen table, such as tonsillectomies, circumcisions and for varicose veins. Instruments were boiled immediately on returning home and fresh dressings were prepared and stored carefully in a biscuit tin. They were sterilised by being put in the oven for one to two hours.

Extra coupons for coal were given to district nurses as the fire had to be kept in all night for instruments and dressings to be prepared for the next day. A telephone was provided which could be plugged in to the bedroom. Off duty had to be arranged with one's opposite number on another district. A nurse was on call 24 hours a day, seven days a week, though not necessarily working all that time. District nurses cared for their patients from the cradle to the grave.'

THE COUNTRY CHEMIST

'In the shop window were large carboys with elaborate glass stoppers, containing brightly coloured liquids of red, green and amber. The counters and fitments were in gleaming mahogany and brass. Behind the counter, rows and rows of bottles and jars, all with glass stoppers and labelled in Latin. Below those were square box-like drawers with brass knobs, again labelled in Latin. They held powders and dry goods like sennapods, liquorice sticks and spices.

People came to the chemist for inexpensive remedies for their ailments and for cuts, bruises and other injuries, in the hope that they need not have to pay the doctor's fees. Any prescriptions from the doctor came to the chemist to be dispensed. Usually these would be for bottles of medicine made by measuring out powders and liquids which were thoroughly mixed in water. They were sent out in bottles with corks deftly tied on with fine string and then wrapped neatly in white paper, folded over and secured top and bottom with a dab of sealing wax. Each bottle had the chemist's own label on it with dosage and instructions. Most skilful of all, perhaps, was the making up of ointments. Powders, oils and liquids were worked into the basic creamy, greasy ingredient with a spatula on a sheet of thick glass. The ointment was then transferred into a round box. Tablets and pills were also sent out in circular cardboard boxes, always known as pill boxes. A record was kept of all prescriptions sent out.

The country chemist also dispensed remedies for animal ills, sometimes foul smelling concoctions and various pills and pellets to be administered. He was chemist, doctor and vet. Rhubarb and sweet nitre was a cure-all for country people and was in constant demand. Red ochre was purchased in considerable quantities by farmers and drovers for marking cattle. Large tubs, of Glauber salts and Epsom salts stood constantly to hand.'

THE LAST JOURNEY

'The same lady who helped at home births was usually also called upon to nurse the sick and tend the dying and prepare the corpse for the undertakers. Family mourning went on for months. Villagers at Burgh le Marsh would call to view the body in its coffin, offer sympathy and bring small gifts of food or flowers. Relatives would dress in severe black for almost a year, then graduate to grey and mauve. Where more than one death occurred in a family, they seemed to dress in black for years. There was very little help for those bereaved and times were hard for those who were left to provide for a family. Many poor and elderly people lived still in constant fear of the workhouse. However, families did support each other as much as they were able, and in spite of their poverty and hard work few felt really deprived.'

'The passing bell was also called the Dead Bell. When there was a death in the village, the bellringer at Market Deeping tolled the bell to announce the passing. The big tenor bell with its mournful tone was struck nine times in three groups of three for a man, and six times in three groups of two for a woman. There was also a toll for each year of the deceased's life. When a child died, the third bell, a much lighter one, was used. The bell could be heard all over the village and all would be anxious to know who had left the community.'

'The tolling of the passing bell seems to have disappeared from village life, as has the delivering of death notices. When my grandmother died at Holton le Moor, I can remember delivering death notices to her friends in the village. They were a simple card edged with a black border, showing the place, date and time of the funeral.'

'When council houses were first built at Ropsley in the early 1950s, with a combined diner/living room, people's first thought was "where will they put anyone who dies?" At a death in the village, the local undertaker came to measure etc but did not remove the corpse. He brought the coffin, having made it himself, about a day before the funeral. Funerals were walking jobs – a long procession would follow the coffin carried on a bier.'

'In my young days you could always tell when there had been a death because you could hear the coffin being made in the shed at the joiner's. The body was kept at home in the front room until the funeral. Funerals from Heighington were always at Washingborough because the boys' school was attached to the chapel of ease and it would have meant disrupting the school to have had them there.'

'Funerals were often grand affairs for the better-off. It was something of great show to have black horses with feathers and a hearse and cab. It was quite a status symbol to be able to say, "We buried him with ham and a seed cake."'

WEDDINGS AND FUNERALS

'The village where I lived was almost like being in a cocoon, there was always sunlight, safety, friends, family, rabbits and relatives,

A bridal gown for three guineas! Pennington & Son of Spalding would also supply 'family mourning'.

everything seemed to be there for my happiness. My friend Anne and I were rather like the old men in *Last of the Summer Wine*. After washing, dressing and eating, mostly lots of bread (home-made) and either eggs or cheese, we both hung about waiting for something to happen and most days something did, if it was only a ride on the hay cart.

But oh dear! I had a weakness for weddings and funerals. Funerals were the best, the Royal Air Force band coming in a bus, all shining and sparkling, the boots, buttons, gold braid and the bandsmen's shining instruments. Then the coffin draped in a Union Jack on a gun carriage, and all the way from outside my home to the church, young airmen and cadets, arms reversed, heads down. The coffin meant very little to me as a three year old, but the music, oh! the music, the grand drum roll, and the heavenly sound of the Funeral March, the men slow marching to church. How my soul sang, the first "live" music of my life.

It seemed to be all for my enjoyment, all outside my house, with its curtains tightly closed, and my mothers admonishment "not to look on grief". So when the cortege started to move along the road, we went on the other side of the hedge, leaping and dancing to this fabulous sound. We would then crouch behind the churchyard wall, and listen to the solemn words and the gunshots over the grave. We didn't look because I thought that was "the grief", so we stayed well hidden until all the mourners had left, and then we could dance up the road behind the band as they played what my mother said was "Life must go on". We would then spend an hour or so looking at the flowers, mostly ones we had never seen growing in gardens, and we would marvel at the colours and the way the wreaths were made.

Other great days in our lives were the weddings. This you must remember was during the war, when there was very little dressing up, tinsel or cake, when a girl in a white dress and flowers, even if they had been worn the month before by a different bride, had all the magic of Yves St Laurent, Hartnell or Chanel. We would get as close as possible to look, and to hear the Wedding March, prayers and hymns, and in great excitement wait for the happy couple to come out of church.

A big problem was caused when I, harum-scarum child, was on everyone's wedding photos – not just as an interested bystander, but in the main group holding the bride's hand, even my head between the happy pair, there I was grinning. None of my family knew about this until the mother of the bride came to my mother in great high dudgeon, to complain that I had "spoiled" all three of her daughters' wedding photos. I now understand her grief and despair and dread to think how many other photographs were ruined by "that damned kid", but they could never take away the joy that shone out of my face. I loved weddings, still do! I will go a long way to watch a wedding. I was 16 before I went officially, that seemed to be the loveliest thing I had ever seen. Now, funerals have become a totally different thing, but I still get a tingle in my back, and the smell of those warm days, whenever I hear that Funeral March.'

CHILDHOOD &
SCHOOLDAYS

GROWING UP IN LINCOLNSHIRE

Perhaps it is true that the sun did not always shine, but growing up between the wars in Lincolnshire we did have a secure and happy childhood. Times were hard for many, but we seemed content with less and found entertainment all around us.

ORANGES TWICE A YEAR

'I was born in Hatcliffe and started school there, one of a family of eight. My father was a farm foreman. We had such fun in harvest time. My mother cooked hot meals to take out in the harvest fields and one of the men would fetch it. She would make hot tea in a can and put an old man's stocking round it to keep it warm.

Then we moved to Barnoldby le Beck. We put the furniture on a waggon and horses. They put a table upside down on the waggon and my sister and me inside it and we rode all the way to Barnoldby with our dolls so we didn't break them.

When we lived at Barnoldby we used to play fox and hounds. One of us hid in the woods and the rest had to find them, but all the farm men used to play with us so we all enjoyed ourselves.

We only had oranges twice a year, at Christmas and in the summer when a beggar came selling them. We called him Orange Billy. Mother gave him a dinner and he would give her another orange. We only had half of one, we had to share everything. My mother could cut a boiled egg in half very well. We used to take turns in what plate it was cut on so you got a bit more yolk.

We all had jobs to do on a Saturday before we went to play. I had to scrub the toilet seat and flour the fire shovel, handle and brush. We had over two miles to walk to school, and three fields before we got to the village.

I remember when Woolworths opened in Grimsby, my mother bought us a flask for sixpence so we could have a hot drink at school for dinner. We were so excited we had drinks before we got to school to see if it was still hot. When dinner time came there was none left.

We never answered our mother or father back. She had a piece of strap hung up by the mantlepiece. When she went for that you had gone. We would say it wasn't me, she would say that will do for when it is, but we all had a wonderful mother.

May week was a big week when farm men would have a week's

holiday and change jobs. Mother always stuffed the chine, she told us it was tradition to have it and rook pie, which I still do now. Mother and Father were married in May week and for their reception they had roast beef, stuffed chine and rook pie.

I wonder how many children kneel before their father to say a prayer before going up to bed, we all had to.'

NEVER BORED

'How did we manage not to die of boredom, we who were young children in the 1930s and early 1940s? The tedium of growing up in rural Lincolnshire with not even the merest thought of a computer in our young minds, no television and in the early days, not even a wireless.

We used our legs much more than children do today; with just over three quarters of a mile each way to school or back, we had to. After lessons we made our way home, first along the village street, then over a five-barred gate, through a grass field, over a stile and along a narrow footpath with farm crops growing alongside. All this was very pleasant on a lovely summer's day, but not so good when it was pouring with rain and water squelching in your shoes.

Children in our day had much more freedom of movement. Many's the time I went wandering round our fields, some with high hedges and not a house to be seen, often with one of our pet cats, who just loved to go for a walk with me. In summer friends and I made mud pies, swung over five-barred gates, climbed straw stacks when partly used and slid down them, and used trees as our climbing frames. My father bought us an old wooden pigsty with a thatched roof to play in. After my elder sister and her friend had worked very hard on it and a kind gentleman put a window in it, we spent many happy hours playing there in the corner of our stackyard.

One day during the war years our father bought us a brougham cab, which had previously been used in Gainsborough for taking people to funerals in style. The cab was beautiful, its exterior being in black and green, while inside it was done with thick buttoned upholstery, and a green carpet on the floor. There was room for two adults to sit side by side in the direction they were travelling, and two children to sit on a hinged seat facing them. The windows were very interesting too, one either side, each having a leather strap which pulled up and down like those on the old-fashioned steam trains used to. Father purchased the cab for £2 from a local auction, later when it was showing signs of deterioration, he sold it for the princely sum of £4. We never even had a photograph of our very unusual playhouse which gave us many happy hours.

The wide drain which was very near to our house was always a source of interest. In the spring we would look for small fishes, eels, and most interesting of all, the toads. In the summer celandines grew along the banks. When it was brimming full, sometimes my brother would row up and down it with an old salting tub, and once during a very hard winter, ice hockey was played on its frozen surface.

On Saturdays we had a penny for pocket money, this was greatly looked forward to and mostly spent on sweets at one of the five village shops.

On a Sunday we usually went to Sunday school both morning and afternoon as did many of our peers. Once a year it was our Sunday school Anniversary, when we were all given recitations to learn for the Palm Sunday. On the following Good Friday the chapel gave us a tea in the schoolroom, after which we all said a poem of our own choice. We were quite poor but even so Mother always found money for a new dress and shoes for this special occasion.'

OVERWHELMED BY THE GENEROSITY OF NATURE

'I grew up in Horncastle during and after the Second World War. Each year seemed to be dominated by the harvest. There was an arable field behind our house and I used to go with my grandfather to help with the harvesting. When we started going away on holiday after the war, as soon as I got home I would go straight away up the back garden to make sure that the field had not been cut – but I never hurried, in case it had. The odd year when some other crop was planted was a grave disappointment.

For a long time two horses, a grey called Prince and a chestnut called Charlie, pulled the binder that cut the corn and tied it in sheaves. When I was very small I was held up to see them in their stalls; their great heads seemed to be as long as I was.

As the binder cut round and round the field and the square of standing corn grew smaller, rabbits would run from their shelter and be killed to make a delicious pie. Then the sheaves would be propped up three against three to make stooks so that the corn could dry. Once, at sunset, I stood at the top of the field and saw the pattern of stooks, each with its shadow; as I ran down the field I seemed to fly.

When the sheaves had dried they were tossed on to a growing stack on the cart, Prince and Charlie stopping by each stook without any command; then they were taken away to be dustily threshed – a noisy operation that I watched from a distance. I would go with my grandmother to glean grain to feed the chickens for many months.

I was almost overwhelmed by the generosity of nature, beginning in the spring when there were snowdrops, coltsfoot, aconites, and

A brother and sister from Swineshead, dressed in their best for the camera in 1920.

violets (which reappeared just in one place year after year). And so throughout the year this wonderful free garden that needed no labour. We also found plenty of free food – young hawthorn leaves which tasted as lovely as they look (although I can't bring myself to taste them now!); sweet nectar sucked from dead-nettle flowers; the nutty seeds of mallow; beech masts which we only found some years; crab apples and wild plums; and of course brambles. These were official, as the whole family went out gathering them so that when we returned home Mother could cook a blackberry cake. The only disappointment were the bitter sloes – several years I was tricked into eating them by older children because I couldn't believe that such delicious looking fruit could be so sour!

We took a picnic when we went blackberrying: picnics were another highlight. Sometimes we went in the car, but I enjoyed it more when we all cycled – although I had to pedal very hard on my tricycle to keep up. Sometimes I went with friends or my sister; I am so glad that my own children were able to go off together with a picnic to explore the countryside when *they* were eight and nine years old. I don't think my grandchildren will. But the best picnics of all were when I went on early Sunday morning cycle rides with my grandma and we took a picnic breakfast; we never saw or heard a vehicle, only the birds and the bees and the breeze in the leaves and it seemed as if we were the only people in the world.

My world did not need to extend very far. I could walk down past the station, which was still used and had a W.H. Smith's in the booking hall, and along the river, across the stanch, by the place where we went to paddle, and across to the town. It wasn't full of antiques shops then but useful shops such as bakers, butchers, grocers (all of whom delivered orders) and sweet shops – I remember having ice cream for the first time, made in a little shop off the Market Place, served on a biscuit. In the grocer's there was glass squares, protecting patterned displays of biscuits which weren't available during the war. I took all the ration books, the bread units and clothes coupons to be part of normal life and I can still remember going to Lincoln the day sweets came off the ration and seeing counters in Marks & Spencer piled high with bags of sweets. Sometimes I still look round supermarkets and marvel at the amount of things on sale and the freedom to buy what you want – if you can afford to.

Rationing continued on into the 1950s, when I grew up or the world changed. When *Rock Around the Clock* came to Lincoln there were photographs in the paper of teenagers rioting all over the city – until somebody noticed that it was the same teenagers posing in each place. There are still several cinemas in Lincoln. I don't know when the Victory Cinema in Horncastle closed, but I remember going to watch films there – and the boys outside asking to go in with strangers, to bypass the eagle eye of the cashier.

I don't remember if there was a coffee bar in Horncastle but there was one near Woolworth's in Lincoln which sold the frothy coffee that was *the* drink for teenagers, and, with the novel juke boxes, the coffee bars gave teenagers a more salubrious meeting place than the public houses where they meet nowadays. But my teenage years weren't such fun as my childhood – nor did they seem to last so long.'

THE CITY BEWILDERED ME

'One of my earliest memories was of Christmas 1926 when I was four years old. Life on a smallholding at Brattleby was not very prosperous, the first Christmas tree I remember was a bunch of holly hanging from a bacon hook in the kitchen ceiling. And Father's sock I hung up for Santa was filled with an orange and some nuts.

I enjoyed being in the country with the animals and collecting wild flowers in the meadows. I had the occasional trip to Lincoln on the carrier of my mother's bike but the city bewildered me. I never did get to ride on the trams in the High Street. If there was a crate of chickens to go to Lincoln market the carrier would take them on his bus. Indeed, he took many things on that bus, even my billy goat when he fell from favour for butting me over.

My next Christmas was much more exciting as an aunt gave me an old artificial Christmas tree complete with some trimmings; I still have one glass ball left today, it must be 75 years old.

I started Scampton school when I was six years old because of a bad attack of whooping cough. My grandmother made me some stays and a black plushy coat from one of her old ones, truly a labour of love. A pair of black lace-up boots completed the outfit. Off I went to school on the service bus, the fare was twopence but we had to walk home. We learnt our tables parrot fashion but, my word, I never forgot them.'

DOLLS AND WOODBINES

'My twin and I were born on 8th February 1922, the fourth and fifth children in a family of eight, seven of whom survived. When two of the children caught whooping cough the baby caught it too and died, the family were devastated.

On a Sunday afternoon we went visiting in the village and woe betide you if you spoiled your Sunday clothes. Sometimes we were given a penny. It was lovely when we had saved up sixpence, we could go and spend it at the Village Shop. One day my sister and

I each bought a celluloid doll. They were completely naked but wrapped in tissue paper. When we got home I went to the toilet across the yard; there were two holes so I sat my doll beside me. Alas, my sister opened the door and the wind blew my doll down the toilet. I ran to tell Grandma who said, "There, you've done it now." However, after tea my uncle took pity on me and got it out with long brass tongs. Grandma washed it in disinfectant before giving it back to me.

At home in Dunston we often wandered down the green lanes. There was always something provided by Mother Nature for us to collect. Sometimes my brothers came home with water hens' eggs for tea. At Washingborough we once saved up till we had enough to buy five Woodbines from the machine outside the post office. Sitting in the summerhouse with my friend we tried to smoke but on hearing Uncle's footsteps we put them under the seat among the dead autumn leaves. When the smoke began to rise, Uncle pulled them out with his walking stick and put out the fire.

One day the school organised a trip to Liverpool to look round a luxury liner, the *Duchess of Bedford*, and the cathedral. We longed to go but there was no way my parents could afford it. My sister talked about it in bed that night and the next morning we went to see Farmer Applewhite in Fen Lane to ask him if we could pick potatoes on his land for a few days. He said we could try but it was much too hard work for us kids. Our Mum didn't want us to do it either but we were determined. We stuck it for two hard weeks, earning £1 each. We were rich and were able to go to Liverpool with our teachers and friends. What an exciting but tiring day, hard earned but long remembered.'

WE LIVED IN ISOLATION

'I was five years old and my sisters were three and seven when we went to live down a lonely lane near the gravel quarries, where my father worked. I was stubborn, quick tempered and naughty. I exasperated both my father and my mother with my determined nature and daring behaviour. I had a strong sense of adventure for my age and I was sturdy and agile. My hair was as unruly as my nature, so it was scraped back into two plaits and tied with ribbons.

My younger sister was a bonny toddler, she had a sweet round face, fair curly hair and was stockily built. My elder sister was the kindest, gentlest person I knew. Although she was thin, with straight fair hair, and looked as if a slight wind would blow her over, she was tough enough when it came to protecting us from outsiders. This she did unfailingly, all the scrapes I got us into, she managed to get us out of.

My mother, who was loving and patient, found us a handful. But when we moved to live out in the countryside she knew we would have plenty of spare space to run around in, to be free and to grow up happily. Little did she know the strong bonds which would grow around us in the years we spent in our wilderness home.

For a wilderness it really was, the gravel quarries having filled with water over the years to become a natural home for birds, insects and small animals. Beyond them the fields and woods stretched as far as we could see, with only the railway line cutting its way through the trees and bushes. Tall willows, alders and the beautiful flowering rushes grew around the silvery water's edge. In summer the whole scene was painted a blazing yellow with the blossoms of the broom and the air was rich with heavily scented gorse flowers. Skylarks sang their long unbroken songs, rising high into the air, circling, then drifting down, filling our ears with their sweet melodies.

On long warm evenings our father would guide us on walks to the places we could not visit on our own, for sinking sands and steep-sided gravel pits were not ideal places for lively youngsters. Our play areas were well away from these dangers. We saw swans nesting surrounded by brown rushes. Kingfishers darted from the steep rat-proof banks, swooping low over the water, a flash of brilliant green and blue light. Dragonflies and water beetles glided noiselessly over the rippling water. Rabbits scuttled into the long grass, water voles "plopped" into the water as we approached. Peeping through the tall bulrushes we glimpsed herons, ducks and wild geese busy at their task of catching fish.

As dusk fell we would make our way wearily down the winding pathways to our home in the clearing. We tried to arrive back there around 8.15 because at that time the Royal Mail train would steam past hooting loudly. This was the cue for us to join hands and dance round in a circle, singing a song my elder sister had created for this occasion.

Then as owls started calling out, dusk turned to dark, and as the night fell we took to the safety of our strange home. Strange it was, for our home had been made from the carriages that steam trains had pulled along years ago. Two carriages adjoining stood on large wheels which had sunk slightly into the ground. Five large wooden steps took you up to the door. The wooden door and outside wooden walls had been brightly painted and white sash windows had been fitted.

The door led into a cosy living room, and to the right of this was a small kitchen with a stove, sink and cupboards from floor to ceiling. To the left of the living room, leading on from another, were three large bedrooms.

The Stickford troop of Cubs and Scouts off to camp in 1936. Many children found their horizons broadened through organised activities.

My younger sister and I slept in a large double bed, my elder sister had a high single bed which was in the room adjoining. There wasn't any door between our rooms, only an archway where a door had once been. Sometimes at night we would all clamber into the double bed and lie listening to the night noises, imagining the terrible creatures that roamed the quarries at night. We called my sister's smaller bed the raft, we clung to it as it floated across dangerous waters. Shadows danced across the ceiling, the trains outside would roar by, and when we heard these we felt safe. Our own train took us to many imaginary places. We would stare out of the carriage windows at our make-believe destinations.

We lived in isolation, it was us against the world. Visitors were few. When our aunts did arrive on the occasional Sunday afternoons, we would hurry our cousins out to see our treasure trove of hiding places. We had secret tunnels and hidden pathways through the broom bushes, only we knew our way in and out of. Our cousins would scramble to keep up with us, not wanting to be left out in the jungle of half light.

I was eight years old when we left our home to move into the village where we had been going to school. We missed it sadly at first, but then we each made our own friends, discovered new pastimes and grew up.

When I look back to the time my sisters and I spent together in our curious home, a deep feeling of warmth and contentment comes over me. All the happiness we shared, the dreams and make-believe we created, will stay with us forever. We truly were the Railway Children.'

A FAMILY OF FIVE

'We were a family of five children, so Mother was kept very busy caring for us all. We lived at Healing, in a house near the railway station at first. There were only a couple of shops originally, including a greengrocer's kept by a Mr Carrott!

While I was a very young child I made friends, as he passed the gate each morning, with the man in the signal box, a Mr Amery. He would take me with him into the box with all the heavy levers and I spent many hours watching and being fascinated to see the signals turned to the 'up' or 'down' position or to give the trains the right of way. He was called up in the First World War, from where he sent me a silk card embroidered with a Union Jack and forget-me-nots, which I kept for many years.

Dolls were quite a feature of life in those days and girls spent long hours playing "house" and dressing their little families, almost until they attended the higher classes at school, or went to a grammar school. Other games played were snakes and ladders, snap, old maid, draughts, and later "sorry" – mostly board games. Outside it was rounders, hopscotch, skipping, whips and tops, hoops and conkers in the season. As children we were able to wander freely over the fields without fear, fishing for struts and tadpoles in the stream and climbing trees. There was one old man we were a little afraid of and he would come over the fields from town collecting mushrooms, but I am sure he was perfectly harmless, and was seen quite regularly.

Holidays as a family were almost unheard of but as a treat we were taken by tram to the seaside for an occasional day out, packing up large quantities of sandwiches, cakes and fruit in a basket, enjoying rides on donkeys, helter skelter, lighthouse and big dipper, Punch and Judy, and there was always music from a piped organ which played all day.

We took it in turns to stay with a grandma who seemed very old to me at that time, even further out in the country where no traffic was seen in the lane except a farm cart, possibly, and I helped to "tent" cows in the lane, while they ate grass on the side of the road. The postman delivered mail on a bicycle and as the next farm was nearly a mile away he would blow a whistle when he was approaching so that we could meet him at the gate for any mail and to give him any letters we had to post.

The Grimsby Sunday schools were brought to Healing to the recreation field for *their* treat, arriving by train about 2.30 in the afternoon when donkey rides, races, and scrambles for fruit and sweets were organised. After tea they left for home and some of us children would stand at the gate with bunches of fresh flowers from our own gardens to sell for a few coppers which the parents were delighted to have to take home. I have since had a very guilty conscience about this, being one of those on the selling end!'

BUT TIMES WERE HARD FOR MANY

'There was real poverty in the 1920s. I have seen poor little children at Barrowby sitting in the gutter outside the food kitchen waiting for it to open, with very poor clothes and boots. We wore boots in those days, laced ones and brown buttoned ones for Sundays.'

'We lived in Skegness in the 1930s and while we were there my father lost his job. My mother took in lodgers to help out financially. I vividly remember the day we went to get soup from the soup kitchen and how I hated all the questions that were asked. After this episode my mother decided to make her own soup with bones from the butcher costing a shilling.'

'I got polio when I was two and they sent me to the Harlow Wood Orthopaedic Hospital at Nottingham to be sorted out. In those days the treatment was to lie down and keep still. I was strapped on to a basket-weave spinal carriage on big wheels – like a big tomato box with handles. I went to Sturton primary school for a year, pushed there flat on my back. Then in 1936 I went to a special school in Manchester. I had calipers and back support then, they were locked together but when you wanted to get up, you had to unlock them. Unfortunately my dress would get caught up and torn, so Matron made me a red dress with a lace collar, with only half a skirt so it would not get ripped. The boys used to snigger, "We can see your knickers." Bacon was a luxury, you had to be a prefect before you got any – other children used to beg bits of bacon bone to suck!

There was no coming home for the holidays then, so I did not see any of my family for ten years, until after the war in 1946.'

GAMES, CHORES AND TREATS

Games came in seasons and we all knew when to play with our hoops or tops, or start playing marbles. There were always chores to do at home, often without any pocket money, and holidays and other treats were very special to us.

THE GAMES WE PLAYED

'At playtime at Allington school we had to go out into the playground whatever the weather. Only in really inclement weather such as flood or snow deep enough to reach the top of your wellingtons were you allowed to stay in.

Whips and tops came out after Easter along with a new packet of chalks for colouring patterns on the top. The chalks were also used for drawing hopscotch diagrams. These were of two types, the ten-squared oblong or the spiral. Every girl had a skipping rope, which was usually a length of clothes line but if you were lucky you had a shop-bought one. The really posh girls had ropes with wooden handles with ball-bearings in them so the rope could turn without the handle turning in your hand.

Hoops and sticks were popular with the boys. Iron hoops were best but were not easy to come by. They were very difficult to start but once on the move they needed only a touch with the stick to guide them. The lighter, wooden hoops were much more difficult to control.

Both boys and girls played marbles and snobs. Snobs were cubes of wood or clay which came in sets of five painted red, blue, green, yellow and white. Every school seemed to have different sets of rules for these games.

Out of school, it was every child's ambition to have a bike. We used to go miles on our bikes. The boys used to make trolleys out of wooden boxes and old pram wheels. What happens to old prams now?

Cardboard boxes were favourite toys. The boys made them into forts and dens and the girls made them into shops and schools and dressed pegs for dolls.'

'When I was six years old there was a field at the bottom of our garden with a river running through. Next door lived a family with several boys, some older than me. They used to get the grey clay from the banks of the river and make clay engines. These had a chimney and a fuel box at the back with a flat lid they would put on. The fuel box was filled with "touchy" wood (this was soft, rotten wood) and then lit with matches. They would put the lid on the fuel box and, of course, the smoke came out of the chimney. I don't remember seeing anyone else do this. My mother told me that she used to tie me to the table leg with a scarf to stop me straying off down to the river when she was busy.'

'Many of the games we played were singing kiss-in-the-ring type, in which all could join. Even young adults played on the Monday evening following the chapel Anniversary Sunday. Many a courtship and wedding followed those meetings.

The last "Oats and Beans" I saw was at Tanoats, Metheringham Fen in the early 1920s.

> Oats and beans and barley grow
> You or I or anyone knows
> That oats and beans and barley grow.
>
> First the farmer sows his seed.
> Covers it in and takes good heed
> Stamps his foot and claps his hand
> And turns around to view the land.
>
> Waiting for a partner [twice]
> Open the ring and take one in
> Make haste and choose your partner [boy picks a girl from ring]

Now you're married you must obey
You must be true to all you say
You must be kind and very good
And help your wife to chop the wood.
Chop it thin and carry it in
Then kiss your partner in the ring.

All joined hands in a ring except one lad. They sang the above song and moved round the one in the middle. This was repeated as long as liked.'

'Vehicles being few and far between at Baston, and travelling at a steady pace, we were quite safe playing in the road. Skipping ropes were strung across the road with a turner each side for games such as "All in together". There were ball games such as "Donkey", when the ball was thrown against the wall of a house and had to be jumped over as it bounced; or "Catch" when the ball was thrown at the wall in various ways such as under one leg or round one's back and had to be caught before it bounced. Whips and tops were popular and we would colour the tops with chalk and see whose was the prettiest when set spinning, and who could keep their top spinning the longest. We would play rounders in the street, marking out the posts with items of clothing.'

'The more usual games played by my parents in the early 1920s at Bardney seem to have been whip and top, and hoops made by the local blacksmith. Marbles made of glass were often taken from the tops of fizzy drinks bottles, while others were made of clay. Hopscotch was played by drawing a grid with chalk on the ground. Humming tops some three inches in diameter were spun, producing a low humming sound. Some tops were mushroom shaped and when hit flew through the air – these were known as "window breakers". The girls had dolls made of pottery which had closable eyes and were dressed beautifully by the girls' mothers or a nimble-fingered aunt. Skipping was another popular pursuit, the skipping rope handles being made on a lathe by the local wheelwright.'

'When I was a child, going to the village school at Ingoldsby, everything seemed so cosy, so safe. There were well cut fat-shaped hedges, and paths in the village with wide green edges to them. I remember the spring evenings when we could play out of doors, and the roads were dry. Then out would come the whips and tops; these were of various colours and sizes and some of the boys could make the tops "jump" quite long distances. Then it was skipping and we played elaborate skipping games, involving intricate rhymes or songs. On long summer evenings we played hide and seek in farmyards, and it was great fun if we had tunnels between hay or straw stacks. We also played a game called "Tin can lurky" where you had a tin can on a large flat stone, and whoever was "on" kicked the tin and while whoever was "it" went to fetch it, we all ran and hid. If you could creep out and re-kick the tin everyone could go and hide again! We loved to play on home-made swings and see-saws and invented various games around these. Going for walks occupied much of our time. We used the old field paths and watched eagerly for the first violets and primroses. In the summer, on a Sunday afternoon, my parents would take me and a few of my friends to Ingoldsby wood. There we knew where wild strawberries grew, and we gathered enough for a dish of these each to eat with sugar and cream. These, together with sandwiches and cakes, made a wonderful feast, accompanied by cups of tea after the kettle had boiled on the primus stove.'

BAREFOOT IN THE STREET

'We lived at Waltham and my dad was a fish merchant "down dock" at a time when the docks were full of trawlers. Saturdays were very busy days dealing with fish orders, and my mother would pay a young lad a penny to take the two soup plates of dinner to my Dad and brother so they didn't spend precious time coming home to eat.

In the summer the women, with their arms crossed, would sit at their room windows, while we children played barefooted in the street: hopscotch, marbles, hoops and skipping ropes. What fun we had playing games and singing the favourite rhymes such as: "Rosy apple, lemonade tart, tell me the name of your sweetheart." We would stop at a chosen letter in the alphabet, then carry on to the next letter. Another was:

> "Eight o'clock is striking, mother let me out!
> My young man is waiting for to take me out,
> First he gave me an apple, then he gave me a pear,
> But then it was a sixpence to me he gave."

and then finishing with:

> "All in – a bottle of gin. All out – a bottle of stout."

In the mornings, straight from the bakehouse, there would be hot muffins for breakfast. There was the corner shop where we could get a "lucky bag", or sherbet, and for a penny, into your basin would go some cheese and bread. Happy days!'

A day trip to Mablethorpe in 1925. The hair nets worn by the girls were very popular and were brightly coloured, bought on arriving.

EVERYONE HAD TO HELP

'I was born at Yarburgh, at a time when farming returns were low and there was little money to employ labour, so from an early age all members of the family had to give a hand; being the youngest of eight, I was perhaps more fortunate than some but there were many jobs I had to do at some time between four and 16 years.

These included emptying the ashes, having riddled out the cinders for re-use, and getting in coal and sticks. The latter had to be collected from the hedgerow or under trees, as Father would not allow you to chop up wood – it might come in useful for repairs. Letting out, feeding, collecting eggs and fastening up ducks and chickens included attention to brooding hens hatching eggs – they could be very vicious when disturbed from their nests, so it was advisable to wear gloves.

Fetching in the cows for milking was all right if they were in the home field, but sometimes you had to cycle some half mile down the Fen road to get them – often they were very loath to leave the field and one had to rush around madly to get them out.

I had to help Father harness up the pony into the trap, when he was going to the market and unharness when he returned – oh, the agony of having to lead Ginger to his standing at the far end of the stable past the backs of the cart horses. I was convinced that one would kick out at me.

Feeding young calves with milk, or later a mixture of calf meal, in a bucket, was fine if it was only one, but if there were two or three together, problems. One would finish first then try to get into the next bucket, or become entangled with the handle and rush around with the bucket on his head.

One of the worst jobs was having to take the cart horses about a mile down the Fen road to the Sykes field. This necessitated riding your bicycle whilst leading Dandy with a halter in one hand – Daisy and Blossom followed behind; on arrival at the first field gate the bike had to be abandoned and you walked down a cart track to the grass field – by then the horses were becoming excited at the thought of a weekend's freedom and rest and it was extremely difficult to slip off Dandy's halter without being knocked down by one of the others.

Seasonal tasks included fruit and berry picking; brambling; taking tea to the harvest field; and early morning mushroom gathering (Oh! the embarrassment when at the grammar school of having to cycle to Louth on my way to school with a large basket full to sell to Manty Wilkinson the dealer; he drove a hard bargain and always greeted you with "They are not a very good trade today, I can only give you a shilling"). Before Christmas there was poultry to be killed, dressed and drawn.

Father kept honey bees, so in May one had to be alert for swarming activity. The drill was to rush out ringing a bell, which should encourage the swarm to settle in a tree. If, however, it left the garden then one followed on foot or bicycle and pinpointed where it was hanging. In the evening Father would don his smock, broad brimmed hat and veil, tie his jacket cuffs and trouser bottoms up with binder twine and collect the swarm into a plaited straw skep (a basket without handle) – the bees were then put into an empty hive. At the end of the summer he hired the extractor from the "beeman" at Louth. The full combs were placed into it and you turned a handle to extract the honey. It was then poured into jars and sold around the village. This was a favourite job as you were often given a copper or two by the buyers.

Churning day was a bore. The milk was separated morning and night and the cream kept in large glazed stone pipkins. The separated milk was used for cooking or fed to the calves and pigs. Usually once a week, the large wooden end-over-end churn was scalded out with boiling water, then rinsed with cold and the cream poured in. The lid must be tightly screwed down and then you turned the handle. Sometimes if the temperature was right and the cream thick, the butter would "come" in half an hour, heralded by a splashing sound as the granules of butter parted from the milk. This then was drained off and the remaining butter salted and washed in several lots of cold water before being made up into pound packs for home use and selling. Sometimes you could be churning for a couple of hours before it came and as this took place in the washhouse away from the house it was extremely tedious.

Despite all the outside jobs we still found time to help Mum in the house. From an early age she allowed us to try our hand at baking and we always assisted with the Christmas puddings and mincemeat. We washed and chopped mounds of parsley for stuffing the Whit Sunday chine, and cycled down to Saltfleet for samphire, which then had to be washed in gallons of water to remove the sand before being packed into jars with vinegar and spice, cooked in the oven, then kept until winter time to be eaten with fat bacon as that Lincolnshire delicacy – pickled samphire.

I don't remember being given regular pocket money, just what Mum could spare or my elder sisters, who were working, handed out. Each year I joined at the village shop Strawson's Christmas Club (they had a sweet factory and shop in Louth) – the aim was to have saved five shillings by Christmas. Oh, the delight of poring over their glossy brochure (only two pages, I think) and selecting sufficient boxes of confectionery for presents for my six sisters.'

ALWAYS CHORES TO DO

'I started school at five and by the time I was seven I had a milk round in the morning before school. I fetched milk from the manor, Woolertons, at Woolsthorpe and delivered to both shops – Simms and Burton's. When I was older I had to fetch four buckets of water from the pond late Sunday night or early Monday morning, for washday, besides my daily two buckets for drinking water.'

'Saturday mornings I had to clean the brass and the stair rods and fire irons, wash the back kitchen floor and run errands for Grandma, all for threepence.'

'Our next door neighbour had a red tiled floor, and before I started school, I went every morning to polish it for her, usually with a weather eye on the high corner cupboard where she kept the sweets for my reward.'

James Cullen of Billinghay tending cattle on Kyme Common in 1905. The wind/water mill behind him drained water from the fens into the river Skirth.

'We got our milk from White Hall Farm at Bigby and I walked a mile there and back before school every morning. In October we worked in the potato fields at Kettleby and earned four shillings a day to buy boots for the winter. Any spare money we spent at Alfred Kirkwood's shop – three caramels for a penny, and as we got older, five Woodbines for twopence.'

SIMPLE TREATS

'I often went with my mother and a friend on the bus to a park for the day in the summer. We took our swimsuits and a towel and played in the paddling pool, in the sandpit and on the swings. We always had a picnic of egg and cress sandwiches, cakes and pop, and returned home happy, tired and dirty.

As we grew older our favourite treat was a penny packet of broken crisps in a small greasy bag! We also had fourpenn'orth of chips from the fish shop with a bottle of dandelion and burdock pop to follow. Sometimes we went for an evening walk with Father to a pub and we sat in the garden enjoying the sunshine and a glass of lemonade while he enjoyed his pint.'

'We were a family of twelve, living at Blyton. Sometimes it needed a lot of work and pulling together to survive and get through the hard times. As the family grew older we were all allotted our own tasks, which had to be carried out or woe betide us. If we were caned at school we had to report back to Dad, who then caned us again for being caned in the first place. You can imagine that ten of us needed some watching and I remember one day, the family all dressed in their Sunday best and went to Blyton Feast. But they must have miscounted the heads, because I was left locked in the house unable to get out!

With things being so tight the smallest treats were a bonus. One day Mum brought a bowl of cherries as an extra treat, but brother John arrived home first, beat us all to it and ate the lot.'

MAKING MONEY

'My father was a shepherd. He used to bring lambs home to be bottle fed and that is how I got my pet, which I used to take up the road with a chain around its neck. My lamb grew to become a fully grown sheep and my mother took it to Sleaford market to be sold. A butcher bought it for £3 9s 6d. Making the sum up to £5 with saved threepenny pieces, my mother took me to the post office to open a savings account. The cashier had to be assured by my mother that I could write, and I was lifted up to the counter to sign my name. That was my first bank account.'

TREATS THROUGH THE YEAR

'Our toys were mostly home-made. When spring came we played marbles, spinning tops, skipping and ball games. We also sang country songs and played games accompanied by rhymes.

On May Day the girls at school danced around the maypole making patterns taught by the teacher. Girls would also come round Osbournby village carrying clothes baskets filled with wild flowers which they had gathered in the fields.

Easter Sunday was very special, we went to church wearing new clothes, and later competed in egg and spoon races. On Whit Sunday we always had gooseberry pie made with the first gooseberries of the season.

In the summer months I went with my parents and younger sister for long walks in the lanes and fields around the village. I collected wild flowers and spent many happy hours pressing them, arranging them in books, naming each flower and recording where and on which date it was found.

In July the village feast was held. A fair was set up in the market square with roundabouts, swings, coconut shies, skittles, and various other stalls which sold water pistols, balloons, windmills, sweets and rock. There were also darts and hoopla stalls. The village sports were also held at this time, and consisted of flat races of half, one and three miles, bicycle races and jumping hurdles for children and adults. The winners received prizes. There were also competitions for decorated bicycles, prams and waggons. Once a year a circus came to the village and a tent was erected in the football field.

Each summer, when my cousins came to stay we held a concert in our grandparents' garden. We wrote the little plays ourselves, made the costumes and rehearsed for weeks before the day of the concert. We invited friends and relations to come, and the money raised we gave to charity.

Oak Apple Day, on 29th May, was dreaded by the girls. If we were not wearing oak leaves we would be chased by the boys with stinging nettles.

After the harvest had been gathered in women and children were allowed to glean the remains of the corn. This helped to feed the hens and chickens which most people kept to provide eggs for the table.

November 5th meant fireworks and bonfire parties with baked potatoes, and going round "guying". I do not remember any accidents in my time. We went from house to house, dressed as Guys or Guy Fawkes. Most householders gave a penny or two, which was spent on sweets or saved for Christmas.

Christmas was very exciting too; we enjoyed waking up on Christmas morning to see what we had in our stockings. This was usually apples, oranges, nuts and a small game or toy. Mummers came to perform their plays in the village at Christmas, and were given drinks and money.'

THE ADVENTURE THAT WENT WRONG

'Great excitement! Today we were going on a trip to take a load of corn to the station. In 1930 that meant hitching out with the big waggon and two shire horses. Blossom, the steady mare was yoked in the shafts and the waggon drawn round to the barn. With the aid of a hickin barrow the 18-stone sacks of wheat were loaded, "Big Tony" my cousin winding the sacks up and carrying them to the waggon where Leonard the farmworker was loading them.

My twin brother and I watched with growing excitement as we were going with the load. This was the highlight of our holiday on the farm and at seven years old was a great adventure. Punch the other horse was fetched and the long gear attached to the shafts. We

At the village fete, near Grimsby, in 1949. Bowling required great concentration!

were lifted onto the load, and with a shout of "Hang on" and a shake of the reins we were off. Down the lanes and through the village all went well, but as we left the village to go down the hill there was a crack. A wheel had broken. The waggon lurched to a halt. There was nothing to be done other than unhitch the horses, leave the waggon where it was and go home.

Everyone wanted to know what had happened, as we rode home on the back of a horse, stopping off at the wheelwright's on the way. A friend of Big Tony was in the street with his motorbike. The trace chains caught the handlebars of the motorbike, it fell on Blossom's foot and she reared up depositing Michael on the motorbike. She then cantered off with me hanging on for grim death. A man on his bike saw what was happening and he threw himself off his bike, caught the reins and brought her to a halt. In the end Michael came off worst with considerable cuts and bruises, I was just scared.

We eventually arrived home safe and sound and looked forward to going to retrieve the waggon. It had been a real adventure – much more than we could have anticipated.'

CHILDHOOD HOLIDAYS

'When we were small children we spent a week's holiday each year at Ingoldmells at the site which later became Butlin's Holiday Camp. It was then owned by the Mastin family, and known generally as Mastin's Corner. Some guests stayed in the farmhouse, there was a small self catering bungalow, and on the field leading to the sand dunes were all manner of huts and tents. We stayed in the bungalow, but how I longed to be in the more romantic huts or tents. My mother disagreed with the romantic theory; I believe she and several of my father's sisters holidayed in these just after the First World War.

My father had a motorcycle and sidecar combination; he would take us one Saturday and return for us the following Saturday as he had poultry to look after and no other labour. With my mother riding pillion and my brother and myself in the sidecar I cannot imagine where we put our clothes and provisions. No toys were needed, we were quite happy playing hide and seek in the sand dunes with other children who came there each year and having competitions to find the largest hairy caterpillar, which were in abundance on the gorse bushes.'

'We never had family holidays, but every year in Allington there were two treats for the children of the village. In the summer the Women's Institute would organise a bus trip to Skegness or Mablethorpe; children went free but grown ups had to pay. We would save up all year for our spending money for that day out. We would run errands for a penny or halfpence or even a farthing. If you were lucky a farmer would pay a shilling a week for feeding his cows. Our parents could never afford pocket money so we had to work to earn every penny, which was hoarded for the annual outing. I remember feeling very rich one year when I had managed to save five shillings which I spent in one day.

The other treat of the year was the Christmas party given by Sir George Welby up at the Hall. We had tea and played games and at the end each child had to go to Sir George and sit on his knee and say thank you.'

SCHOOLDAYS – THE BEST YEARS OF OUR LIVES?

Schools changed very little until the 1950s, and memories of wet clothes steaming round the fire, inkwells and slates, reciting tables and long walks to school are common to generations of Lincolnshire children. The teachers often battled poor conditions to give us a good basic education.

SCARTHO IN THE EARLY 20th CENTURY

'At the beginning of the century Scartho did not have a school and the children from the village had to walk over the fields to Waltham, the next village, to either the church or the Wesleyan school. It would have been a long walk for the five year olds. The children took sandwiches for their lunch and drank water from a pump in the playground.

In 1910 the council school was built and Mr Holdsworth was the headmaster. The school consisted of two rooms separated by a glass panel with an open grate at each end with large fireguards protecting the children. These made a good place to dry their clothes on wet and snowy days. The children wore warm clothing with boots on their feet and gaiters in the winter. The girls wore pinafores over their dresses. There were two teachers and the children were divided into seven classes with the older pupils being taught by the headmaster. The teachers wrote on blackboards and the children had slates and wet rags to clean their slates. The younger children had sand trays and practised their writing with their fingers in the sand. The subjects they were taught were drawing, spelling, dictation, mental arithmetic, reading, writing, poetry, composition, English, arithmetic, geography, handwork, history, scripture and drill.

Children would be taken into the nearby fields for nature lessons and to draw flowers. Favourite games in the playground were football, skipping, hopscotch and whip and top.

Scartho was one of the villages where the boys were able to sit an examination for a free scholarship to Clee Boys Grammar School.

There were also a few dame schools. One was run by Mrs Sarah Brumflitt in her cottage, where the children sat on forms in the parlour and learned the three Rs and were thoroughly taught for a penny a week.

As the years passed and the population increased and transport became more widely available, some children went to schools in Grimsby and new and bigger schools were built in Scartho. One lady told me that she and her five year old sister walked to Wintringham school in Grimsby.'

A LIFE IN EDUCATION BEGINS

'My early school days, from 1904, were spent at Park School under the headship of Mr John Turner, where the three Rs were of great importance. He retired in 1911 when Mr G H Bird was appointed. He was the first certificated teacher to be appointed in Boston, after the formation of the School Board, at a salary of £70 per year. I passed the scholarship exam that year and had the choice of attending the high school (Allen House) or PT Centre (Pupil Teacher), in the Old Blue Coat School – Laughton's Buildings. I opted for the PT Centre, as even then I knew that I wanted to teach and hopefully in the school where I had been a scholar. At Centre, eleven to 16 years were the preparatory classes, but from 16 to 18 years for two and a half days a week I was taught and for the rest of the time I learned how to teach and handle children at Shodfriars school, for the magnificent salary of £10 for the first year and £14 for the second.

Mr Jacques was headmaster at Centre, Miss MacGregor headmistress, a young, enthusiastic person who taught History and English, and Miss White, Science. Miss Mac tried to make us into ladies, but we all loved her. Mrs Gray, whose husband was an umbrella mender, was the caretaker. I remember several of us being scolded by Miss Mac for fraternising on the school steps with Mr Gray, and Hilda Waddington indignantly stood up and remonstrated with her that surely "all men are brothers"? We were all horrified and a blushing Miss Mac, dumbfounded.

We wore no special uniform, only a tie, orange, yellow, green or blue, depending on the group we were in. The only game we played was cricket in the yard. Mr Jacques used to bat and if someone got him out we all had to go in for lessons, so the idea was to let him bat.

I left Centre at 18 years and went to Furzedown Training College in London for two years. It was 1917 and the First World War was still being fought. Places at Furzedown were greatly coveted. Mostly pupil teachers from Boston went to Lincoln Diocesan Training College but you had to be Church of England and attend church services. At that time I was proud to be a Congregationalist and so thrilled to be accepted at Furzedown. I had a wonderful two years there and left with the General Teaching Certificate.'

110

I STARTED SCHOOL IN 1911

'I had my fifth birthday on 23rd January 1911 and started to school at the end of the month. Children started to school as soon as they were five, there were no set times to start. The statutory school age then was five to 13 years. I remember I left school on the Friday I was 13 and started work on the Saturday.

The school day was from 9 am to 3.45 pm from Monday to Friday. There were, of course, no secondary schools so everyone stayed at the village school until they were 13 unless parents were able to afford to pay for their children to be educated at the grammar school at Horncastle. Anyone going to the grammar school had to cycle. I remember they used to have Wednesday afternoons off but had to go to school on Saturday mornings.

Whilst at school I lived in a Revesby estate house at Moorside, Mareham le Fen. I walked to and from school every day in all kinds of weather, often getting very wet on the way, and it was a case of staying in wet clothes at school when that did happen. I wore strong hobnailed boots. The girls wore boots too.

When I attended school there were three classrooms and six classes, ie two classes in each room. There was no partition to divide the long room in those days. The girls used the corridor at the south end as a cloakroom and their toilets were outside – near the school house. The boys' cloakroom was at the other end of school and their toilets were also outside, across the playground. There were no handwashing facilities. There was a pump near the double gates for us to get a drink of water.

The school bell (in the roof) was rung by pulling a rope at the beginning of each session. Girls and boys lined up outside their respective cloakrooms. Sandwiches were taken for lunchtime. There were no fancy drinks to take – we usually took cold tea in a bottle. We sat at our desks or anywhere possible to eat our lunch.

School was heated by large open fires surrounded by a fireguard. There was no other heating system. It was very hot sitting in a desk near the fire and very cold sitting at the back of the room!

There were six teachers at the school; Mr Eddles was the headmaster and his wife also taught. There were between 95 and 110 children on roll whilst I was at school. We sat in desks for two. The lids lifted up and gave storage space for our books. There was a hole in the desk to hold an inkwell. Pens and ink were only used by older children, younger ones used slates and slate pencils or books and pencils.

The day started with the marking of the register and then prayers and a hymn. This was followed by arithmetic, handwriting, scripture, geography, history, reading, drawing, English and singing. The girls used to have sewing lessons. Older boys used to garden. We had a strip of garden from the school lane to what is now the field. There was no playing field when I was at school. The boys' playground was at the front and side of the school and the girls' at the rear of school. There was no equipment with which to play, we just played tig etc.

The rector used to come for scripture lessons and would sometimes give us a test. I remember I once came first in a test! When the rector, inspector and other visitors came we always stood and said "Good morning, Sir" and then immediately sat down again.

Discipline in the school was good, there were not many very naughty children. Anyone who misbehaved was caned on the hand and if anyone tried to pull their hand away, they were then given an extra stroke! It was no use expecting sympathy at home because if our parents found out we had had the cane, they hit us too!

We could wear what clothes we liked (or had), there being no uniform. Our trousers were below the knee and tucked into long socks. Some of the boys' shirts had celluloid collars and these were most uncomfortable.

We did not have school outings and parties like the children do today but some days were a little different and looked upon as a treat. We were taken to church on Ascension Day and then given the rest of the day off. Mrs Eddles used to take the older ones for a walk to Revesby to see the hounds meet, once a year. We were away from school from about 11 am to 1.30 pm and once three boys took the rest of the day off (I was one!). We had six weeks' holiday during the summer.

I was at school during the year of the coronation of George V. Mr Eddles had been given five coronation mugs to give to boys living in Revesby estate houses (the mugs had been given by the Honourable Richard Stanhope). I was very proud to receive one of these mugs and I am pleased to say I still have it in my possession.'

THE BLUE COAT SCHOOL

'There was a Blue Coat school in Spalding until 1919. The school had only seven pupils and to qualify for admission you were interviewed by the Spalding Town Husbands (a charitable group). If selected, you were taught reading, writing and how to knit, sew, embroider and crochet. The pupils were admitted at seven years of age and left at 14. One pupil was given a sewing machine by her parents and was thus able to earn a living making shirts, trousers and skirts etc, with the skills she had gained at school.'

VILLAGE SCHOOLS IN THE 1920s

'At Burgh le Marsh the school building was of red brick, very solid and rather grim looking. It had an extremely high ceiling and the interior was painted brown for the lower half and cream for the upper part. Windows were high so pupils could not be distracted from lessons by outside activities – though I do remember our class being allowed outside to watch a very early bi-plane slowly make its way over the treetops. We sat in long desks, three or four to a desk, which had grooves in for pen and pencil and holes for removable inkwells. Timetables were very rigid, and because this was a church school scripture was an important part of the curriculum. The then curate of the living came one morning each week to give instruction and we got a half day holiday after the scripture exam.

It always seemed so cold in school in winter as the only heating was a large and temperamental black stove at one end of the one and only classroom. Strict discipline reigned throughout and the cane was in frequent use, but I was never aware of any child not being able to read and write at an early age.'

'I started school at five and walked four miles to school in all weathers, rain-blow-snow. Took sandwiches for the midday meal made up with home-made jam, or even chutney – no cheese, just chutney. A lot of people were poor at Friskney, and the vicar's wife gave her clothes to the poorer villagers, and frequently rabbit pies or an extra game bird.'

'The headmaster at Colsterworth was Mr Ball. He was very strict but fair. He demanded respect from children in the street – boys had to touch their caps and get off the path when they met him.'

CHALK AND TALK

'In the 1920s there was no public transport, cars were rare and not everyone had bicycles, least of all children, so scholars walked two miles to Stixwould school. First, there was the ferry crossing the river Witham, then over the railway lines. Punctuality was the first lesson. Several scholars gathered at the ferry, and were taken over to be at school in good time. There was high praise one day when we reached school, for we had crossed the river in an eel boat, rowed by "Dubby" North, as the ferry boat had sunk, and the Witham was very high and choppy.

Teaching was chalk and talk, for there was little apparatus, only a map of the world with the Empire in pink, a modulator, and two pictures after a scripture examination of St Paul in prison and St Peter trying to walk on water. The library consisted of a few books on a shelf, very small print and unabridged – *Around the World in 80 Days, The Wide, Wide World* etc. The infants had coloured counters and cardboard coins, and much learning was acquired by chanting the alphabet, tables and counting aided by a large wooden abacus. Slates and slate pencils were writing equipment. The slates were lined on one side for writing and squared for sums on the other, as were the heavy blackboards, on easels. There were a few wax crayons and water-colour paints. Following a visit by the "drill" inspector, Miss Terry, a box of skipping ropes and balls arrived at school, but they had to be used on the road, as the playground was gravelled. There was very little traffic then, so it was safe to play on the highway. Copper-plate writing was taught from the start, first on slates, then with pencil and paper. When Standard Two was reached steel nibbed, wooden shafted pens were used with ink from wells set in the desks. Some pupils were very inept with these new tools, with disastrous results, inky fingers, ink stains on pinafores, crossed nibs and ink spatters on pages. Special books were used weekly for copywriting from the blackboard and great attention was paid to detail and quality of writing. A page could be filled with "June is the month of roses".

When the school doctor or dentist visited, the infants vacated the small room and doubled up with the older pupils in the large room, so routine work was abandoned. Infectious diseases were rare, but there were cases of rickets and consumption (tuberculosis). Many eye defects were not corrected, as most parents could not afford to buy spectacles. There was no National Health Service in those days.

One winter the children gave a concert to raise money for a Christmas treat. Much was left to the imagination for there were no costumes, or scenery and very few props. For some children it was the only party of the year, and some needed that meal. In 1923 there was an outdoor concert, when pupils performed at the old vicarage. The funds raised paid for a bus ride from Stixwould to Skegness. For some, it was the first time they had seen the sea, or ridden in a bus.

In March each year, children who attained the age of eleven years sat the Lindsey Junior Scholarship Examination, regardless of academic attainment. If that hurdle was passed, there was an oral test at Lincoln, where being successful meant gaining a place at Horncastle grammar school, with books and tuition, until the age of 16 or 18 years.

Apart from Christmas and Easter, school holidays varied according to the farming year. A month's holiday for harvest and three weeks for potato picking were allocated and the dates fixed by school managers according to local crops maturing.

Most pupils of that era were destined for domestic service, or work on farms, but a few with more ambition and parental backing became teachers or nurses, railwaymen or members of HM Forces. Many of us owe immense debts of gratitude to those dedicated teachers who gave us the "Open Sesame" to the vast treasure house of learning and we still derive pleasure in remembering our spartan but sound early education.'

SCHOOL LIFE AT NORTH SOMERCOTES

'There were around 150 attending the school at North Somercotes in the 1920s. There were four large classrooms each housing two classes, divided by wooden partitions (the top half being glass), five teachers and the headmaster. The vicar called weekly, visiting each class to give religious instruction. Children living nearby went home for midday dinner, but the other children took a packed lunch, washed down with cold water from the outside tap. The infants and the girls all played together at playtime, the boys in a separate playground.

Reading, writing and arithmetic were the main subjects taught, with a little history and geography thrown in. The girls were taught sewing and in the spring and summer the boys worked in the headmaster's garden for two half days a week. There was an additional garden, divided into plots for the boys, the seeds being provided by the school – lettuce, radish, beetroot, etc, which they were allowed to take home, but the produce from the headmaster's garden was much appreciated by himself and his wife.

The toilets were in a large block – earth closets, of course, girls' and boys' toilets back to back. The boys delighted in throwing stones over into the girls' section as there was no roof on the toilets. PE consisted of the boys playing football, and the girls played at skipping and throwing balls. The "nit" nurse came round each year and any unfortunate scholar had to stay at home until the problem had been dealt with.

One teacher was known as Lacy the Lugpuller. A boy misbehaving or his work not being up to standard, Lacy the Lugpuller would drag the boy from his seat by one of his ears. Any really bad behaviour amongst the boys resulted in the cane. These were kept in a cupboard, and one boy – the most frequently caned – when the right opportunity came along would take a cane, make a cut in the end and insert a horse hair. This produced extraordinary results as the cane, when used, would split all the way down.

The boys all wore short trousers up to leaving school and their boots were studded. After the harvest holiday, when money was more plentiful owing to the harvest overtime, many of the children had new clothes and boots. The girls wore soft leather ankle boots and plimsolls in the summer. The headmaster complained bitterly about the boys' studded boots as the noise on the wooden floors was quite deafening, much to the boys' amusement.

Most of the children walked to school – a few had cycles. Those children living over three miles from school were not expected to attend during very bad weather. My husband and his sister lived over the three mile limit but in bad weather they were taken to school by horse and cart covered with a tarpaulin along with other neighbouring children. There was a four week holiday in the summer, but at potato lifting time the older boys were allowed two weeks off school for potato picking. For this they received two shillings a day. At 14 the children left school, most of them to work on the land, the girls to go into service, the more fortunate ones finding employment in one of the village shops.'

SCHOOLDAYS AT FOTHERBY

'Our village has never had a school, and in the early 1900s and before, children had to walk from Fotherby three miles to Louth school and three miles home in the evening, or walk along footpaths through fields three miles to Covenham school and walk home again in the evening. They all had to carry their packed-up lunch. If parents could afford to buy bicycles some of the children were lucky and arrived at school much quicker.

In 1919, when I and many other children were five years old, our parents with the help and encouragement of our Member of Parliament who lived locally, approached the Education Authority to provide some form of transport to take us to school and home again. So my age group did not start school until the authority decided to pay our fares to go to school at Louth.

The train did not leave the halt until after 9 am and we had to walk from Louth station so it was well after 9.30 am by the time we reached Kidgate school. On rainy days we arrived rather wet, and we always missed prayers and the beginning of the first lessons. At dinner time we sat at our desks to eat our sandwiches, during the winter months our teacher would make us all a mug of hot cocoa. Then it was out in the playground to play games until it was time to resume lessons. There was not a suitably timed train at the end of our school day, so we were brought home in a horse-drawn waggonette. It had wooden seats along each side with a door at the back. It was open during the summer time, in winter a wooden frame covered with a green tarpaulin was put on to keep out the cold. The older boys always wanted to sit outside alongside the driver. In winter time it was always dark when we arrived home.

This method of transport lasted for some time, then the Education Authority decided if we went to school in the waggonette we would arrive earlier. We had to leave home very early in the morning. One cold frosty morning near to Cordeaux Corner the horse slipped, the waggonette going into a dyke, but we were all more frightened than hurt. We then progressed to motorised transport provided by a local garage. It was a long narrow bus with a door at the back, wooden seats along each side, with the driver sitting in a small cab at the front who had great difficulty controlling the really naughty boys. The bus did not travel at a very high speed and it took almost as long as the horse. The bus did break down quite often, then taxis were sent to pick us up. We felt very important on those occasions. As time passed the buses did improve, but I cannot remember that we got to padded seats before I left school.'

AN EXCITING DAY IN 1926

'One very exciting day in 1926, several of us entered Denton school as four year old pupils. We had three classrooms, a headmaster and two "Misses". We were packed in like sardines. Both the aforementioned "Misses" are alive today and reasonably well, one now a nonagenarian and the other advanced in her eighties, so our antics couldn't have harmed them in any way.

On being introduced to the arrangements for the "little people", we were absolutely thrilled. The contraption was known as "The Gallery", and comprised a huge set of wooden stairs which filled one end of the classroom from floor to ceiling. We sat on one step and planted our feet firmly on that below, and the lap thus formed was our desk. We were proud of the issue of one slate, one small piece of white chalk and a piece of clean rag. The slates were really a very good idea, for any error was at once erased. The rags were in constant use!

The school's day was long compared with the present time, and we would play many singing games during our breaks, ie "In and out the windows", "The farmer wants a wife" etc. Some of the children walked long distances to school, and would arrive wet through and cold, but the school fires would be stoked up, and their outer clothing hung on the guard to dry.

We wore a great deal of clothing. There would be a substantial vest, then a fleecy liberty bodice (which garment would support black woollen stockings), navy blue fleecy-lined pants with two very useful pockets, a woollen jumper and a pleated tunic. There is little wonder that I have no memory of feeling cold!'

A MEMORABLE DAY

'One very memorable day an airship flew over Mount Street school and all the children were told they could go into the playground to look at it. I remember feeling very apprehensive about it as it was very large and very low and made a strange whirring noise. This was in fact the German airship *Hindenburg*, which flew over Lincoln on Friday 26th June 1936 (eleven months before its destruction at Lakehurst in the United States). The aircraft had crossed the Atlantic and strong winds had blown her off course. She was heading for Frankfurt and passed over Lincoln at 11 am coming from the direction of Newark, and then followed the course of the river Witham.'

EARLY DAYS AT STEWTON SCHOOL

'In 1930, at four years and ten months, I started my schooling, having already learned to ride my two-wheel bike. At that time it was an all-age school from five to 14 years, but changed to a junior school the next year when the seniors went to the town to school, travelling by bus.

There were two rooms plus a cloakroom. Heating was by tortoise stoves and on wet days coats were dried round them – steamy wool still reminds me of those days. Pinafores were going out of fashion then and I never wore one, but I did have a handkerchief pinned to my dress by a safety pin. I suppose they were too precious to lose. I always went home for my dinner except on pigkilling days, when like those who lived further away I took sandwiches. I did not like to hear the pig squealing or see him hanging from a tree. I liked to help bake in my fashion, and once when I was five I invited the whole class home for tea without my mother's permission, but she managed to feed us all somehow.

When free milk was introduced we had Horlicks to drink, the milk being heated on the stoves. We also learned to knit, but I found this very difficult and never did master the art of using four needles. Physical education was called drill and consisted of marching and arm stretching exercises.'

WILSFORD MYERS SCHOOL

'I moved to Wilsford with my parents before the war. Memories of this time come clearly to me, it seems incredible that it is over 50 years ago. My father was the village policeman, a tall, fair, giant of a man, or so it seemed to me. My mother was ambitious and immensely proud. It was decided that I start school at Wilsford

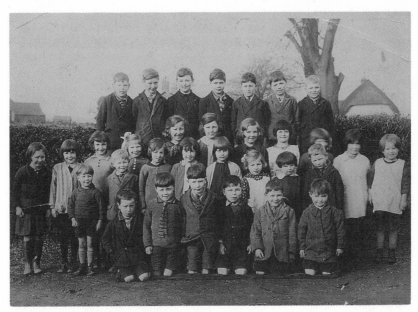

Stewton schoolchildren in about 1930.

Myers, which I have always considered my first school, although I believe I may have attended a nursery school before we moved to Wilsford.

The school was up on a hill to the south of the village, quite some distance from where I lived at "Town End". School transport did not exist so we all walked or biked. As far as I remember most of us went home at midday so that was four journeys a day. School Lane was lonely then, two houses only, right next to the school and a cottage on the south side of the lane, now demolished. "The plots" over which we took a short cut made the journey easier but once planted with a crop, country children did not cross it. This is now built on. I remember the steep slope to the Main Street and how we were warned never to run out of the end. Walking through the Main Street was no hazard. Cars were few and far between.

The school had two teachers, Mrs Stevens in the "big room" and Mrs Peggy Sheffield in the "little room". Mrs Stevens lived in the school house. The big room was for the seniors. Some remained at the school for the whole of their educational career. Some took the "scholarship" and the few who passed went to Carres Grammar School or Sleaford High School.

Nature walks in orderly crocodiles to collect specimens were much enjoyed, especially as the sun always shone! We returned with grasses, flowers, fruit, twigs and birds nests for the nature table. The ultimate deterrent was not to be allowed on a nature walk. Reading was from Beacon Readers – about a farmer, "Old Lob". Amongst his animals I remember was Percy the bad chick, I quite liked him!

This brings me to punishment. It was meted out regularly, usually I think deserved, and certainly expected if limits were exceeded. The big boys had the cane, kept hanging for all to see in the "big room". One seemed to have his fair share and the yells as the cane thwacked across his bottom could be heard in the little room (and also seen through the glass door). Needless to say a naughty boy was held in awe. The big boys put pins down the cane so that it split and rendered it less painful. Our punishment was "the corner". To this we were sent for minor offences, while a slapped hand and a ruler across the calf of the leg were the increasing penalty. I had the ruler once, the reason well remembered. Both rooms were heated by large tortoise stoves. I melted some plasticine on the top of ours. The smell was terrible, the retribution worse!

A country custom was taking a May Garland round the village on May Day. This consisted of a washing basket with a doll dressed very prettily and surrounded by flowers; a few pennies were collected. The 24th May was Empire Day, we all had to march past and salute the flag which flew from a pole near the end of the little room.

Oak Apple Day must have its origin in antiquity. It is certainly related to the story of King Charles and his hiding in an oak tree. Everyone gathered a stinging nettle and chased anyone who was not wearing an oak leaf. Needless to say there was a mad rush up the hill towards Kelby, where an oak tree grew. This was right next to the watermill, now no longer there. I remember gathering my oak leaf the night before in order to avoid those horribly nettled legs. Yes, we all wore short white socks in summer and three-quarter length socks in winter. The boys wore short trousers, the girls kilts or pinafore slips. Jeans came 30 years or so later!

Playtime was a welcome break. The "pit" was used for play, perhaps not so hazardous then as now. There was a cave where we were told there was a snake. That kept us away from there. I remember other fears. Bill Cook's bull, which kept us away from Waterloo Farm. I don't think any of us ever saw it. Then there was Ben Liddard's pointer dog, equally elusive, but it kept us from disturbing his pheasant rearing pens.

For reasons you will understand I did not fear the policeman! It was he who promised me a fruit pastille if I could recite my seven times table before we got to Ancaster. There were so many happy days riding beside him on my little bike as he made his progress round his beat. Naturally we stopped to talk to my friends en route so they did not fear him either. We all had a respect for the rules.

Wilsford Myers school provided me and many others with a basis of education and a preparation for life. I returned to the school in 1965 as school doctor. The school medical was held in the "little room", it did not seem to have changed.'

TOILETS AND SHEEP'S HEAD

'Immediately prior to the Second World War there were about 20 of us pupils at Cranwell, boys and girls ranging in age from five to eleven all in the one classroom. Our teacher was a real dragon and anyone who stepped out of line received a caning on the hands.

While I was only there a few terms, it was the toilets that made a lasting impression on me and I never forgot the odour! These were the old-fashioned vault type with wooden bench seating and were situated at the bottom of the playground. I believe that someone emptied them with a ladle once a year. There was no running water. A bowl of cold water, soap and a towel were placed by the entrance to the school – I cannot remember them being changed during the day!

At Sleaford County Senior School we were asked to make a special meat dish for Parents Day. Mother bought me a sheep's head for sixpence and the butcher took the eyes out and chopped off the snout. Mother showed me how to trim it and we put it in salted water overnight. The next day it was washed and simmered for about two hours, when the meat was taken off the bone and put through the mincing machine. The following day I took the meat and flour and lard and a round pie dish to school and on Parents Day I could have sold the resulting pie many times over.'

HIGHLIGHT OF THE YEAR

'The highlight of the year at Whaplode school was the school outing to Skegness, paid for by the school committee and organised by the headmaster, the local vicar and the policeman. The meal was paid for and consisted of fish and chips in a cafe. The children were also given a shilling for tea and a shilling to spend at the fair. They met at the school and then marched to the station, where their parents met them and looked after them on the train, which was free for the children.'

BINDO AND DICK-BOD

'Kirton Holme school had four classrooms, a headmaster who lived in the adjoining school house, and three teachers. Some lodged locally, though one lady teacher came on her motorcycle.

The cane was used on the unruly, a warning to others – and sometimes the culprits got more when they got home. In my husband's time there, boxing was supervised by the headmaster. The school day commenced with prayers, and a grace was said at dinnertime and a prayer at home time, though it was not a church school. Good manners and discipline were instilled into us.

The dentist's van came regularly, putting fear into most of us as you never knew when it was to be your turn – he was an ex-army dentist with little patience for children. The school nurse came occasionally to check our health and our hair for lice (her nickname was Dick-bod, because of the lice). A school attendance officer was another regular visitor, nicknamed Bindo, but he was very keen and liable to get into trouble with parents as he often went to homes where the children weren't even old enough for school!'

'ALL-AGE' SCHOOL

'The retired headmaster of Pinchbeck school remembers that 50 years ago it was an "all-age" school of 200 children between the ages of five and 14, housed in five classrooms. He was given the job of teaching 48 pupils in the eight to ten age range, housed in a room 22 foot by 20 foot. There were two small windows and the artificial lighting was provided by two 60 watt bulbs. There was a classroom either side of his, the partitions not being exactly soundproof, and he often had to compete with a class rendering *There is a lady sweet and kind* on one side and a class chanting the four times table on the other side.'

FIRST IMPRESSIONS AT BURGH LE MARSH

'First impression of a timid, delicate child of five in 1934 was this very high room with regimental lines and rows of desks, dark solid furniture which had already withstood years of kicks, scuffs and scratches. On each one was a small tin containing dainty shells for counting, later to be replaced by colourful counters depending on progress. What great glee when a child was lucky enough to be allocated new ones!

The day began with the calling of the register, with the teacher perched on a high chair at her desk. Everyone was in her sight and everyone was required to sit up straight with arms folded behind their back, thus preventing "fiddling fingers".

A scripture story followed; then sums, first on slates, then into small squared sum books with the emphasis on neatness being almost as great as on accuracy! Playtime was preceded by a beaker of Horlicks made by the teacher using a shining copper urn for the price of a halfpence per day. A visit to the outside toilets proved to be an adventure as well as urgent; to keep the door closed was an art in itself.

On returning to the classroom, writing first took the form of copy writing with lines indicating letter size and "pot hooks" to help with letter formation, all this with the blackboard in supposedly prime position but proving to be somewhat neck-aching for a tiny tot. Reading was sometimes a class ritual, individual attention a great treat.

Lunch time (still seated at the somewhat restrictive desks) was heralded by grace and consisted of tempting sandwiches and a piece of home-made cake or pastry, gobbled quickly otherwise it would be pinched. Everyone had to go into the playground after this with no supervision and a certain amount of bullying took place, general pushing and shoving around and taunts about attire. I remember one occasion of being "sent to Coventry" for several days for treading accidentally on an unfortunate snail!

The afternoon session was more relaxed with plasticine, pastel drawing on sugar paper, wax crayoning in white drawing books and modelling to suit the time of year. Story time to end the day I enjoyed most of all, *The Elves and the Shoemaker* being a firm favourite.

Physical training was a formal affair with teams of six to eight pupils wearing the still-used coloured bands, and one privileged person to be captain responsible for any apparatus to be returned to its box. In school a monitor was selected to give out pencils, paper etc and he or she would choose someone to sharpen pencils with a mounted contraption on the cupboard side. Imagine the favouritism possible with this order!'

TEACHER AND COOK

'I got a job in Alkborough in 1953 as the school cook. There was only one drawback, I had never cooked before! I followed the departing cook around the kitchen during her final week, writing down everything I could. I ended up being able to cook sponge puddings for 60 but not for two. It was fortunate that the school was very close to the vicarage, where we had a flat, as I often got into bed only to remember that I'd left the meat on in the oven and we would have to get up and go and turn it off. School meals were the norm by then and cost about one shilling and ninepence a week. A school cook then was able to write her own menus and order her own provisions. Meals had to cost out at tenpence. Once, when oranges were cheap I bought a whole crate. The children had them every which way.

My husband taught at Winterton and we eventually moved to the school house in West Street. This house was very old, with three storeys and many little rooms. It had water and sanitation but no electricity and we were glad to pay 14 shillings a week for it. It had been a coffin builder's, and in the cellar under the kitchen were the stone shelves where the coffins were kept. It was very eerie if you were in the house on your own at night.

There was much building of secondary modern schools at this time and they were generally well equipped. They were also a reasonable size, at 200 to 300 pupils. There were school houses for staff or preferential council houses to attract teachers. Salaries were low, about £44 a month as a starting salary for an honours graduate in 1952. The annual increment was at the discretion of the headmaster. Teachers were paid at the end of July and then not again until the end of September. You either had to budget wisely or go hungry.'

THE WORLD OF WORK

THE FARMING YEAR

When farming was labour intensive, and horses provided the power on the land, the years had their own rhythm which was felt throughout the community. Everyone would lend a hand at harvest time, and children's school holidays were planned around the potato picking fortnight. It was a slower way of life, but a satisfying one that involved the whole family.

SHIRE HORSES AND MANUAL LABOUR

'I lived on a farm on the Fens which catered for the greengrocery trade as well. Most of the work in those days was done by shire horses and manual labour. My father was the stockman on the farm, so we were with the horses from an early age. They looked so huge to me. There were chickens, pigs and two cows, one for suckling calves and the other for milk and cream for butter. Most farms were self-sufficient in eggs, milk, butter, pork, ham, bacon and chickens. The horses were kept in a large stable with a granary above where the corn and hay was stored. My father, being the stockman, had to get up at 5 am to see to the stock and get the horses ready for work. Modernisation came late to the Fens, so horses were used up to and during the war.

In the autumn when the crops were all harvested, the muck (manure) was spread. This was all forked into carts and spread by hand. This caused an awful smell for a while. The dilly carts were also emptied out onto the land. Fortunately this was not a job I had to do!

The land was ploughed by a one or two furrow plough, which took a long time. When the horses were ready, my father took a snack and off he went. My mother used to take his dinner down to him. We walked miles in those days. I often stayed down the fields and came home with my Dad on horseback. All the land was worked in the same way, ploughed, worked down with harrows, chisel harrows, discs and rolls. Everything done by man and horse.

Wheat was drilled in November, oats and barley in the spring. I used to go with my father to do the harrowing etc, because we had no play schools or baby-sitters, so we had to go with either parent. The chisel harrows broke up the soil ready for drilling. If it was wet, I have seen my father scatter the seed by hand from a big hopper he carried round his neck and just threw the corn about. If it was dry

Threshing time at Coningsby, a busy time for farmers. The boy on the left is carrying water on a yoke for the steam engine.

they could use a horse drill. Tractors were starting to come onto the farms, but the farmer for whom my father worked still believed in horses. The corn was all hand-hoed to get the rubbish out. When the corn got taller it was a job to see the labourer, especially when he was pulling wild oats at the end of June. When I turned five and went to school, I only went to the fields after tea. We all had to work, because when the war came all the young men went away.

The corn was cut two weeks before it was ready and put into stooks. A binder was used to cut the corn which tied it into sheaves. After about ten days, weather permitting, the corn was ready. For about six weeks horses and carts carrying the corn to the yards was part of village life. The sheaves were then thrown onto "mofferies", special high sided carts, with a pitchfork. They were taken to the yard, where I loved to watch the men throwing the sheaves onto the stack which was shaped like a house. When it was high enough, along came the thatcher who was a joy to watch. The stacks, lovely when they were thatched, looked like a row of cottages.

Later in the year the threshing machine came into the yard. Men on the stacks threw sheaves to the man on the threshing drum. He used to take the string off and feed the sheaves into the drum which separated the chaff and straw. The corn was bagged into 18-cwt sacks which were carried up to the granary where they were left open to dry. The chaff was also bagged to feed later to the animals. The straw, as I remember, was made into another stack until the baler and a batter came. The batter used to tie the straw into bundles which was used for covering potatoes. It was a very dirty job and everywhere was dusty and dirty. Then of course there were the rats! Two men and their dogs stood by to catch them as they came out of the stack, but I stayed as far away as I could.

It was always a happy time at harvest, men whistling and singing. Mother kept them all supplied with tea. Later, of course, the corn was let down from the granary and taken by lorry (our farm had one) to the mill in the village. The corn harvest was a very long and labour intensive period. Farmers helped each other in those days. We all had to help move the bales as soon as we could lift them. The first combine harvester I saw was in the 1950s.

The land was prepared in the same way for the potatoes, but ridges had to be drawn in which to set them. Setting potatoes was either done from a bucket or a chitting box. If you were lucky you would have someone to fill the bucket, otherwise one of the women did it. Chitting boxes required three people, two to carry the box and set at the same time, and the third to set the middle row. I started by setting the middle row. The boxes were left down the rows and as one finished you picked up the next. The potatoes were covered up straightaway. As soon as there was room a horse and ridger was brought into action. The rows were filled in by splitting the row in two, so half filled in one side and half the other. Thus when they turned round the other half was filled in making a full ridge. Weeds were hoed by hand and as soon as we could hold a hoe we had to help. Come harvest time they had to be picked, either by bucket, a "mollie" (a special kind of deep basket) or an ordinary basket depending on your age. As the farm was also a market garden, the potatoes for the market were near the house and dug with a fork.

The main potatoes were spun out using a spinner which spun the potatoes out six feet so it needed two of us side by side. When I was small I used to take a medicine bottle with me and fill it with tiny potatoes. Asked what I was going to do with them I replied that my Mum would do them for my tea! After the spinner, the hoover left them in neat rows. They were picked up, thrown into the cart and put into heaps, called graves where they were strawed and soiled down to be riddled in the winter. When I was old enough I also had to help with this. The riddle consisted of a tripod stuck in the ground with two riddles on top; a small one at the bottom and a larger one on top. The potatoes were thrown into the riddle, shaken and the large potatoes thrown into a hopper which held a one-cwt sack, which took some lifting when one was not very old, before being carted away to the merchant. The small ones were collected for the pigs. We used to take turns in all these jobs.

Sugar beet is a smoother seed and so the land had to be worked more. The beet was drilled in full rows, not like you see today. This had to be hoed out every seven to eight inches and then we had to single each plant the same distance apart. It was very back-aching! It had to be hoed by hand to keep it clean. At harvest time it was ploughed out before being knocked. You had to pick up two beet and knock them together to get the dirt off. This was hard work. The beet was laid in rows before we chopped the tops off with a knife and threw the beet into heaps. Then the beet was picked up by hand or pitchfork and thrown into a cart. I never got the hang of the pitchfork so I did it by hand. The beet was put into lorries and taken to the factory. Later the coming of the elevator made the loading much easier.

I have seen my father cut the lucerne and grasses for hay with a scythe. It was then forked into rows to dry before being taken to the yards and put into sacks. Later we had a mower to cut the grass and a turner to put it into rows. The hay was fed to the stock during the winter. Because the drill used for the grass seed was much smaller and the seed was fine, it was called a fiddle drill. Grass used for seed was threshed through a smaller machine and was even worse than the corn because neither man nor machine could be seen.

Where my father worked most of the beans were grown for the green market. The seed was thrown by hand and worked in. It was funny to see two or three men going up and down the fields with hoppers round their necks. We used to go with my father at night to pull what was needed for the market next day. The ones that were left and got old were dried for next year's seed.

Peas required a pea drill. Some of these were picked fresh for the market. We used to go and pick a peck of peas for a penny. The rest were cut and dried in heaps before being threshed in the yard and used either for seed peas or dried peas.

Being a market garden as well, we had all the soft fruits, strawberries, raspberries, redcurrants etc. We were able to eat as many as we liked, but we soon got fed up and just picked them!

We had to go to work to help our parents because wages were so low and it was a job to make ends meet. This is only a small part of farming which in those days was very labour intensive, and owed a lot to our good old shire horses!'

WE DID A LOT OF WALKING

'The horses always knew when it was drawing near to home time, and once they were unyoked from the implements they were impatient to be off, often finding the energy to trot. For them the day's work was over, but for the men there was still the feeding, watering, and grooming to be done, and once a week the horse brasses to be cleaned. Every farmer took a pride in his horses and liked to think that his were the smartest and best kept in the district.

Farmers did a lot of walking in those days. I can remember my father sowing the hay seed with a seed barrow. This was one wheel with two handles and a long box attached which allowed the seed to filter out as he trudged up and down the field. Another grass and clover sower was known as the fiddle. It was carried by the sower and was a box with a hole through which a slat of wood was passed backwards and forwards in a fiddling action to distribute the seed.

We kept ducks which would waddle in a line across the village main street to get to the dyke where they spent the day swimming up and down. Then they would waddle home again at night. If a vehicle coincided with the ducks' crossing time it would stop and wait patiently for them to get safely over.

We had a flock of 500 sheep which constantly required a change of pasture. My brothers and I would have to walk them sometimes as far as eight miles to an uncle's farm at Witham on the Hill. When we reached the pub we would hold them up and wait for our father to arrive in his old Morris Cowley car, and demand a reward of a bottle of pop. If Dad was in a good mood we sometimes got a bag of crisps too.'

KEEP PUMPING!

'The farm workers were always going to the pump in Cow Lane at Swinderby when they were thrashing (threshing) on the farms, with a water cart as they called it. It had a square thing at the top and they would put it under the pump and pump it full, as they needed the water for the threshing machine. When they had the cultivators, where you had an engine at each side of the field to pull the plough across on a wire rope, they would start at about four o'clock in the morning when it was light and you would hear them going to the pump to get water. Everyone had their own pump at home in their backyards but the one down Cow Lane was just for agricultural purposes.'

GOING GLEANING

'Late on an evening in harvest time at Market Deeping, some 70 years ago, as the last cart passed along the village street taking corn from the field to the farmyard, word would come that a certain field had been cleared and was available for gleaning. Preparations would be made hastily and the next morning, hopefully a dry one, mothers, neighbours, boys and girls would set off with old prams, trucks and hessian bags to the said field.

Whether it had grown wheat, barley or oats, after the cutter and binder had been at work and the stooks had been removed, it would have been raked. After that there was always plenty left for the gleaners. Ears of corn were cut or broken from the straws and put into the teemer one wore around the waist. This resembled an apron with the bottom half raised and stitched down to make a big pocket. When the teemer was full its contents were emptied into the big hessian bag.

Sometimes one made gleans by placing the straws together and holding them below the ears before securing them by a twist. Gleans were put into heaps and all watched to see who could make the largest heap. At lunch time all met together in a corner of the field and out came the jam turnovers, the apples and bottles of drink. Some of the adults drank cold tea out of pint sized glass beer bottles with their big heavy screw corks. Heads were protected from the sun and some mums wore men's caps. One lady always wore a pink sun bonnet with a big frill that went over the back of the neck.

By mid afternoon all the prams and trucks were loaded up and the trek home began. On arrival the hens in our backyard were given some of the new corn and they scratched and clucked in appreciation. From the nesting box in the henhouse there were new laid eggs for tea in return. The corn collected was stored in an old outhouse and it provided food for the hens for many weeks to come, plus an occasional feast for a few uninvited mice from time to time.'

HARVEST TIME IN THE 1940s

'The harvest usually started in August. The first job on farms around Boston was opening out the headlands which was done by hand with a scythe. These cuttings were then bundled and hand tied using straw. The horse-drawn binder followed cutting the corn, bundling it into sheaves and ejecting them in rows alongside. Numerous rabbits invariably took up residence in the corn, and the method of binding meant that they were gradually confined into a smaller area in the centre of the field. With the aid of a shotgun my father killed some of the younger ones, which were shared out with employees. Boiled rabbit with white sauce accompanied by fresh vegetables was a commonplace harvest time evening meal.

The next operation was "stooking" ie grouping the sheaves in a standing position with an equal number (usually four or five) each

Charlie Hutton, farmer at Tumby Moorside, in the early 1900s with his horse and horse-rake.

side so the structure allowed any rain to flow downwards and any drying winds and the sun helped to further ripen the grain. After a few days, dependent on favourable weather, the sheaves were gathered by fork, placed on horse-drawn carts (with suitable side extensions for a bigger load) and taken to the farmyard and awaiting the ultimate arrival of the threshing machine. Pleasant memories are revived on writing this of my sister and I perched on top of the load riding back to the farmyard and occasionally losing sheaves en route, due to the uneven nature of the track, much to the disgust of my father.

The final highlight was the harvest festival held in the local chapel, singing the familiar harvest hymns and on the following day the harvest supper and auctioning of the varied produce originally on display.'

THE OLDEST STACK?

'Farming was the main industry at Aisby and an interesting local story achieved international fame. Mr Selby, in 1881, stacked a nine acre field of wheat and vowed he would not sell it until wheat reached a certain price, but died before this was attained. On the outbreak of war in 1914, his son was asked to thresh the wheat stack, now 34 years old, and the grain "was found in remarkably good condition" and was bought by Henry Bell, millers of Grantham.'

DAIRY FARMING

The dairy farmer was often also the local milkman, with his own round, and was a well known figure in the town or village. He might be helped by his family, or by a dairymaid, and one lady recalls a life which took her from dairymaid to civil servant.

THE LAST DAIRY FARMER

'A. H. Martin, my father, was the last dairy farmer in Barrowby. Born in 1905, he spent all his working life as a dairyman. He started milking cows when he left school at the age of twelve years for a local dairy farmer, Mr Pell. Mr Pell sold the milk around Grantham. My father delivered milk with Mr Pell until he was 21, then his father purchased a milk business for him in 1926.

When he started as a dairyman he purchased the milk from local farmers. To increase his income he had permission to shoot and catch rabbits on Mr Wakefield's North Lodge Farm. He sold these for threepence or sixpence. He also went to local auctions and bought chickens for a shilling and eggs for a penny and resold them.

In 1935 we moved into our first smallholding and he slowly built up his dairy herd. He also kept chickens and pigs. At that time local people kept one cow for home use to make cream, butter and cheese. Around June and July there would be a glut of milk and these people would come into Grantham and sell their surplus milk for a halfpenny or penny a pint. The dairymen called them Cuckoo Milkmen.

When war started in 1939 he was not allowed to sell milk where he wanted to. The Ministry of Agriculture allocated zones to dairymen. His zone was Barrowby, Market Place, Westgate Grantham and the roads off. From the start he delivered milk from a pony and cart. Dolly the pony would also do light jobs around the farm. With the war came petrol rationing, and because of this cars and vans were cheap. His first was a three-wheeled van. At times during the war he would buy cars for £5 and just take the wheels and axle to make a trailer.

My husband joined my father in 1948. He did the milk round and my father worked on the farm. The land was mainly between Barrowby and Grantham, but he also had fields down the Vale of Belvoir. In the 1950s milking machines were introduced on the farm, but my father would still milk by hand. Relations would visit and the children take cups to the milking shed to be filled with milk straight from the cow.

The Grantham by-pass was built through the land that my father farmed. He retired in 1970, and although he had finished with the farm he still kept chickens and rabbits up to his death in 1987.'

£1 A MONTH AND MY KEEP

'I was born in 1915 at Haxey, one of a family of seven. When I left school I was paid £1 a month and my keep on a local farm. I got up at 6 am to get the fire lit to make the men's tea, and the horses had to be fed and watered before starting their daily work. I also fed the poultry.

After milking I would strain the milk and take it to the cellar. This was done twice a day – there were no refrigerators then, of course. Each time all the utensils had to be washed. Butter was made on a Thursday, always using a wooden bowl. I would shape it into half pounds and the lady of the house would put a special mark on it. All goods, including the butter, had to go by train from Haxey station to Doncaster.

There was a little jug which had to be filled with cream each day and they had cream in their tea. Any milk surplus was fed to the pigs. If anyone called at the farm for milk the farmer would sell it; it was not pasteurised or sterilised but just kept cool in the cellar. The milk that was separated from the cream was called old milk and it could be bought cheaply and used in puddings. A newly calved cow produced rich milk known as beestings and this was made into a beautiful custard tart.'

FROM DAIRYMAID TO CIVIL SERVANT

'I started my life-long career in "dairying" when I went to the Midland Agricultural College in Nottinghamshire in 1925 (it is now the School of Agriculture of Nottingham University). There I learned the practicalities of cheese and butter making as well as the theories of Dairying and Agriculture.

In those days part of the course consisted of six months' practical work and I went to a private cheese dairy in Leicestershire where I learned to make both Leicester and Stilton Cheese. Conditions were not very rosy for students in 1926 – I arrived on 26th April and did

134

not have even half a day off until August Bank Holiday! Working from 6 am and when the weather was hot finishing sometimes around 11 pm, all for my keep and ten shillings per week. That was the year of the General Strike and as all transport was affected we couldn't get rid of the mature cheese and finished up with every available space full of cheeses weighing at least 40 lbs. We even had them under our beds!

I then spent some time in a stately home near Nottingham as a private dairymaid to Sir Stanley Birkin. A pleasant job but not very challenging. I simply made butter, cream cheese and clotted cream for the family. There was a very strict order in the range of staff. Chef, housekeeper, butler and dairymaid lived and ate together. The head housemaid ruled the servants' hall with a rod of iron and was treated like a lady – tea in bed every morning! The footman and chauffeur, together with the under-housemaids, ate in the servants' hall, then the two kitchenmaids and odd-job boys ate in the kitchen. A staff of approximately ten to twelve for one widower!

I then moved to a farm near Grantham as head dairymaid of four, where we had a large herd of Friesians and Guernsey cows. This farm was one of the first in the country to produce TB-free milk and we despatched small consignments by train all over the country to rich families for their children. We also had several shops in Nottingham to which we delivered milk produced on the farm that morning, as well as Cheshire cheese, cream cheese and butter. To enable the lorry to leave the farm by 6 am every day, we started work at 4 am on two mornings and 7 am on the third. Great joy if the 7 am shift came after a dance! I stayed there for six years, during which I bought a car at the great cost of £17 and this enabled me to travel home to Carlton more frequently. My highest wage all the time I was there was 17 shillings per week, plus living accommodation and food. A colleague and myself made ourselves extra income by making and selling ice cream in the evenings and at weekends.

Then came the war. I moved to Suffolk (out of the frying pan into the fire) to make Cheddar cheese in 1940; for me a glorious memorable summer, despite air raids, fire watching and very good views every day of the Battle of Britain.

After some time life became too hectic so I contacted my old college and found that many jobs were available, and could not believe my good fortune when I was offered a job by the War Agricultural Committee to go round the dairy farmers in Lindsey advising them how to produce clean milk, so in the end all my hard practical work was paying off. As a bonus, I was asked to work in the Louth, Alford, Spilsby and Horncastle districts, so after a period of many years, from 1925 to 1944, I was back living in Carlton.

Eventually the War Ag Committee was taken over by the Ministry of Agriculture, Fisheries and Food and I became an established Civil Servant. During these years I was approached by the Dairy Council with a request to publicise English cheese and as a result I travelled all over the county giving talks to all kinds of organisations, urging people to buy English cheese.'

LIFE ON THE LAND

Farming employed by far the majority of Lincolnshire men and women in the past, many of them living in tied houses and bringing up large families in primitive conditions. These men were skilled at their work and proud of their abilities, starting in a hard school at any early age.

FROM AN EARLY AGE

'It was a bad harvest in 1912 around Coningsby and Tattershall. The fields were so wet that the sheaves of corn were carried on to the hedges to dry. There was little mechanisation, all implements were horse-drawn. Horses had to be fed, watered, groomed and taken to the village blacksmith to be shod. Harness was cleaned and kept in good repair. The "Stallion Man" walked his charge around the farms to serve the brood mares. Prancing along with his groom, the entire horse as he as known, had his mane and tail plaited and entwined with woollen braid in his owner's colours. This braid was about an inch wide, red, blue, green, yellow or white and was still on sale at a penny a yard in the 1930s, at the saddler's. It was a fine sight to see the Frithville stallions of Tommy Balderston being exercised by their grooms.

From an early age, a farm child acquired physical and mental skills unconsciously, as he or she was given small tasks to perform. A tin seaside bucket held water or corn for the sitting hens. When the chicks hatched, it was pleasant to hold the fluffy chicks and detach the egg tooth, which they had used to break the shell, from their beaks. The chicks were then put in a wooden coop with their mother, 12 or 13 hopefully in a clutch. Eggs were gathered from the nests in the fowl house, soiled ones washed, and counted into crates for sale. Weighing and measuring were learned from milk, butter making and baking. Sticks had to be gathered, or wood chopped for lighting fires. Turning the cream separator handle relieved an adult for other tasks and could be a counting exercise. Tending cows was a child's job; the roadside verges provided grazing, there was little traffic and it was safe for a child to be out unaccompanied. I was about four or five years old when I tended cows. This conserved the meadow grass. Potato setting often coincided with Easter holidays from school and children picked potatoes in October to earn money, often for new winter clothes.

When harvest was ready, the outside of a corn field was mowed with a scythe. I remember making bands of cornstalks and tying sheaves which Mother had gathered with a rake. The dry straw and thistles were not very kind to small hands, no weed killers then. When Bardney factory was built in about 1927 farmers in the area began to grow sugar beet, which was sown with a horse-drawn drill. The plants were too thick, so men hoed out plants at two-leaf stage, leaving space for the beet to grow. Children went after school to single, pulling out plants to leave one only.'

'In 1949 a young lad of 14 regularly had to be up in the morning before 5.30 am to help with the milking on the farm at Stickney. There were normally two house cows so that when one was dry the other would produce enough milk for the family. The boy milked one and his Dad the other. They had to be all milked and had their breakfasts before the farm labourers arrived to commence their work at 7 am. One winter's morning there was a light covering of snow over the frozen puddles in the yard and as the lad carried his bucket of milk back to the house, his feet slipped from under him and he fell flat on his back. Dad did not ask if he had hurt himself, he just told him off for the milk he had lost in the fall.'

'In 1928 my husband's family "flitted" from Sutterton to Kirton Holme, the furniture and some of the family coming on a horse-drawn trolley, Mother walking behind with the baby in the pram. His father was a farm foreman. At 14 years old my husband was paid seven shillings and sixpence a week, hours being 7 am to 4 pm Monday to Friday and 7 am to 1 pm on Saturday. Being a foreman's son, he also had to help in the night for no extra pay, if any stock was due to be born. At 16 years old his pay was ten shillings a week, and by now he was carrying corn in 18-stone hessian sacks and beans in 19-stone sacks, up the granary steps.'

THE MAIN EMPLOYMENT

'Even on a small farm like ours at Stallingborough (125 acres), there were the waggoner, the garthman and the shepherd. We had three shire horses and two waggons for working on the farm – the garthman looked after the cows and pigs and did the milking. The shepherd must have been Welsh because he taught us the old Celtic numbers for counting the sheep. The groom, who came in to the house for his dinner, looked after the horse and pony, and polished the boots and shoes, including my father's leggings.'

'I had an uncle who was a farm labourer living at Langworth with my grandmother. Come 6th April each year he moved from one farm to another, my mother and I assisting in packing their home onto a tractor and trailer. They moved in turn to Snelland, Stainton, Barlings and Langworth on a regular basis. April 6th was always a significant day in the farming community, when the farm owners settled their debts.'

'Years ago in Owersby and Osgodby villages, the men were mainly employed working on the land. There were working farmers and gentleman farmers, and their sons followed in their father's footsteps. The gentlemen farmers would employ a cook, housemaid and kitchen maid, as well as a nursery maid if there was a family of young children, and possibly a governess. There might also be a house boy who cleaned boots and saddlery etc, and of course a groom-gardener. Single men and girls had a week's holiday in May, May Day being on the 14th, and wages for the year would be paid on that date.'

'A horseman's weekly wage in the 1930s was 30 shillings. This was increased to 37s 6d in 1934, and to £2 0s 4d in 1938. He would have four days' paid holiday a year, and worked 14 hours a day, with one and a half hours' break time. The rent of tied farm cottages was two shillings and sixpence to three shillings a week. Women went potato picking from 8 am to 3 pm for two shillings and sixpence a day. Large loaves of bread cost sixpence then and small ones were twopence. Butter cost sixpence a pound and coal cost two shillings for a hundredweight bag.'

'My father worked on a farm between Ludford and Louth as a "seedsman"; this meant that he was next in line to the farm foreman, and his main responsibility was to ensure that when crops were sown the right amount of seed for each field was procured, the seed drills set so that the rows were the correct distance apart and that the seed went into the ground in the right density. In the 1930s all the work in the fields, ploughing, harrowing, drilling, muck spreading and reaping was carried out by horse and manpower, as there were no tractors in use on the farm at that time. A lot of my father's time was spent in looking after the horses, getting up around 5 am to make sure that they were fed and watered, and harnessed, before the work of the day could begin.

On a large farm such as this, there would be a blacksmith's shop in the farmyard and a blacksmith would come at regular intervals to shoe the horses. I have in my possession a rather tattered piece of paper on which the farm foreman set out my father's contract for the year 6th April 1930 to 6th April 1931. It reads –

27 shillings per week
35 stone bacon
House and garden
40 kids (bundles of firewood)
40 stone potatoes
Piece work – leading in harvest time

There is a piece missing but so far as I can recollect, it referred to payment of overtime when threshing was in progress. The bacon referred to in the contract would be from a pig killed on the premises, and large sides of bacon and hams adorned the walls of the living room.'

CASUAL WORK

'Most people at Freiston worked on the land, and many families lived in tied cottages. A lot of the casual work was done by women, who were paid by the day or by quantity, i.e. sacks of potatoes picked. The gangs of women often took pre-school children with them. The women were paid about ten shillings a day, but if the weather was bad they got nothing. All planting and harvesting was done by hand, as was hoeing and weeding. Large quantities of cotton waste was brought from the mills of Yorkshire and Nottingham and used as fertilizer. It became very smelly if left in heaps before spreading, but often contained buttons and needles which the bigger children would remove for their mothers to use. School children would often spend their lunch breaks picking a bag of beans or peas for one shilling, the only pocket money they had. Soot and farmyard manure were the only things, other than cotton waste, added to the land in those days.'

'School holidays at Kirton Holme were spent potato picking, and with the horse and spinner chasing you it was hard, heavy work for the few coppers you earned, which usually went towards shoes and clothes. We also went pea pulling – for 40 pounds of peas you would be paid one shilling. Women could pull 19 bags a day and mind their children in the fields. With strawberry pulling children were seldom encouraged as they ate more than they pulled and trampled down the plants.'

'Landwork for women paid about three shillings and sixpence a week around Hibaldstow. The workers were paid by the acre for lifting sugar beet, which had to come out of the ground complete with the tops on. The beet was then knocked on the ground to remove the soil, then it was topped and the beet laid in rows. When the tractors came along the beet would be loaded by the women onto the trailer. It was very wet work. The women were kitted out with wellingtons and trousers and had hessian sacks tied round their middle with binder twine. Children could obtain a blue card at twelve to enable them to go potato picking. Stone picking was soul destroying and back-breaking work. The stones were hand picked from the fields and put into baskets which were emptied onto a trailer. The fields were just as bad the following year after ploughing.'

'As gas and sewerage came to Haxey, the trenches all had to be dug by hand. The money was a little more than farm wages and there was a drift from the land. The men were not paid if it rained. They could not do both jobs at once so they had to choose between farm and trenches.

When there was no work in the winter the men would be put to sough ("suff") the pipes draining the fields.'

THE WAGGONER

'My husband was employed in the early 1930s as a waggoner at a farm in North Somercotes. The farm was owned by a landowner – a bachelor who lived locally but had a farm foreman, his wife and family living in the large farmhouse. The foreman's wife was expected to board the four waggoners, or horsemen, employed on the farm, also a single farm labourer. They were known as the first, second, third and fourth waggoners. The men were paid yearly, the first waggoner receiving £100, and second £80, the third £70 and the fourth £60, but the labourer was paid weekly.

The men never strayed beyond the kitchen. Access to their bedroom, a large bedroom with two double beds, was by means of a wooden ladder-like staircase from the kitchen. Each man had six horses in his care. In the winter the waggoners had to rise at 4.30 am as their horses had to be fed and watered before the men breakfasted ready to start work at 6.30. The men never ate with the family and breakfast consisted of the same thing day in and day out – cold, very fat home-cured bacon and bread, no butter and certainly no marmalade. It was the first waggoner's duty to carve the meat

Frank Foster and his horses on Euriah Spratt's farm at Scrivelsby in 1911.

for breakfast, and also for the men's sandwiches for their midday snack which each man had to pack for himself. They were given a raw onion to eat along with their sandwiches, but there was no cake or biscuits. They had a bottle of cold tea to wash it all down. Flasks didn't appear until the mid 1930s.

The waggoners worked in the fields until 2.30 pm and had to be in the farmhouse ready for a hot meal at three o'clock. Only the harness would be taken off the horses at this stage. For dinner the men were always fed on fat boiled bacon, with vegetables cooked in the same pot. Occasionally they had rabbit. This was followed by spotted dick pudding or treacle pudding. They were given half an hour to eat this meal and immediately afterwards they had to go out to attend and feed their horses. The time was then more or less their own until six o'clock, tea time. This consisted of bread and butter and jam, and usually a scone, this being considered quite sufficient, it not being long since their last meal, nor had they done any hard work. After tea the men went out once more into the barn for a natter and a smoke. The men were not given room to relax in the farmhouse.

All the men took great pride in looking after their horses and polishing the horse brasses – they were expected to pay for their own polish. Some of them used to buy oil with which to oil the leather. Also in the winter months the sheaves of oats had to be cut up for horse feed by a cut-box, turned by hand which the men always called "nodding". Much of this was done in the evening, and no extra pay was given for this. By eight o'clock the men were ready for bed. There were no half days on Saturdays, the men worked as usual until 5 pm, but later, when Saturday half day became the rule the men only worked until 3 pm.

Those men who could not get home on a Sunday were given a treat of beef or mutton for dinner. The family would partake of their helpings first and the men were passed the remainder in the kitchen. Consequently, if it happened to be a fat joint, most of the lean meat had gone, but the Yorkshire pudding was always fresh. On Sunday they always had Quaker oat pudding with raisins. For tea on Sundays it was bread and home-made butter, no jam – there was always a scone to follow. The foreman's wife never did the men's washing, it was always up to them to find some kind woman in the village to do this and they would pay her a shilling. It was not expected that the men would have baths, the most they could hope for was a good wash down.

The owner of the farm allowed one pig to be killed for each man living in the farmhouse. Seven pigs would be killed at intervals during the winter months, one for each of the waggoners, one for the single labourer, one each for the foreman and his son. The men always used to say that they bred pigs without hams as the foreman and his wife and family ate the hams and the men the fat bacon.

One of the most hated jobs on the farm was lime spreading. The lime was delivered by lorry and tipped into a heap in the field. The men had to fill the carts with shovels and spread it on the land. They wore goggles for this which they had to provide. The men's faces became so sore and red that they couldn't shave for many days. Another hated job was spreading what was known as basic slag. This had a soot-like appearance and was very heavy – coming in eight-stone sacks standing about two feet high. Up to the outbreak of war and only fertilizer used on the land was "guano", which was imported into the country in twelve-stone sacks.

Every man took great pride in his work. Every Sunday during ploughing time the men would cycle round inspecting each other's ploughing. It was not unknown for a man to suffer such pangs of jealousy that he would alter another man's plough making it impossible for him to plough a straight furrow. A man in harvest time would be insulted to find his stack had acquired a few props overnight. No farmer or his men, however busy or hard pressed worked on Sundays.'

IN THE FAMILY

'When I was a child growing up on a farm in Lincolnshire, I had to help my parents and life was hard. There was no refuse collection, so all household swill was fed to the pigs and my Dad used to bury all the rest that was not edible. I used to go about three times a day to the fields to check the stock and prime the pump for water for the troughs. I also used to help with the sugar beet crop which had to be taken up by hand. All handwork on the farm had its own special tool, such as the one which "thatched" the cornstack if it was to stand (pegging in the extra straw to keep it weatherproofed). There were winter jobs which kept the farm labourers in work, things like cleaning out the dykes, which was done by hand, or draining water from the fields. My Dad never gave my mother any money, farmers' wives kept hens to cover their housekeeping. I well remember that always at the end of each harvest, my Dad would throw his hat up in the air and we would all relax with a well earned drink.'

IN SERVICE

For many young girls, going into service was the only work available to them when they left school. From the 'big house' to the local farmhouse, servants were still part of everyday employment until after the Second World War. It could be hard and ill-paid work, but if you were lucky enough to have a 'good' family, it could open up a new world.

A DIFFERENT WORLD

'On my 13th birthday in 1915 I left Gonerby school. Although very young I was well equipped at reading, writing, spelling and arithmetic. I immediately went into domestic service at Grantham House. The staff consisted of just two of us, cook and myself, so that the work was very hard indeed. I remember that every morning the steps at the entrance to the house were swept and scrubbed before 7 am. I became rather homesick.

My second job was with the Public Benefit Shoe Shop in Grantham Market Place. I had to walk the three miles there and back, but in those days I managed this in about half an hour each way. On Saturday the shop didn't close until 10 pm; thank goodness it was

Sunday on the morrow. During the war the shop was extremely busy, but after the soldiers had left business declined, and I found myself out of a job.

This time I went back into service at Allington Hall; this was a large household and I was very happy there. The hours were long, we were on duty from 6.30 am until 10 pm, and our time off was just one half day per week plus a half day every other Sunday. It was my job to look after the bedroom fires for, of course, there was no central heating; however, the odd-job man did carry the coal buckets upstairs. Occasionally the bachelor Sir George Welby would hold a ball, when his two sisters, Lady Mostyn and Lady Dallas would act as hostesses. This meant a deal of work for us, with perhaps ten bedrooms in use, but extra help would be employed from the village.

At Allington Hall we were paid £18 a year, and out of this we provided our own uniform of print morning dress and a black skirt and blouse for afternoons.

I saw little of my family, but my brother Harry delivered the meat every Friday, and I would be called for a few minutes' chat with him, and that is how I kept up with news of home and events in Gonerby. When I was able to go home I did not go empty handed; there would probably be a rabbit or a pound of butter for my family.

The day came when I took tea to the men working in the harvest field and my eyes came to rest on a very good looking curly haired individual, Bert Hill, and we soon became friends. Bert was an engineer by trade, but had suffered redundancy in the recession of the 1920s, and was therefore working as an assistant gamekeeper. We would meet whenever possible, but romances were disapproved of in the big houses, this despite the fact there were three very separate staircases, one for the gentry, one for the maids and another for the male servants. I can assure you there wasn't any "hanky panky" in those days; we wouldn't have dreamt of such things! However, the relationship advanced, and one of us had to leave; it had to be me because I was able to find other work. Lincolnshire had to be left behind and I went to Bawtry House in Derbyshire, but Bert and I were married in 1929.'

LIVING IN ON THE FARM

'My mother who will be 90 years old this summer, can remember her life in service as a young woman in the 1920s. She lived in at a farmhouse in the village of Blyton. The household was made up of the farmer, his wife, their small child, two farm boys and my mother. She had to be up in the mornings at 5 am, light the fire and make the breakfast. It was an old fashioned farm kitchen with a cooking range which comprised of two ovens, a boiler and a fire grate. This range had to be blackleaded once a week, this was done each Saturday, and was my mother's job.

The farmer's wife dealt with all the cooking. My mother was responsible for the housework, washing, ironing, and some shopping, and also work in the dairy. She had to separate the milk and put the cream into a pipkin, for making into butter later. The butter was made on Wednesday of each week. It was then her task to load it into the baby's pram and transport it to the shop in the village for sale.

Wages were paid out weekly, and often the farmer and his wife were out on Saturday afternoons at the neighbouring market town of Gainsborough. On these occasions the farmer would leave a cheque with my mother to cash at the village shop, she would then pay the farm boys their wages and take her own.

She was allowed out in the evenings if the work was completed, but she had to be in by nine o'clock. She worked there for three years then the farmer and his family emigrated to Australia. My mother was invited to go with them and continue working for them, but she was very much a "home bird" and declined their offer.'

'I left school at 14 and was a housemaid for a farmer's wife near Friskney. I helped on the farm measuring out milk and making churn butter. I springcleaned the damned house all the week and then started all over again the next week!

A day's menu started at 6 am with fat bacon, bread, pickles and mustard. At midday we had fat bacon and vegetables, rice pudding and fruit in season, followed at 5 pm by fat bacon, mustard and vinegar with bread and no butter.'

UNDER-HOUSEMAID

'My job was under-housemaid in a large Hall. The staff consisted of nine and I had to get up at 6.30 am each morning to waken the head housemaid, the cook and the lady's maid with a cup of tea.

There were fireplaces in all the rooms, both upstairs and down, and in winter time I had as many as 13 fireplaces to clean up before starting on the bedrooms, which had to be cleaned out every day.

Also in winter time, if there were visitors to the Hall, I had to help in the unpacking of their suitcases, light a fire in their bedrooms and take brass cans of hot water to their rooms. The water was kept hot by covering the cans with towels.

In the evening, I assisted the head housemaid to put out the visitors' evening clothes. Dances at the Hall were quite frequent and we received good tips for looking after the visitors' coats. These tips helped to eke out our wages which, before the war, were very poor.

At Christmas time, the lady of the Hall would look after herself and her daughter. The staff enjoyed Christmas Day and the stable men used to come up for dinner that day. The lady then went away for a holiday whilst we cleaned her rooms. This was very hard work as floors had to be scrubbed – there were no modern cleaning facilities.

Any mending was done by the head housemaid and myself. This included sheets, towels, and I remember even patching an oven cloth!

We had one half day off each week – this was well earned and much enjoyed.'

'I left school at 14 years of age. My first job was under-housemaid in a large house; there was a lady and two teenage daughters – all hunting people. There was a staff of ten and all lived in. I had to get up at 5.30 every day, 6.30 on Sundays. I used to have four grates to blacklead; tongs and pokers were brass and were cleaned every morning. When there were visitors in, bedroom grates were used and had to be cleaned while the visitors were at breakfast. The young ladies went cub hunting three mornings a week so I had to be up at five o'clock as they would want their baths and breakfast at 6.30. Then there was the bathroom to clean and everything had to be all ready for when they came in from hunting.

I had to use a hard sweeping brush for the carpets, long-handled soft brush and dustpan and brush. There were no fitted carpets, just big squares so I had to polish all round them with beeswax polish and that was very hard work. The big front steps had to be scrubbed in all weathers. The servants' quarters were all lino and scrubbed stairs. I had one half day a week off from one o'clock and had to be in at nine o'clock in the summer months and 8.30 in the winter. We never had lunch hours.

We had three meals a day. Breakfast at 9.30, lunch at 1.30, high tea at six o'clock. As soon as the meal was over you had to go and get on with your work which lasted till about 7.30 every evening. The only time we could go out on a Sunday was if you went to church morning or evening. My wage was £1 10s a month.

I was married in 1926. My husband was a farm worker and our wage was 29s 3d a week. He had to work all day Sundays for the cottage and one pint of milk a day. I had seven children. The youngest was born in 1941 and our wage then was only £3 10s a week. I had to make do and mend all the time.'

'I started work in 1904 at the age of 13 as an "in-between maid" for a wage of £8 per annum, paid quarterly. The day started at 6 am and my first job was to scrub the front steps. After two years I moved on to be a cook for £12 a year and saved up to buy a bicycle for 30 shillings. I met my future husband, a waggoner, while I was doing this job and we bought a wedding ring from Ince the jewellers in Brigg, costing £2. The lady of the house gave us a counterpane and a pair of sheets as a wedding present.'

THE ONLY SERVANT

'Women worked in service on farms or in large houses from the age of 14. Around Hibaldstow, women were working from 8 am to 8 pm for three shillings a week in the 1930s, doing everything from the washing and cleaning to plucking chickens. One lady in service in a household in Brigg was the only servant and did all the household duties. On washday she had to carry all the washing to Scawby Brook, about two miles away, where the washing was done at a relative's home where there was a big kitchen and a wash room. She would spend all day washing and ironing. There was a table there large enough to iron a bed sheet spread out completely flat. The big kitchen floor had to be scrubbed at the end of a very tiring day and the washing then carried all the way back to Brigg. She was allowed half a day off on a Thursday (market day) but had to be back in time to put the tea on the table. She also had Saturday afternoon and evening off, when she could visit the cinema, but she had to be back by eight o'clock.'

TRADES AND CRAFTS IN THE VILLAGES

From the village shop to the miller, the blacksmith to the saddler, every village had its craftsmen and businessmen. These were busy and self-sufficient communities, providing employment on the doorstep.

THE VILLAGE BLACKSMITH

'Quincey & Sons of Bardney were the village blacksmiths, wheel-wrights and undertakers. Their work included shoeing horses, filing and pulling horses' teeth, ringing bulls' noses, making carts, cleaning wells, sawing timber by using a saw driven by a steam engine, and making coffins. The yard at their premises was fitted with a railway track (narrow gauge) for ease of transporting wood etc. It was said that on one occasion John Quincey shinned up a six foot wall (himself being a small man of about five foot six inches) in order to get out of the way of a bull which was showing the whites of its eyes – this being a danger signal! A local farmer owed Quinceys a sum of money and not wishing to pay in cash he handed over one of his pigs instead. A few weeks later the pig produced a litter of piglets thus increasing the value considerably – the farmer was not amused as he had no idea that the pig was pregnant!

The business changed from blacksmithing to motor car trading and repairing as the needs of the community changed. The family's horse and trap of the 1920s was replaced by a motor bike and sidecar about 1930 but as the size of the family increased (there were eight children in all) this was replaced by a car in about 1932. This car had a cab for two people to sit in, which was under cover, and a dickey seat at the back where three passengers could sit but which was out in the open.'

'At one time there were two blacksmiths in Wragby. One employed by the woodyard had four teams of six horses which he looked after and they were stabled adjacent to his home. These were used in the felling and transporting of trees. There was also a general blacksmith in the village.'

THE SADDLER'S SHOP

'During the time of which I write, commencing about 1914, there were three main places where the villagers of Owston Ferry gathered together in the daytime. In the evening some went to the pub but in the daytime the cobbler's shop, the blacksmith's shop and the saddler's shop were the centres where those people not at work assembled.

As one walked along the High Street of our village, on the right you passed the blacksmith's shop with the sound of hammers ringing on anvils and the smell of burning hooves as the hot shoes were applied to the horses' feet and burnt on to fit before being nailed into place. On the other side, a little further along, was the saddler's shop with its large window displaying boxes of

Billy Quincey was still working as a wheelwright at Bardney in 1950.

leggings (pigskin ones to be worn on market and special days, and a rougher pair for everyday wear), dandy brushes and currycombs for grooming, bridles, trap harness collars and whips, all set out in orderly fashion so as to be attractive to the eye of the beholder from the outside, and to be easily accessible from the inside of the shop.

Upon opening the door, especially in winter time, one would be greeted with a blast of warm air from the tortoise stove burning at one end of the shop, a fug of tobacco smoke and the smell of leather, wax, Stockholm tar and collar checks. Inside the door one stepped on to the boarden floor where on the right stood the small office where the books were kept, and on the left the long bench with a loose thick plank, about six feet long, on top of which the cutting out was done. Underneath the bench were three compartments, one for waste paper and legging boxes etc, the middle one a large deep drawer into which off-cuts of leather were dropped against the time when such a small piece was required for patching or for stiffening. The end compartment held rolls of various leathers stored on end, cowhide, sealskin with a gloss on it like patent leather, used chiefly for the fronts of traps, and horsehide, not tanned but cured with a greenish white look to it and salt showing in places, from which were cut whiteleather laces for sewing parts of horse collars and any semi-exposed part where it would wear better than hemp.

In front of the bench were two sewing horses. These were stool-like pieces of equipment mounted on four stout legs. The seat portion was well padded, and to the front a pair of jaws were secured. One jaw was firmly fixed and the other hinged. A leather strap passed from the anchorage in the moveable jaw through the fixed one and down and through a slot cut in the front part of the seat and pedal which was hinged to the left front leg of the horse and extended about four or five inches beyond the right front leg. On the rear side of the right front leg was a rack of strong teeth, and when the work was tacked ready for sewing the saddler, with the toe of his boot, tripped the iron pedal free of the rack which freed the jaws, these were then opened, the work inserted and the pedal jammed under one of the teeth in the rack. This tightened the jaws together in the form of a vice. The work could then proceed.

For use on the farms, where saddlers sometimes carried out work, they used clams instead. They were easy to transport being simply two pieces of wood about four feet long, so cut as to have a curve along about half the length. These pieces were fitted so that when bolted together they formed a spring vice. The tips acting as jaws were forced apart, the work inserted, and with the saddler sitting on a chair holding the clams between his knees he could work quite well.

When making the threads for sewing he would take the end of

The saddler's shop at Owston Ferry in about 1900.

the hemp, usually hanging from a drawer in which it was kept, pull off sufficient to pass around a hook fastened to the bench, take a few paces backwards so as to roughly measure the length required, then holding the double strands in one hand give a rub to the piece extending to the drawer on his small leather apron, worn over his white working one, give the hemp a sharp jerk and snap it off, then repeat the procedure until he had the requisite number of cords passing round the hook and held in one hand. He would then spit into his palm and rub his hands across the threads on his leather apron, and after a few turns the hemp strands would be twisted into the thread required. This was then well waxed from a ball of black wax for sewing black leather or beeswax for brown leather and was ready for threading through the eye of the two pointless needles which saddlers used.

The scene confronting anyone entering the shop on any day of the week except Saturday afternoon, which was half-day closing, was of the saddler and his apprentice working away in the shop, most probably with a small number of onlookers. There were the genuine customers who came in with a piece of harness to be repaired, or to collect a piece already done, and who stopped on for a few minutes to chat with my father, who was the saddler, this especially on days when farm work was held up owing to inclement weather conditions. There were also a number of village ancients full of knowledge who came along to while away the hour.

A FARMING COMMUNITY

'Scartho in 1900 was a farming community growing crops and some farmers keeping sheep, pigs and cattle. These farmers would employ farm labourers and some would have servants. The Drewery family were blacksmiths over many generations and Mr J. H. Drewery from 1903 held the ancient office of pinder or guardian of the village pound. This is where stray animals were kept. The Freshney family were the wheelwrights and built and repaired the carts and carriages. Mr Robinson was the joiner who did the repairs in the village and also made coffins. The Kirmans were dairy farmers and were the local milkmen delivering the milk in churns, measured with ladles into the customers' containers.

Scartho had its own mill owned by the Colebrook family and situated on the boundary with Grimsby. This was a windmill with five sails and the local farmers would bring their corn to be ground. Mr Fenwick took over the management in 1913 until work ceased just after the Second World War. He recalled the day when the mill was working at top speed and a cog in the top cone snapped and the one-ton sail toppled to the ground, nearly causing his demise. The mill was then powered by electricity and the sails were removed in the late 1930s. It was finally demolished in the 1950s but traces of the foundations can still be seen. The sails were used on other mills to keep them working.

The village had a post office and general stores, also a butcher, and by 1923 a garage and petrol pump had arrived. Small shops were opening in the 1920s and 1930s. Orders would be collected by the grocer's and butcher's boys who whistled the latest tunes as they rode their bicycles around the village. There was no pre-packing and everything was weighed and wrapped at the shop – butter, lard, dried fruit etc. In 1937 Mr Hartley opened his sweets and tobacconist's shop called "Humphrey's" and at this time was selling 20 Player's cigarettes for 11½d plus a free-box of matches. Later he moved his shop to another location in the village and opened a library. He would travel to London on the train and buy books from W. H. Smith. When they had been well read by his customers he sold them to Grimsby Library. The village was by now well served with shops, which included an off licence, chemist, greengrocer, fish and chip shop and a dairy which sold delicious home-made ice cream.'

'There were several village shops in Scamblesby, including bakers and a butcher. The village had its own windmill where villagers took their corn to be ground for breadmaking, and during the war some had their beans or corn made into their own animal feedstuff. After the war the mill gradually fell into disuse and was demolished, leaving no traces today.

Jobs were mainly local, land work for boys and domestic service for girls. From time to time there would be an opportunity for a boy to be apprenticed to local tradesmen such as the blacksmith, wheelwright, baker, saddler or butcher.

An apprentice wheelwright, for instance, received no pay, just his keep. The work covered many areas, including coffin making in this village. When the apprentice became an "improver" he received 50 shillings a week in 1940. In 1921, prices for some of the work undertaken by the wheelwright included – an ordinary coffin at £4, a brassed one at £6 and an extra-finished one at £7, all in elm (an oak coffin would have cost £10); a five-barred gate, planed and painted, for £2; stairs at 5s a step; sliding Yorkshire windows at 2s 6d a foot; a pig cratch for £1 10s. He might also build new houses.'

THE VILLAGE SHOP

'We sold practically everything in our village shop at Sturton. Provisions on one side, drapery on the other, millinery and a dispensary upstairs. Grandma trimmed hats and my husband was a qualified chemist. Our motto was "If we haven't got it, we'll get it for you".

All goods – lard, flour, cereal, sugar – were bought in bulk, so everything had to be weighed and packaged. Amber coloured treacle was brought in barrels and customers brought their two-pound stone jars to fill. The treacle came out very slowly so customers would get fed up standing over it, they would leave it, the jar would overfill and treacle would be all over the floor, a terrible mess to clear up. We had to make a rule that a customer must stay with her jar!

We baked our own bread. The oven was coke-fired and stoked last thing at night for baking bread early next morning. I believe the bobby on night-beat would sneak into the bakehouse for a warm during very cold weather.

We ran a drapery club, one shilling a week. One lady who collected was handed a bit of paper once with "Don't mention shoes" written on it. The wife was saving up for them and didn't want her husband to know.

Mr Lucas went around on his bike, collecting orders – he took monkey nuts to give to the children. The orders were made up in the shop and delivered. The driver took dog biscuits to pacify the dogs!'

'My father's shop at Ingoldsby was small, but the range of things he sold was truly amazing. I can remember exactly where everything was kept. The "bacon counter" also housed the butter, cheese and lard and it had to be scrubbed each night. Cheeses came whole and had to be skinned. Butter and lard had to be weighed and wrapped, as did sugar and dried fruit, and this in small amounts too when rationing was in force during the war. Along the back of the shop were attractive mahogany fixtures full of things like tea, cocoa, sugar, tins of fruit and salmon. Small drawers opened to reveal spices, cloves, mustard, peppercorns, cinnamon etc. There was the cigarette area, and I liked to fill this up as I could peep inside a packet sometimes if I was saving for a set of cigarette cards!

Thursday was half-day closing and I often helped to restock the sweet counter which was built up at one end of the main counter. I'm sure I ate too much chocolate, Cadbury's Milk Marzipan was my favourite, no longer made. You could get a good bag of sweets for one penny, and a small bag for a halfpenny. Along the front of the counter were biscuits, tinned and loose, and fruit and vegetables. We also sold things like brushes and buckets, shoes and dresses, skirts and stockings. There was a "chemist's" section behind the door with packets or cards, things like Carter's Little Liver Pills and Vick. When it was King George and Queen Elizabeth's Coronation in 1937 I remember making a large cardboard model of the procession of carriages and horses and my father made a road and trees, and we set it out in the shop window, together with a display of brassware and Union Jacks. I thought it was very fine!

Paraffin, batteries and cycle parts were kept in the "bottom shop", a small building at the bottom of the drive. The shop was open until 8 pm each evening, and 10 pm on Saturdays. Men often called from the hamlets of Hanby or Keisby on their way to the Heathcote Arms public house at Ingoldsby. The shop was quite a meeting place and there was often much hilarity. I could write much about various village characters, but one stands out in my mind, Miss Coddington. She was small and precise, wearing a black bonnet and long skirt. She visited the shop at 3 pm each Saturday afternoon. Bacon was rationed from 1940 to 1946 and it was two ounces a week for each person. Miss Coddington never did get the hang of it and always used to say, "I'll take my bacon in a piece, Mr Park"!'

OTHER WAYS WE MADE A LIVING

There were, of course, dozens of other ways we made a living in the past and some of them are remembered here, from working in the ironstone quarries to training to be a nurse, from catching moles to making chairs.

THE IRONSTONE QUARRIES

'The most important iron ore deposits in Britain are found between Corby, Northamptonshire, and Scunthorpe in Lincolnshire. During the Second World War production was accelerated to meet the war-time demands.

The history of the quarries around Harlaxton, Denton and Knipton is of great interest to those of us who live there. Most of the ore was obtained by open-cast mining, the areas were small and as a section was worked, the land was quickly returned to agricultural use. Sometimes imported top-soil was brought in to replace the original stony surface. The farmland was then better than the original, and a year later was being grazed. Quick-set hedges were planted, parcels of land were re-afforested with a mixture of sycamore, larch and fir trees.

About 1938 the ironstone producers co-operated with Government departments to ensure the successful restoration of the land, and the beauty of the countryside. This restoration also contributed to the improvement of the farmlands, more viable farm units, and shorter roads; a good example of this latter can be seen at the top of Swinehill in Harlaxton. Subsequent statutory obligations were introduced which made land restoration even more effective. We can accept with gratitude that the ironstone mining has enhanced the landscape, land has been drained, hedged, ploughed, woods planted, and roads built. At Harlaxton, some most interesting Roman remains were uncovered, a tessellated pavement, a deep well, and other fragments of Roman occupation.

Mining continued in the Harlaxton, Denton and Knipton areas until the late 1960s, and a dispersal sale was held at the Harlaxton Quarry in about 1972.

The men who worked in the quarries hold strong memories, and deep affection for friends, and the life as it was. At Harlaxton about 1957, 93 men were employed at the mine. Only two had cars, ten had motor cycles, and the others either rode bicycles or walked to work. Ironstone was extracted by a giant drag-line operating boom shovels. These modern machines were made by Ruston Bucyrus, and Ransome Rapier; it is impossible to realise their size from illustrations. The base plate of one measured 48 feet by four feet and weighed 227 tons. The walking mechanism could be put into operation and with steps of seven feet could move 200 yards in an hour. In spite of the huge weight of these machines, it was distributed so evenly over the base plate that the overall pressure was only slightly heavier than that of a human foot.

The ironstone was loaded into tippler trucks, the contents weighed at the Casthorpe weigh bridge, then these trucks were taken by railway lines to join the national rail system at Bottesford. The locomotives were an assortment of many styles, some saddle tankers, others which looked even older, their drivers taking a great interest in their engines. The railway lines have gone but the track can still be seen at Denton, where it runs under the Denton to Woolsthorpe-by-Belvoir road. Many of these great little steam engines went for scrap but some can be seen in the Nene Valley collection, and at the Rutland Railway Museum at Cottesmore. They had some exciting names – Gunby, The Marquis of Granby, Juno, Jupiter Jenny, Betty, Bagnall – all well remembered, later to be replaced by Rolls Royce diesels.

As the cost of rail transport was high some of the ore was set alight in large fires by the quarries which reduced the waste material, and the weight. Eventually, lorries were used to transport the ore on some journeys.

The quarries at Denton and Harlaxton continued into the late 1960s. The spell of prosperity was expected to last until about the year 2000 but imported ore contained less wastage and its use contributed to the decline of the British iron ore production. At the site of the buildings at the Harlaxton mine the concrete bases of the huts can still be seen, used nowadays I am told for sugar beet awaiting collection by lorries.

Before the use of the heavy mechanical diggers most of the work was manual. Knipton was a central village for the quarries, and 600 men were employed at the peak of production. The work was heavy, the over-burden of soil up to a depth of three or four feet at this point was removed by men with barrows. Once opened, the area of ore exposed would be about six yards wide by 500 yards long. The men who took off the over-burden were called "toppers". These were followed by "fillers" who actually loaded the ore into 20-ton waggons. This was considered to be the hardest work in the country. It was dangerous work, using wheelbarrows along springing planks, and by today's standards the men did everything wrong. They drank too much beer, smoked and had large families, and nearly all had an allotment, kept a pig and lived on boiled bacon! In a day's work a filler had to load eight or nine trams, each holding about two tons. The men had the use of a hut for their meals which they brought with them, but there are tales of the engine drivers frying eggs and bacon on shovels at the engine fire-door.

Early in the 1970s the ironstone mining in this area finished, the quarries were levelled, the hedges were planted, the railways removed, and the men made redundant. Never again will the giant drag-lines operate here, there is nothing left to see except the lovely country, but the memories of the comradeship and the working lives of the men who were there remain.'

WIND AND WATER MILLS

'I was born in a water mill, where my father was the miller, in a Lincolnshire village in the 1930s. For me the mill was a curious mixture of excitement and fear.

Firstly, there was the mill dam, which ran alongside our garden, ten foot deep in places, swirling and rushing beneath the mill through an iron grating. Inside the mill the water seemed even more fearsome, giving me nightmares of being sucked down into a bottomless abyss.

The mill building was five storeys in height, and on special days my father would go to the top and hoist the Union Jack on the flagpole; this was one of the tallest buildings in the village, and the flag would be seen quite a distance away. My father was a very patriotic man, and having fought in the trenches in the 1914–18 war this was his way of celebrating peace time. The top of the mill was reached by means of wooden stepladders from floor to floor, each one becoming narrower and seemingly more rickety as it neared the top. Workmen would run up and down these steps with the utmost ease, usually coming down backwards, but to me the ladders were another source of fear – if a worn step was going to give way I was sure it would be when I was creeping nervously up or down.

Watching the millstones turning slowly as the grain trickled down, I could feel the building vibrating, and as the wooden floor had worn away in places I was certain that one day before long the building would give an extra big shudder and fall to the ground, millstones and all.

One thing I did enjoy was when my father or a workman weighed me on the sack weighing machine. As I stood on the platform it moved gently to and fro, as weights were hung on the balance, and a slide moved along to determine an accurate weight reading. This procedure was great fun.

My brother or father would often give me a ride on a running barrow – this was exciting, especially where one part of the floor was lower than the other, and we had a run downhill at top speed.

The most scary thing of all I recall was the sack hoist. This chain ran through a series of trap doors, which would come crashing open to allow the loaded sack to be lifted up. The trap doors were of course constructed in such a way that one could walk over them when they were closed without any chance of them opening downwards. But this was something my child-like brain could not understand, and I was always very careful never to go near the trap doors for fear of falling through. In another part of the mill there was a chute, where sacks of grain could be slid down into a lorry or cart beneath. I always thought it would have been fun to slide down there and end up in the vehicle below, but I was never brave enough to try it.

The mill may seem to have been a very hazardous place for us children to play, but no doubt we were always well supervised by adults, and never in any real danger.'

'Our unique eight-sailed windmill at Heckington originally had only five sails. In 1890, during a thunderstorm, lightning struck the fantail causing the mill to rotate backwards and the top to be blown off. The tower was gutted by fire.

A chance meeting in Boston in 1891 between a Mr Pocklington, who had just purchased all the movable parts of a mill which was soon to be demolished, and Mr Nash, the owner of the empty tower at Heckington, resulted in Mr Pocklington acquiring the gutted tower. With much skill and ingenuity the work was carried out to transform the gutted tower into a magnificent eight-sailed windmill to grind wheat for flour and to drive two circular saws. Grinding wheat for flour ceased in the mill about 1907 due to the popular demand for white flour produced from American hard grain. However, white flour was "bought in" from Boston and packeted for sale until the end of the 1930s.

After the death of Mr John Pocklington the mill passed to his eldest son John, who with his son worked the mill until the Second World War. The absence of his son in the forces and John's increasing infirmity led to the shutters being removed from the sails. The mill began to deteriorate and the Kesteven County Council purchased the mill in 1953 for the sum of £2,000.'

CHAIRMAKING

'In these days of cheap, flat-packed disposable household furniture which you buy directly from the shelf and assemble on your sitting room floor, I like to recall a time when furniture was practical, sensible, good looking and made to last, a source of great pride to

Cutting timber with a portable steam engine in High Hall Wood, Woodhall Spa in 1908. As well as timber for fences and gates, Woodhall provided pit props for the coal mines.

the craftsmen who fashioned it.

My father, Richard Marshall, learned his trade from his own father, Thomas Marshall, who came to Market Rasen from Yorkshire in 1890 to start up a chair work business.

Thomas bought, under mortgage, some property consisting of four cottages and a piece of land adjacent to the local railway line. He converted the cottages into a single house and built on a new workshop which contained a steam engine to run his lathes and saws.

Outside there was an area for storing his raw materials – the oaks, ash, elms and beech which were delivered whole. My sisters Nancy, Hilda and I used to love watching these huge trees arrive on their long trailers, pulled by magnificent shire horses.

Once the trees had been unloaded by crane they were taken to the woodyard on a bogey rail and cut up by circular saw into planks. These were stored in a nearby shed, maturing and seasoning for at least seven years before they were ready to be converted into chairs and suites.

At that time the fashion was for seven-piece suites – a sofa, two arm chairs and four small chairs – although this changed later into the three-piece suite of modern times.

Marshall and Son, who employed several men, also had facilities for varnishing and upholstering so that they were able to produce finished furniture. The completed suites, packed in hessian and hay, were sent by rail to shops all over Lincolnshire or delivered locally by hand cart. Waggons would take them to nearby villages.

Nowadays it is fashionable to recycle everything, including your rubbish, but this is not a new practice – Marshall's were doing it 50 years ago! Business people in Rasen would send their waste to Marshall's for disposal – old boxes and paper, bits of rubber and the like – to be burnt in the hungry belly of the great steam engine.

In 1936 my father developed heart trouble which left him handicapped and unable to continue his heavy, arduous labour at the furniture works. The business closed three years later on the outbreak of war.'

A SEASONAL TRADE

'Pre-war Mablethorpe was in some respects the same as it is today, in that most employment centred on seasonal trade. The brickyard, gas works, railway and local council did employ some men on a permanent basis though not in great numbers, so in the 1920s and 1930s just about every home was turned into a boarding house. They just squeezed folk in somewhere, giving up their own beds to earn a few shillings. Apartments were the most popular with the visitors – that meant the landlady supplied the accommodation and the visitors brought their own food and the landlady cooked it. These people arrived mainly by train, a few by coach. Various works and factories had special weeks for holidays and these were busy times. There were also daily excursion trains and on Sundays especially there would be trip trains and evening trains from Grimsby, and the shops and pubs would stay open to serve them.'

THORNTON HALL INDUSTRIES

'Thornton Hall Industries was a family firm started by Mrs Helen Smethurst and later joined by her cousin, Miss Gladys Mawson in the 1920s. It was an exclusive works providing needlework and drapery items for the rich upper classes. As the demand for the merchandise outstripped the supply the workforce expanded, drawing on young female school-leavers from the surrounding villages.

During the Second World War, a contract was obtained from the Admiralty by Miss Mawson and five girls remained embroidering officers' badges. After the war business boomed again and it was in

1951 that I joined the staff to work in the office, along with 14 girls in the workrooms.

Miss Mawson designed all the patterns for tea cosies, nightdress cases and workbags. She visited the textile manufacturers to buy rolls of chintz, taffeta and satins. The floral chintzes were quilted around their designs but the taffeta and satins had to be drawn on by hand. The desk lamp was laid down on the desk and a piece of glass, resting on two bricks, provided the workbench. The light shone from underneath the patterns and I was able to trace it onto the material. Luxury babyware was developed with padded baskets and satin-lined cribs being produced.

At the beginning of the year new stock was made and fresh ideas tried out ready for the Spring Show when buyers from exclusive shops like Harrods would come to see the merchandise set out in one of the large rooms transformed into a "shop". The Industries would then get into top gear, employing part-time old "hands", to produce the ordered goods in time for the Christmas trade. It was part of my job to do all the packing. Each article was pressed and wrapped in tissue paper after careful inspection for nothing but the highest standard was allowed to leave the premises. Our goods were also sold on board the ships of the Union Castle Line. We had special orders at times and we were quite proud when an article was destined for the Royal household.

We cycled to work for eight o'clock in the morning, some having to travel three or four miles each way. We left at 5.30 having had two quarter-hour breaks and half an hour for eating a packed lunch. We didn't work on Saturdays. The pay was very poor and at the time when the Industries closed down in 1960 the girls were earning, on average, about £4 a week. At one time a group of the senior girls threatened to resign unless they got a pay rise and, as a result, were awarded a farthing an hour increase.

Heating of the rooms was by means of a temperamental boiler looked after by the gardener. The large windows, under which the machinists worked, were draughty. We used a lot of wadding for quilting and juniors would sit "fluffing" wadding to make cosy pads so that everywhere was covered in fine fluff, including hair, eyebrows and clothes. But, in spite of these hardships, we were a happy "family".'

TRANSPORT AND PUMPING

'The Pinchbeck Transport Company had a depot in the village for several years until 1929. A driver with them for some years recollects: "Lorries were ex W.D. three-ton Thorneycrofts on solid rubber tyres. Seats were wooden bench type and you had to provide your own cushion. There were no side windows and the driver's windscreen was split into two parts, one of which could be opened for ventilation in summer and to give better visibility in fog. The speed limit was 12 mph and police used to set speed traps but most drivers learned where to expect them. The usual journey time to the London market was about seven hours but it was possible to do it in six hours by slipping out of gear downhill and getting a good run at the next uphill. These runs to London were usually made after drivers had worked locally through the day and it was necessary to leave Pinchbeck by 8 pm to catch the early market, they would then pick up a return load and deliver to its destination."

The Pinchbeck Marsh Pumping Station and house were built in 1833. The station drained the whole of Pinchbeck and part of Spalding and was vital to their existence. It was run for an average of 180 days a year from mid October to mid May. The volume of water drained each year varied between 1,093,000 and 3,690,000 tons, drained into the river Glen. Mr Seymour who was appointed Superintendent of the Drainage Board in 1909, manned the engine, which in flood time ran continuously for weeks at a time. This engine was the last of its type to work in the fens, most of them had disappeared in the 1920s. Mr Seymour was taken on at a wage of £2 a week, with a house to live in, which was quite primitive with no water laid on. Heating was from coal and paraffin and candles. Mr Seymour often had to work for 16 hours at a time.

One of the jobs the men had to do each summer was to crawl up the flues of the large boiler to clean them out. They would perhaps take a fortnight to complete this dirty task. Each day they could be seen standing in a tin bath in the yard scrubbing each other down. The pumping station is no longer in use, but happily is preserved on its original site as a museum.'

THE RADIO SHOP

'Robert lived in Grimsby from his birth in 1919 until university and then his army service in 1939. He remembers delivering accumulators for radios on a bicycle for his uncle when he was eleven years old. They were made from glass and filled with acid and were held together with a rubber strap when being transported to prevent breakage. He had one on each handlebar and two wooden boxes on the back containing three more. His uncle Emil recharged the accumulators returned, in the pantry of his house. The customers were charged sixpence for the large ones and fourpence for small ones and Bob received two shillings a week. The round was over most of the town. If the customer had a high tension battery it would last about six months but a low tension one needed recharging every week. He began his round on Saturday mornings at nine to be back for eleven and then go out with the recharged batteries. Much care was needed as too much rattling about meant acid spilling onto your clothes or skin.

Later, but still a schoolboy, he worked for his Uncle Alf who had a radio shop in Pasture Street. Here he swept the yard which was made up of granite slabs and became covered in straw from the boxes that the equipment came in. Another job was to run up into the loft to get valves etc to refill the shelves. A more dangerous task involved opening the accumulators by melting their pitch seal with a bunsen burner and refitting new plates. At first they had to be replaced but now they only needed a new set of plates thus saving his uncle a lot of money and earning himself a bit extra pocket money. The batteries were charged up in the loft and needed topping up with distilled water contained in carboys. Another carboy contained sulphuric acid to replace that lost by evaporation, so great care was needed not to mix them up as the way to get fluid from them was by sucking it up a glass rod! If the accumulator ran out in the week the customer had to get it to the workshop themselves or forgo their wireless programmes.'

TRAINING TO BE A CHEMIST

'My father was an apprentice pharmacist with Boots the Chemists in Lincoln in 1933, after leaving school, and required four subjects at School Certificate to enter the profession. He then served a four-year apprenticeship working from 8.30 am to 7 pm each day and attending night school for four nights a week for two years until 9.30 pm, then two nights a week for two years. His wage as an apprentice was ten shillings a week.

The chemist dispensed mostly mixtures, pills and cachets for human consumption but also dealt with veterinary medicines such as batch lots of horse conditioning powders. A mixture for acrine disease in bees was distributed nationwide. On average 40 prescriptions per week were dealt with on National Health Insurance and about 30 were "private" prescriptions which the doctor wrote and the patient paid two to three shillings for. "Over the counter" medicines included sweet nitre and tincture of rhubarb for cold cures, syrup of figs to keep you regular and Barrack Sergeant drops to aid backache. Thirty dozen eggs were bought from time to time from the local market and put into waterglass for preserving then sent to Nottingham to be made into white oils embrocation with camphor, ammonia and turpentine. Tar was fetched from the gas works to be made into ointments.

On Fridays a local carrier came from Coningsby through Horncastle to Lincoln and collected orders for goods required on his way. These were packed into parcels, priced and then collected by him. He paid for them initially and received a penny in the shilling discount then charged his customers the full rate on his return journey. The chemist also delivered goods on a tradesbike anywhere in Lincoln in approximately a three to four mile radius.'

TRAINING TO BE A NURSE

'It was in 1951 at the age of 16 years that I applied to Boston General Hospital hoping to become a pre-nursing cadet. I had always wanted to nurse and intended to gain experience in hospital before starting training at 18 years. Matron Bowler invited me to her office for an interview; my mother was to accompany me. After introductions I was sent off to complete a short written test, while Matron explained to Mother what my duties would be. After a quick glance at my paper Matron looked up and asked, "When would you like to start?" I can still recall the joy I felt at the prospect of starting work on my chosen career.

The Boston General Hospital where I was to work was a cottage hospital situated by the river near the site of the old park and swimming baths. On my first day I had to report to the sewing room to be fitted out in uniform – green dresses, white aprons and an oblong starched linen piece to be made up into a cap.

My first stay in a nurses home was a short walk from the hospital in a fine old house called Greyfriars in South End. I felt desperately lonely as I waited in the big front bedroom for the two nurses sharing the room to come off duty. The home came alive just before 9 pm when all the junior nurses came in. In those days all students were single females and had to be resident in one of the nurses homes. It was strictly no visiting. I was soon made welcome and had my hat made up for me. It was so intricate I didn't undo it for weeks! Whilst sitting on someone's bed drinking coffee, Sister Eustace the Sister Tutor came into the room looking for me. All the girls got to their feet but I remained seated and so got my first lesson in hospital etiquette. Always stand when a Sister enters the room; open doors for senior members of staff and allow them to walk in front at all times.

The hours of duty were long and tiring, we worked split shifts, which meant starting at 7.30 am and then having three hours off duty, at either 10 am till 1 pm or 2 pm until 5 pm or finishing at 6 pm. Discipline was strict. We had to be in our rooms by 10 pm. One late night pass per week with Matron's permission was allowed. We queued at her door and she liked to know where we were going, some places were out of bounds!

Meals were taken in a pleasant dining room with waitress service,

Matron and Sisters at one table and others according to their year. The juniors sat at the bottom of the table and were served last. Breakfast was served at 7 am and you had to be there. Night Sister sat in and checked that you had a full meal.

Just after my 18th birthday I started my training for State Registration. The first nine weeks were spent at Preliminary Training School at Lincoln County Hospital. Only two of us went from Boston on this occasion and for both of us it was our first time in Lincoln.'

THE BOSTON DAY NURSERY

'Boston Day Nursery was in Bank Street, where the most recent County Hall buildings are sited, and it had been for some years a voluntary nursery, founded by Miss Ryan, who was sister to the late Councillor Mrs Alice Johnson.

The Borough of Boston took over responsibility for the day nursery in 1935, and the permanent staff consisted of a matron and sister, who were resident, and a cook and cleaner who came daily. There was an intake of four student nursery nurses each year, for one year's training, at a premium of £25, and students had to provide sheets, pillowcases, towels and uniform, also paying for laundry at one shilling and sixpence a week.

Children were admitted to the nursery from the age of one month to five years and the majority of mothers worked on the land or were employed in the local canning factories or Fogarty's Feather Factory. The charge was sixpence a day, and for this the children were fed, clothed and well cared for from 7 am until 5.30 pm when they were collected by their mothers. As the children arrived they were bathed and changed into nursery clothes which were a knitted vest, cotton smock and trousers or knickers to match, and a jumper. It was not at all unusual for children to have fleas and head lice and heads were combed daily, though of course some children were spotlessly clean.

At 9 am the children had cocoa and a rusk. Rusks were fingers of bread, baked hard. Lunch was always a good nourishing meal, nicely served, even though plates and mugs were tin or enamel in those days, and the children had sandwiches, cakes and milk to drink for tea. Nurses prepared the morning drinks and tea, and they had always to be dainty and attractively presented.

There was a small walled garden for a play area, with a paved section leading from the nurseries where meals could be served if the weather was fine. The children were also taken into the central park, and usually they had a rest after lunch on stretcher beds, outside if the weather permitted.

The nurses' day began at 6 am and duties were on a week's rota;

165

cooking breakfast, taking tea up to Matron and Sister, preparing the nurseries and the children's clothes, opening windows and lighting the gas copper in the children's bathroom! This was to heat the water for the baby baths or sink baths, where hot water was not laid on.

The students were responsible for cleaning the nurseries, for care of the children's clothes, i.e. laundry and repairs, also for making garments. Ironing was done on Saturday mornings and the clean clothes put in the children's numbered bags on Sunday, and clean towels and face cloths hung on their pegs.

Lectures were on two evenings a week and students had 20 minutes for meals and one hour off duty each day. In addition they had one weekend off each month.'

THE TAILOR

'Mr John Fidell was a tailor in Worlaby from 1870 until about 1926. He died in 1929. He was born at Croxton in 1847. He received little schooling and commenced life by picking stones off the land to repair roads for threepence per day. At the age of 14 he was apprenticed to a tailor for seven years, his father paying a premium of £7. During this period he improved his education by practising arithmetic and writing in the evenings. When out of his apprenticeship he received eight shillings a week. When he came to Worlaby he set up in business on his own. He met his wife in Worlaby and in 1876 they were married and moved to Chapel House where they lived all their married life.

May, his granddaughter, born in 1914, can remember him sitting cross-legged in the window of his workshop sewing suits for farm workers in the village. They would purchase one a year and the tailor had to wait for payment until they received their wages at the end of a year's labour. Waxed cotton was used for sewing on the buttons and the tailor guaranteed the suit would wear out before the buttons dropped off.

At the beginning of this century there were two tailors in Worlaby, both making a good living. However, by the 1920s trade had diminished owing to ready-made clothes which were cheaper and available in the towns. Travelling was also easier.

Mrs Fidell was a dressmaker, both before her marriage and after. When her children were small she sewed a christening robe for a well-to-do family at Wrawby. When it was finished, she walked the four miles with a pram holding two or three of her children to deliver the robe. She also sewed for the people in the big houses in Worlaby. It was common practice for dressmakers to spend a whole day in these houses making or mending garments. This (like her husband) was during the period up to the 1920s, after which ready-made clothes could be bought at Brigg or Barton.'

'This is an edited transcript of a conversation with Mr Hought, mole and rat catcher.

"'I was twelve when the war started in 1914, so I should be about leaving school. I started catching rabbits and moles, and all that. I catched a few (moles) in me time. When I was ten year old my Dad gave me two traps, showed me how to set 'em and says, 'There, I've finished giving you pocket-money now. You'll earn your own, with these two traps.' And I'd allus plenty o' money when I went to school. The two traps kept me in money.

I skinned the moles and sold the skins. Moleskins was 2s 3d each during the '14 war. A man's wages was only 2s 9d a day then. And I'd get 3d for catching it, so I got half-a-crown a piece. All the lads envied me when I went to school 'cos I'd allus a pocket full o' money. I used to send them (skins) to John May at Grantham, and another one down at Wisbech. The reason moleskins was making so much was all the young women round here was on munitions in Lincoln; and they wanted a fur coat. When I used to go Lincoln sometimes, and I used to see all these young girls that was on munitions, five or six hundred o' them, all had these moleskin coats on. I used to think to m'sel that maybe I catched some o' them."

(Skinning) "I laid them out on board and laid them out square, like, and when they got dry I sent 'em. Postage was not much in them days, you know. Not like it is now. They're not worth anything now. Postage is too much, by the time you get your money back it hasn't been worth yer trouble."

"I went to Binbrook airdrome and catched 'em a lot (of moles) off the landing-ground and all round. Anyway the Clerk o' the Works come to me, and he say, 'Do you catch rats?' And I say, 'Well, I can do. I've all m'father's recipes, and 'e was an expert.' 'Well,' 'e says, 'Will you go down and see the Group Captain. He's some in his house. When he gets home from bombing at three or four o'clock in the morning he has to get out of bed and rattling on the wall with his shoe to stop them from gnawing. The bedroom is boarded about halfway up all the way round, and they was behind there gnawing.' So I went down to see the Group Captain and tell him what I'd come for. There was an airman there doing his jobs, and 'e says, 'Take him anywhere 'e wants to go, Luke. If 'e wants to look round anywhere.' So I says, 'I want to look in the box-room, that'll be where they're coming in.' So we got up in the false roof, and there was a board about that square, with about a handful stuff on. Supposed to be rat-poison, I expect; but my Dad allus tell me, if you wanted to poison a rat you had to give 'im sommat 'e would eat, or you wouldn't get on very well. I says, 'E's never eaten none 'o that. You'll never kill 'em with that. I'll bring you a bit o' stuff in the morning; see how we get on.' 'I took a bit stuff next morning and said, 'I'll give you a call in two or three days; see how we're getting on.'

So I went back. I went down the road in two or three days. His house was across the bottom. When I got within about 20 yards, he put the window up. He said 'Come in. I've never had so much peace in my life. I've never heard another thing. Are you going to have a drink?' I said, 'Yes, I'll have a pot with you.' He said, 'Yes; and you can have another anytime when you come into the house.' I said, 'Thank you. That's worth knowing.' He said, 'Will you do the Camp?'

I had a look round the Camp. The first thing I thought was: Well, where do I want to be? I want to be where the grub is. I want to be across at the Airmen's Mess. That'll be where the rat is. So . . . It was about three o'clock in the afternoon and I went to the door o' the Airmen's Mess and I just opened it with a little stick . . . and there was about 1,500 rats under the tables picking the crumbs up! That was the middle of the afternoon.'''

WATERCRESS BEDS

'We came to live in Aby from Hertfordshire in 1911 when I was nine. My father worked the watercress beds at Belleau and these were later left to him. It was a good living. I used to take the hampers of watercress up to the station with a donkey and cart. The cress went as far away as London, Manchester and Liverpool.

The donkey died so we got another one from Mablethorpe but it wouldn't work for us. Somebody took it back and it galloped all the way back to the sands. We got a pony then.

In 1970 the plants got a disease. This could have been cured, but the railway closed down and we went out of business.

When the Great War started a lot of the men went into the army so I left school when I was twelve, and I went to work for Mr and Mrs White at Croft Farm. We made butter, cheese and cottage cheese to send to a stall on Louth market.'

GOING SHRIMPING

'My Friskney Grandad had a pony and a trap that had two wooden wheels with metal rims. He would go shrimping and cockling down on the shore at Friskney. The fishermen and the horse and cart followed the tide out, the horse often being up to his neck in the sea still drawing the cart. The fishing net was thrown out to trawl the shrimps, one end still attached to the cart and the other end in deep water. The pony often *swam* back to the shallow water. The shrimps would be tipped into wooden tubs and the process started again.

DEEP SEA FISHING

Many Lincolnshire men went out on the deep sea trawlers from Grimsby, or worked on the docks or the fish market. It was not an easy life, for them or for their families.

MEMORIES OF A FISHERMAN'S WIFE

'After my future husband left school he had worked on a farm at North Coates; his home was the Fleece Inn in that village. In 1920, at the age of 19 he arrived at the farm one morning ten minutes late. He was accosted by the boss who said, "You are late, Salt." His reply was, "I am not too late to go home again." On arriving home at the pub, he found his elder brother preparing for a fishing trip on a Grimsby trawler. He was soon on his way to the dock offices with a view to signing on a trawler. He was allowed to sail on his brother's ship as a deckie learner. It had taken only four hours from leaving the farm to be on the way to the fishing grounds at Iceland.

I met my husband through a relative, when he had moved to Tetney. He was, by then, well established in the fishing industry, and was at that time sitting for his skipper's ticket at the Nautical School in Orwell Street, Grimsby. Shortly after gaining his certificate we were married at Tetney church. On the morning of the wedding he arrived in port at 7.30 am, the wedding being on the same day at 2.30. He sailed again for the fishing grounds the following morning after only having been in dock for 24 hours.

There was no telephone communication in those days, and when a ship left the docks nothing more was heard until they arrived back in port. All the woollen clothes worn at sea were hand knitted with white Abb wool, and heavy hard wearing trousers called "Fearnaughts" were worn under oilskins. It was hard work washing sea clothes, and difficult to get them dry. One saying was: "The clothes are dirty but the money is clean." The food aboard the ships was basic. Fish for breakfast and tea, meat only once a day at dinner, no fresh vegetables at all. One favourite cake which I baked was the "Cakeoma" mixture, baked in a bread tin. On being told to butter well, my husband remarked "Will Taylor's margarine do?"

Living out of town, my allowance was £3 a week came by registered letter. In the 1930s times were very hard and many of the fishermen were unemployed. There was no dole money for skippers and mates, as they were classed as shareholders, and after a poor trip was landed sometimes no money was paid out. Often this carried on for several trips until the debt was cleared.

Although time in dock was short, a popular evening out was to visit the Palace Variety theatre in Victoria Street, where many well known artists performed. The Prince of Wales theatre, or Curry's as it was known, was in Freeman Street where dramas or comedies were presented.'

WE CAME FROM YARMOUTH

'I was born in 1920 at Yarmouth. When I was about six years old the big coal strike of 1926 happened. Of course all ships were coal fired so it did an awful lot of damage, my mother used to say that's what made them poor. Skippers, mates and engineers couldn't pay insurance stamps, they were classed as "sharemen" so when they were out of work they could not claim any labour money, all they were allowed was food tickets, which was very demoralising. When my father got a ship, after the coal strike, he served as a mate. He managed to save enough money to sit for his skipper's ticket. My poor mother had to plan every penny to see us through and also by that time there were two more children. He got his skipper's ticket and then could not get a ship. Finally he got one at Lowestoft, which is about seven miles from where we lived, so he cycled there.

In the meantime my grandfather who was a mate on a trawler came to try his luck in Grimsby. He found they liked North Sea skippers from Yarmouth as they knew that area of the sea better, so he lent my father the money to come to Grimsby to try his luck. By this time my mother had had five children. Father soon got a ship. As I got older I was sure of one thing, I would never marry a fisherman. As the eldest I used to hear all Mother's troubles and worries, and many a stormy night I heard her walking the bedroom floor with worry, and there was always a shortage of money. The children never got to know their fathers very well, as they were never at home but always at sea. The women had to be both father and mother. Father saved enough money for us all to come to Grimsby. My poor mother had all the home to pack and bring to Grimsby, on her own. It was the first time I had ever been on a train, I was 13.

Grimsby was a much bigger fishing town than Yarmouth. On a Friday afternoon the schools closed because the children had to go down dock to collect their father's wages. I was one of them. I must say things were a lot easier by now, a skipper's wage was £3 per week and a mate's was £2 10s. If they had a good trip they were all right but if they had a bad trip things were different. They "settled up" every three months and if things had been bad the wages had to be paid back.

My father's ship was the *Rodney* and he skippered it until the war started. It was then taken for mine sweeping. When he was fishing he was at sea for seven or eight days and home for 48 hours then off again. It was quite a ritual the night he came home, always with a lovely "fry" in his kit bag, that was our supper that night. He would send someone for a bottle of beer and a bottle of cheap wine and we would all play cards. Next morning he would get dressed up and go down dock to the office. My mother would meet him then it was into the "Humber", the pub all fishermen used, for a drink, then on to the local market for a bargain or two and then home for tea, then to the Prince of Wales Theatre to see a show. The next day it was off to sea again. By this time Father was able to buy Mother a lovely radiogram that had a waveband on so that he could talk to her sometimes. Mother used to play for hours with her radiogram, listening to the fishing. One day she heard a May Day call, it went on and on. Suddenly she said to my sister, "That's your father, he is in trouble. Go down dock to the office and tell them." It *was* my father, the ship had lost its rudder, but he brought the ship safely home. He was awarded £80, which was quite a good sum.

By this time I was 14 and Father had persuaded me to work in a braiding room as the pay would be good. I left school one week and started work the next week. I don't think I will ever forget that first day as long as I live. When the nine o'clock buzzer went I thought it was home time, my hands were swollen and full of blisters and the palm of my right hand was red raw, but we stuck it out. We were able to buy an ointment containing Laudanum to rub on our hands, we also used Friar's Balsam to harden our fingers. The nail on our first finger was always worn away. We sometimes wore a wrist strap as braiding was very heavy work. For two years we worked as needle fillers learning our trade. We worked from 7.30 am to 5 pm for ten shillings and threepence per week for the first year and twelve shillings and six pence per week for the second. At 16 years of age we were set on making nets. After a few weeks we were earning an average of £2 per week, that was as much as some men were earning.

During the war we made camouflage nets and spliced ropes for putting around shells. My father stopped fishing to go mine sweeping, as did lots of fishermen. After the war ended there was a few good years' fishing. My eldest brother was an engineer in the Navy, but he also went fishing when the war ended. Icelandic fishing was hard work, they had to chip the ice from the decks to keep working. The fishing in Grimsby is very poor now and none of my family are fishermen, it ended with my father and eldest brother.'

ON THE DOCKS AT GRIMSBY

'My father was a ship's husbandman and worked near the fish docks in Grimsby. This was about 60 years ago. We used to visit him there and the policeman on the gate knew us and let us in. There were three docks in Grimsby – the fish docks, the Alexander dock for private boats and the Royal dock for passenger boats.

The wives of the deep sea trawler men were always knitting. They knitted underwear, seaboot stockings and pullovers, all in oiled wool to keep their menfolk dry and warm in the fierce weather they encountered. They had a leather pouch fitted under their left arm to hold the needle and support the heavy wool. When the boats returned to harbour the women met them to take the heavy canvas bag which contained the woollen worn during the trip. Their job was to wash and dry these garments ready for the next trip, with no washing machines or spin dryers and only cold water on tap if they were lucky.'

LOSS

'The loss of a vessel and its crew was always an occasion of great sadness, shared by the whole community. Newsboys ran through the streets with newspapers bearing the tragic story, even if the news came through at night. It was the dread of every fisherman's wife and involved a great many families. Sympathy and kindly support were there but financial help and compensation were poor, mostly dependent on the generosity of the townspeople. The port missionary would go round to all with help and support and a joint service would be held in the fisherman's church, St Andrew's in Freeman Street. The church is no longer there.'

'Between the two world wars, 120 Grimsby trawlers were lost at sea. After the Second World War, from 1946 to 1960, a further 45 never returned to port.

So far as Grimsby is concerned, fishing reached its peak in the 1970s. The smaller vessels were still fishing the North Sea, but the larger boats were heading for the Faroes and Iceland, and others, when circumstances necessitated a change, as far away as Greenland and the White Sea. In 1976, following a settlement of the Icelandic troubles, Grimsby boats could not fish within 200 miles of the coast. This and similar fishing limits meant the loss over a short period of all Grimsby's deep sea trawlers, and the port today has a comparatively small fleet of much smaller vessels.'

172

WAR & PEACE

THE GREAT WAR 1914–1918

Every town and village in Lincolnshire was touched by the war, as the men marched off and those left behind faced bombing from the air for the first time. The end of the war was greeted with heartfelt relief, tinged with sadness.

YOUR COUNTRY NEEDS YOU!

'My earliest memories date from around 1910 when I was living with my parents and much older brothers and sisters at Sutton on Sea. I remember them as glorious summer days on the sea shore among the high sand dunes, now sadly gone. We played hide and seek along the golden sands and were entertained by the Clements, old friends who came every summer. How handsome they were in their cream trousers, bright blazers and straw boaters, and how we children laughed at the antics of Tommy Reno, the comedian. Sometimes a kind gentleman would buy us an ice cream cone – there were no sinister warnings given or needed in those days.

Then in 1914 there was the announcement that we were at war with Germany and soon pictures of Kitchener appeared everywhere, with his finger pointing, saying "Your Country Needs You". My 19 year old brother came home from his job in London on a three shilling return ticket from Kings Cross, and told us that he thought it was his duty to enlist in the army at once. When I realised he might be killed, those summer days were over for good.'

PUT THAT LIGHT OUT!

'During the war the special constable at Haxey Carr was the only local person with a telephone. He would get warnings of air raids and go out patrolling to see if any lights were showing. If he saw a light anywhere he would shout, in a broad Lincolnshire accent, "Put that light out. Zeps are out!"

Before the war there was a lot of talk about the Germans coming. The Hammond's photographic shop at Haxey went up in flames and the owner thought the Germans had arrived! The only foreigners who actually came to the village were Belgian refugees, who were given a house to live in free of rent, furnished by the villagers.'

'THE CAMP'

'In 1916 a "bombshell" descended on the quiet hamlet of Cranwell for it was in that year that Mr Usher Banks, the tenant of Lodge Farm, heard that the land he farmed was being taken over by the Royal Naval Air Service. Altogether, some 3,000 acres were acquired under the Defence of the Realm Act. Towards the end of the year three officers arrived and stayed at the Bristol Arms Hotel in Sleaford. They were followed by the first 35 men and supplies.

Mrs Alice Gant (who then lived at Cranwell Lodge) recalls in her memories: "Sometime in February 1916, Mr Sutherland came running to the school to tell the teacher that there was an aeroplane coming in the distance. School was quickly closed down and we ran home. It landed in the field at the end of our garden – I know that it was a BE2C biplane No 3999. We had a good view. Several more arrived one Sunday at the beginning of April. Before that date, one moonlight night, my parents heard a funny noise. They went out to look and saw a German Zeppelin flying over. Evidently, the Germans had heard about Cranwell and had come to look it over. No bombs were dropped on this occasion but, sometime later, another Zeppelin did bomb the camp."

Construction continued apace and the road soon became deeply rutted. A railway line was laid from Sleaford to transport both men and materials. This was finally closed in 1956. On 1st April 1916 the Royal Naval Air Service Training Establishment at Cranwell (HMS *Daedalus* as it was known to the Admiralty) was officially opened.

The original farmhouse, The Lodge, was enlarged to become the residence of the Commanding Officer and it is still used for this purpose. In July "The Camp", as it is known locally, received a visit from George V and Queen Mary. The village organised a hay waggon to transport the children, who cheered themselves hoarse. Both George VI (when he was Duke of York) and Prince Charles served at Cranwell. In 1917 it was recommended that a Cadet College be established and a separate service set up. On 1st April 1918 the Royal Air Service and the Royal Flying Corps were amalgamated and the Royal Air Force was born.

It is now difficult to comprehend that prior to 1915, RAF Cranwell was one farm, with a farmhouse and five workers' cottages.'

OPENING THE FLAX MILLS

'The flax mill in Crossgate at Pinchbeck was built in 1851, and by 1856 there were 100 employees. The mill was closed in 1879 as a result of the agricultural depression. However, on 22nd January 1918 the *Lincs Free Press* reported that: "The government have taken over the old flax mills at Pinchbeck in connection with an emergency scheme for flax production and the treatment of the resultant crop, in order to increase the supply of linen for aeronautical and other urgent war purposes. The flax mill has been closed for a number of years and the proposed reopening has caused great interest in the district."'

LIFE THROUGH THE WAR

'I was six years old at the beginning of the First World War. My father joined the army very soon after it began so my mother, younger sister and I went to live with my grandparents, deep in the heart of the Lincolnshire Fenlands.

We were four miles from Ruskington and two miles from Dorrington, called North Hills. Whenever we visited these villages to shop we walked, for the dogcart was only ever used to carry goods too heavy for us, or the butter and eggs which were sent to Lincoln market every Friday; the horse had enough other work to do.

My two uncles worked on the farm but like many young men, soon decided to fight for King and Country, which left serious problems as manpower was at a minimum. At harvest I have watched my grandmother on top of the haywain with my mother on the ground handing up the stooks of corn to her with a pitchfork most of the day, besides preparing meals for my grandfather, the children and anyone else they were lucky enough to get to help; also milking cows, feeding pigs and chickens, yet they still found time to do lovely embroidery and crochet.

How well I remember the night we were woken by the sound of a Zeppelin overhead and being told to dress quickly while the rest of the family set off to join friends at the nearest farm. Left with my grandfather, I was feeling very frightened with the tension and the fear which came through to me. After he had put out the lamps, locked the door and hidden the key he put me on his back and we set off through the orchard. It was pitch black and suddenly he bumped into a tree and I fell to the ground – it was some little time before we found each other but we made it in the end! The Zeppelin dropped a bomb; fortunately it fell in a grass field but it left a huge crater – we felt the earth shake. Much coming and going next day, people wanting to look.

I was sent the two miles to Sunday school each week, winter and summer. We would also visit my grandmother's cousin: she was always dressed in black, with a lovely white apron, grey hair in a little bun, wearing a man's cloth cap and smoking a clay pipe – but my, could she cook!

I can still close my eyes and feel I am back in the village shop run by two maiden ladies called the Misses Fenley. They sold everything

176

Two hundred soldiers were billeted on one farm at Stallingborough in 1916. The officers had their photograph taken with the farmer's family.

you could ever need, from sweets, cheese, bacon, butter and bread to rope, paraffin and oil lamps. To us children it was magic; how long it took us to spend our weekly penny goodness only knows!

My father came home from the war without a scratch, lucky fellow; both my uncles returned also, but one had been gassed very badly and died within a year, the other joined the mounted police on Hull docks. My grandparents stayed on the farm until they were 80. Wonderful, happy, hardworking years!'

'During the war we went brambling to make jam for the soldiers. We had many scares from Zeppelins at Osgodby but no raids; the one at Scarborough was the nearest. The air raid warden lived in Mill Lane and I can remember his voice shouting: "Lights out!"

Horses from the war were brought back to any farmer to keep for a few weeks to build the poor things up again. Christopher's, a firm in Lincoln, did a very good business in horseflesh for food. There was a song about it:

> Christopher's horse flesh,
> Bob a pound,
> Nice and juicy all around!'

177

'We had 200 soldiers billeted on our farm at Stallingborough, with two officers in the house, all waiting to go across to France. The men slept in the granary and other farm buildings. During the time they were with us, foot and mouth broke out on the farm. Sheets soaked in disinfectant were hung around the farmyard and buckets of disinfectant provided for feet to be dipped into.

My father hunted with the Brocklesby hounds, but his horse was taken to go by sea to the Dardanelles, and died on the way. My father never hunted again.'

ZEPPELIN!

'The war must have been a difficult time for the village people with the men away fighting and the farms and businesses to be kept going. Eight men from Scartho were killed during this war.

On 24th September 1916 after an air raid warning a Zeppelin was heard droning overhead and five bombs were dropped – the first on the west side of Waltham Road, the second near White House which brought down part of a cottage, though the two elderly people living there were providentially in the other half at the time and were not hurt. The third dropped in the churchyard, the fourth just beyond the church hedge and the fifth further on in the same line. The last three caused considerable damage to the church and rectory which were also struck by pieces of shrapnel. The dropping of bombs continued in a straight line for about a mile. One lady remembers as a child sheltering under the billiard table at the White House. Her mother was caught by the blast and fell over cutting her head but was not badly hurt. The only fatalities were two chickens and five sparrows. When morning dawned, Grimsby residents expected to find the village half destroyed but were cheered by hearing the church bells ringing for service as usual despite windows having been blown out. Half the slates and tiles were off, and even the interior sacristan window was ripped out.'

'I remember seeing a Zeppelin come from the direction of Scunthorpe and turn round over Roxby, over the farm in Bracken Holme Road. There was a gun at the top of Sawcliffe Hill, but they said it was a wooden one, and so it couldn't fire. My father was a special constable and did air raid warden duties.'

'One of my earliest memories is of staying with relatives at Cleethorpes during the First World War. There were searchlights at night, and the special constables came round calling "Lights out!" and I would be told to hide under the table. A Zeppelin dropped a bomb on the Methodist chapel in Cleethorpes, killing all the soldiers billeted there. In those days news did not travel fast and it was not until two days later that my mother heard of the tragedy and promptly fetched me back to my home on a farm. I wasn't allowed to go back to Cleethorpes until the war was over.'

IT'S OVER!

'For the peace celebrations of 1919, scholars from Stixwould school walked to Petwood, Woodhall Spa, where Sir Archibald and Lady Weigall provided tea and each child was presented with a peace medal. All the girls wore white cotton dresses.'

'Peace celebrations were held at Worlaby, as in every town and village in Lincolnshire, in July 1919. Flags were hoisted and decorations put out. There was a children's parade from the school to the village green and in the morning a united service was conducted by the vicar. Afterwards, in Mr Robinson's field, games were held and in the afternoon there were children's sports. Everyone then adjourned to the National school where a splendid tea had been laid on. Typically, the rain interrupted the after-tea sports, but they were continued on the Monday night so we did not miss out on anything.

Also in 1919 a committee was formed to discuss the erecting of a war memorial in the village. Eventually a design of Aberdeen grey polished granite was selected and the names of the ten men from the village who had lost their lives were inscribed in gold leaf. The unveiling took place on Whit Sunday 1920, 23rd May, and on that glorious early summer's day there was a large attendance to honour the dead. A parade of the members of the local Friendly Society in their club regalia, headed by a procession of schoolchildren, proceeded from the school to the monument, where a wreath and a beautiful cross of choice flowers was placed near the memorial. Discharged soldiers formed a guard of honour round the monument, which was shrouded by a Union Jack. The whole cost of the monument was £151 2s 4d, and this large sum was collected wholly by local people.'

THE SECOND WORLD WAR 1939–1945

Just 20 years later, we were at war again. Lincolnshire became 'a patchwork of airfields' and we struggled with gas masks and dug out air raid shelters.

LIFE WENT ON

'In 1939, at the outbreak of the Second World War, a barrier was erected across Scartho Road near the Methodist chapel and guarded by the hastily formed Local Defence Volunteers. The Methodist schoolroom was taken over as their headquarters. Men of all ages volunteered, one of them being my husband at the age of 17. The only uniform they had at first were forage caps. The reservoir was one of the places that had to be guarded and this was done by this valiant band who were later called the Home Guard. At first their only weapons were wooden staves but as the war progressed they were fully kitted out and given Ross rifles and finally some ammunition. The only casualty was one of the Home Guard who was sleeping on a bench during his rest period and another guard came in off his spell of duty, caught the trigger of his gun by mistake and shot his sleeping companion through the heel.

Gas masks were issued to the population and Anderson shelters were erected in gardens and people took cover during the raids, but the main targets were the docks. Scartho had a string of incendiary bombs dropped in the village and these were extinguished before any damage was done.

Life went on in the village, everyone doing their bit. Gardens were used to grow vegetables, clothes were darned, old jumpers unpicked and reknitted for children, shirt collars turned, sheets cut down the middle and the sides joined for longer use. Dried eggs were widely used and made a reasonable scrambled egg with the addition of a little parsley. Dances were held in the well blacked-out church hall and airmen from nearby airfields came to join the villagers. Sadly, 17 Scartho men were lost in this war.'

TELEGRAPH POLE GUNS

'The priory at Freiston, until recently the vicarage and dating from the 11th century, was used as a fire station during the war. The Home Guard also used it as their headquarters.

Many families took in evacuees, either children on their own or whole families. There were also a large number of soldiers billeted in the village at The Bull and Dog pub, or in local homes. With the evacuees, soldiers and Land Army girls, the population of the village almost doubled during the war.

Gun emplacements were built along the sea bank. However, the guns were never forthcoming and the local ARP put old telegraph poles through the gun holes pointing toward the sea, in the hope that if the enemy came into the Wash, they would think the poles were guns!'

SANDBAGS AND PIGS

'When war was declared in 1939, everyone in Roxby helped fill sandbags to put round the reading room, thus making a safe haven to go to when air raids took place. The reading room was in the centre of the village, where people came to pay their rent and where the boys' club and the football team met.

There was also a pig club in Roxby during the war where everyone who kept a pig could collect pig food, as this was rationed. Most people in the village killed one or two pigs a year, and kept chickens, and a few people had one or two cows, so none of us went very short of food during the war.'

WOODEN BOMBS

'In the early 1940s an airfield was built at East Kirkby. Sand and ballast were brought in by train to Stickney railway station, where Irish workmen shovelled it from the wagons into sidings and then onto lorries. Later on there were train loads of bombs for the airfield.

There was a searchlight camp at Keal Cotes. The Germans gave us a bit of a pestering. They dropped quite a lot of bombs and land mines. There was also a mock airfield down the Back Lane, Stickford. They used to light it up at night to attract German bombers away from the real airfield. They put dummy wooden aircraft on this field, but one night the Germans dropped dummy wooden bombs to show they weren't deceived.

When the men came back from Dunkirk, some were billeted in the old Primitive Methodist chapel and others in private homes in Stickford.'

A HIVE OF ACTIVITY

'I was 14 years old when war was declared and I attended the Immingham secondary modern school. At school the next morning, our headmaster, Mr Wheatley, took assembly outside where we had a flagpole service and hoisted the Union Jack flag. Another of my memories is that pupils had to file out to the playing field and practice laying face down on the grass with six feet of space between each pupil, this was in case of air raids. Thankfully the training never became a reality. Eventually a large air raid shelter was built adjacent to the girls' playground. I left school a few months after this and I joined the Old Scholars Association. I was attending one of their meetings one evening at the school when we learned that a German bomber had come down at Thorndykes corner in Immingham. The pilot and his crew survived and were brought to the school and put into the medical room where they were given treatment before being taken away under escort.

Our sleepy little village was soon to become a hive of activity. Lancaster bombers were based at the new aerodrome at North Killingholme and the noise of them setting off on bombing raids was something we had to get used to, as they circled round and round in the sky waiting for the squadrons of planes to get into formation and then set off to Germany. It was strangely quiet when they had at last departed into the night but not for long as the German planes came over to bomb the city of Hull, and the four huge guns in a field in the middle of the village fired almost constantly towards Hull in an effort to bring down the "Jerries". I used to sleep at the house of an old lady next door during the war to keep her company and if the "buzzers" went to warn us of an enemy attack my parents and my brother would run round to be with us. My father was a special constable and during raids would have to patrol his "patch" in case of fires being started by the incendiary bombs which rained down on Hull, some of which went astray.

Mrs Hill, my Mum, brother and I would sit in the cupboard under the stairs which had been made as comfortable as possible. Three tall stools had been put in there for the adults to sit on, and the shelves opposite had been cleared so they could try and get a little sleep by putting their arms on the shelves and resting their heads on their arms! At the feet of the adults was a feather filled bolster which I laid on and across the end of the cupboard was another for Charles who was twelve years old at the commencement of the war. The noise of the four guns firing repeatedly was almost unbearable and we would try to keep it out by covering our ears with our hands. I remember one night particularly. The Germans seemed to have gone home and we came out from under the stairs when we heard a lone aircraft overhead and then a loud screaming noise which caused the electric light in the ceiling to swing backwards and forwards violently. Charles and I flung ourselves under the table! Everything after that seemed very quiet, and so it was for the rest of the night, but next morning news of a bomb having landed in Mr and Mrs Leaning's garden in the next lane caused most of the villagers to go down Scrub Lane to view the huge hole.

Searchlight crews were stationed on the outskirts of the village. I think there were four of these and at dark they would practise searching the sky for enemy aircraft. Each would search the sky separately and then all crews would meet up like an "X" and it was in the middle that, if and when a raid was going on, a bomber might be caught in the lights and the guns knew where to shoot to bring it down. It fascinated everyone watching it. Another familiar sight at this time was that of "balloons" down Brickyard Road, Chasehill Road and also in the village. These were manned by the RAF and looked, to a child, like very big fat fishes way up in the sky on the end of a rope or wire.

Down on the Humber Bank at this time was a group of NFS men, National Fire Services, who were presumably stationed there in case of fire among the tanks of black oil owned by the Admiralty and the petrol tanks owned by firms called Celand and Citex. A contingent of firefighting sailors was also based on the Humber Bank. The petrol tanks supplied aerodromes with fuel for the planes, and the black oil tanks supplied oil to the naval ships when they came up the Humber. A friend of mine who lived on the Humber Bank at the brickyard had quite a puzzling experience one morning when she got up, for her bungalow windows were covered in muddy hand prints and there were also footmarks in the garden. Eventually she was told that a Lancaster bomber had come down in the Humber and the crew had managed to get out and swim and later walk on the mud to safety!

I was a member of the Women's Voluntary Services in the village and the old blacksmith's shop had been turned into a Forces canteen. I took a turn behind the counter along with two other ladies. The menu was mainly beans on toast, or jam on toast, and tea and coffee of course. The men (young mostly) seemed to enjoy coming to a different environment, having a game of darts and a chat to whoever there was to chat to, and we quite enjoyed it too.

In 1942 a contingent of the American Air Force arrived at Goxhill to train as fighter pilots and people of the area heard a different sound in the sky, that of Lightning aircraft. These had twin fuselages and screamed across the sky. Another noise to get used to! Jeeps full of Americans, or Yanks as we used to call them, rushed about the countryside making friends, especially, of children to whom they dispensed chewing gum and candy bars. They also gave the children of Goxhill wonderful Christmas parties.'

BUZZ BOMBS

'I lived on the outskirts of Barton on Humber and although only young remember the war years, particularly having to get inside when the air raid siren went and my older brother often missing at the time. We would listen to the "buzz bombs" chugging along over the Humber and hope the engines never stopped because that was when they dropped and exploded.

The searchlights at Barrow Haven scanned the skies for aircraft. Incendiary bombs were dropped to light up the area for enemy aircraft and one did drop at Barrow Haven where the big guns were kept. There were too many big pits full of water for much to burn but shrapnel flew for miles, some near our home, breaking our windows.'

BOMBS OVER GRIMSBY

'My memories of the war days include the sound of that first warning siren one Sunday at the beginning of the war, when we lived in Chelmsford Avenue, Grimsby. We all went into the Anderson shelter and then some silly fellow ran down the Avenue sounding the "Gas" rattle, so we sat in the shelter with gas masks on, but my mother had to take her mask off because she couldn't breathe, and there were we three children – my sister Joan, my brother Ralph and myself crying our hearts out because we thought she would die. Then my father came to see us – he was on ARP duty – to tell us we would be all right.

We had "ack-ack" guns on the farm behind our house, and had to have thick brown sticky paper criss-cross on all our windows. Every time the guns went off the windows and house shook, and one day the guns shot at a plane which came down on Mr Trevor's farm at the back of our house. All the men went running – armed with pitchforks – to the plane and found the poor pilot quite petrified. Another night there was an air raid and a lot of bombs dropped around us. We had to get out of the house in a great hurry and were told to run to my aunt's house, which was on the corner of Gloucester Avenue and Chelmsford Avenue, so my brother and I had to run like mad just as we were in our pyjamas! What a shock when we arrived, as there was a great big crater outside the house and unknown to us we had run through the middle of lots of anti-personnel bombs and it was a wonder we didn't get blown up. The Avenue was closed after we got out, but how lucky we were to get out! Another time my father and brother were delivering coal on Scartho Road, near to a row of wooden shops opposite Kirk's Farm. Father had just got into the cab of his lorry and Ralph was just returning when a plane started to machine-gun them, my brother throwing himself under the lorry.

In the summer holidays we used to do "holidays at home" in the People's Park, and when I belonged to a tap dancing class we entertained the people of Grimsby and the Forces stationed in the town. I remember rolling my hair into ringlets with rags, and then used sugar and water to keep it in – we thought we looked great but our hair was so stiff and sticky!'

'When the war began I was secretary to the school doctor based in the School Clinic, Burgess Street. It was always full of children seeking free medical attention.

One evening butterfly bombs were dropped. The next morning a lady arrived at the clinic with a bomb on a shovel. She asked the staff what to do with it – she was advised to carry it *very carefully* to the police station! Another family sought shelter in their garden Anderson shelter all night, little knowing that a huge bomb had been dropped and nestled right underneath them.

Some colleagues were on fire-watch duty on the flat roof of the council offices in Town Hall Square. The siren sounded and their leader bolted down into the offices below and slammed the roof door shut, leaving the intrepid firewatchers as sitting ducks.

One night three bombs were dropped on Town Station. My sister and a friend sheltered in an office and were covered in soot from the chimney, but those who had gone into the air raid shelter were killed.

Our saddest days were preparing the children for evacuation – those given "healthy" decisions boarded the buses amidst tears, smiles, gas masks and hugs from sad parents.

There were street parties everywhere after the war. Hope Street excelled itself, with bunting and flags down the middle of the street laden with food. Everybody had pooled their rations, and those neighbours who had shared hopes, fears and food now rejoiced together.'

INCIDENTS AND ATTACKS

'Hibaldstow is famous for an incident when a Spitfire took off with a WAAF clinging to the tail. She had been carrying out normal duties holding down the tail before take-off in wind. The pilot should have stopped after taxiing to position prior to take-off to allow the WAAF to get off. Unfortunately the pilot, probably due to fatigue, failed to do this, resulting in a flight over the airfield which has become history. The Spitfire is now part of the Battle of Britain Flight and this story is related by them.

During the war there were many incidents in the area because the airfield on the edge of the village was used as an Operational Training Unit. Quite a number of crashes involved the training aircraft.

Fortunately there was only one enemy attack. A German aircraft had followed a British plane back in. The false runway lights were switched on, diverting the enemy plane away from the airfield. The stick of four bombs that were dropped fell mainly in fields and back gardens, the only direct hit being to a garden shed, but ceilings came down and windows were blown out in property along the main road. The post office suffered some damage and postage stamps could be seen blowing about in the road.

Another incident occurred when twelve American B17s were diverted due to fog. The sight of these huge aircraft was something to be forever remembered. Distress flares were set off, one of which landed in a farmer's stackyard causing it to go up in flames. He did not know until years later that the whole event was witnessed by two young men in the Home Guard, for he had a terrible job obtaining compensation, the Yanks having denied that the flares had travelled in that direction.'

LIFE GOES ON

Whatever happened, we still had to feed and clothe our families and work as well as we could for the war effort. We coped with rations and coupons, and still found time for enjoyment.

WE CAME TO FOSTON

'In September 1939, Muriel and I were married. September was the month the war commenced and we came to live at Foston having bought the shop and bakery from Mr H. Shelbourn. Muriel came from London and I came from Birmingham and we found the conditions were so different from the city life we were accustomed to.

We did not have the luxury of main drainage. Lavatories as we know them did not exist. Not many houses had septic tanks and most had bucket toilets, the contents of which were buried in the gardens. Mains water did not come to Foston until after the war. Water came from wells at various depths from 25 feet to 50 feet. A few houses had a bathroom for which water was hand-pumped to a tank in the roof. Some of us installed an electric pump which was not the best idea, it was so easy in the summer time to empty the well.

We did not have any street lighting, but that did not matter as all lighting was prohibited for the duration of the war. A complete blackout for both business and household premises was rigorously enforced by the police and special constables which every village and town had in plenty.

Going back to the water supply, drinking water was delivered to each house daily, two buckets each day from Mr Johnson's water tanks delivered by Model-T Ford lorry. This service was supplied by the West Kesteven District Council because the well water was of doubtful purity.

The advantages of village life were considerable. The residents were well supplied by local and our own tradesmen. We had a resident butcher's shop with post office, a mobile greengrocer, a cobbler, a saddler who was also the knacker man (dead animal collector), a garage and petrol and paraffin station, and a local milk supplier (door to door). A district nurse lived in the village who was also the midwife as most babies were born at home. Dr Wilkie from Long Bennington held three surgeries in the village each week. I nearly forgot our blacksmith/farrier. Including my own shop and bakery, with three outside bakers and grocers and three butchers, all tradesmen gave a door to door service, and we had a good bus service operated by the Lincolnshire Road Car Company Limited giving us seven services every day to Grantham and Newark. I must not forget Percy Dickinson, our coal merchant with his horse-drawn coal carts, who had his coal yard at Sedgebrook station where his coal was delivered by rail. Our two public houses, the Black Horse and the Black Boy were well patronised for social meeting places, darts, skittles and dominoes, played with considerable skill.

Soon after war broke out we had to carry identity cards. Every person had to register and we were issued with ration books which were on a coupon basis. Village people were better off than town dwellers because rabbits, hares and poultry were always available. As the war went on and Lincolnshire became one big airfield, I obtained the contract to supply the YMCA and NAAFI canteens with bread, flour and bakery goods on Bottesford RAF airfield, which put my establishment under some pressure, especially my water supply. I engaged a water diviner from Melton Mowbray – a Mr Clarke – and on his findings, we bored 150 feet and found sufficient water for our needs but at great expense. I got into all sorts of difficulties with my bank manager! Within a 15 mile radius of Foston there were 20 airfields and landing strips, most of which were operated by Bomber Command.

To supplement the food rationing we had a very successful Pig Club of which I was the chairman. We had about 40 members and we were allowed to keep two pigs, one for home consumption and one to be sold to the bacon factory. A ration of pig food meal was issued by the Ministry of Agriculture and pig killing day was a very busy day of salting the flitch and hams, making the brawn and sausages, rendering the lard and making the pork pies which were brought to me at the bakery to be baked. We had all sorts and sizes, some just swimming in fat which made a horrible mess in our ovens, and we charged threepence per pie.

The farms were very different in the 1940s and 1950s. In Foston, if my memory is correct, there were five herds of dairy cows which meant employment for a number of men. The milk was collected in churns by the daily milk lorry and some taken to Sedgebrook station and put on rail for transport to Nottingham Dairies.

Because of the restriction of travel during the war, we became a very close and friendly community. The Women's Institute Hall (which incidentally was a wooden army hut purchased from Belton Park after the 1914–18 war) was a meeting place for our social events. A whist drive was held every fortnight, very regular dances and any social gathering such as Christmas parties for the children. The local RAF personnel superbly supported any event we put on; no trouble in those days, too many "Redcaps" about.

The Land Army girls from the hostel at Allington did invaluable service as more and more men were called up for military service.

With the building of the prisoner of war camp at Allington, we had both German and Italian men working on the farms; they were good workers and much appreciated. I supplied the camp with bread and security was very tight. Every time, we had to show our pass when going in and coming out to the guard with a loaded rifle. The same applied when the Americans took over Bottesford airfield with the first of the Flying Fortresses. Every time we approached the barrier out came a GI with a tommy gun at the ready. At the same time they were very generous with some of the things we hadn't seen for a long time, such as bananas, oranges, melon, gammon and silks and nylons for the girls as well as Camel cigarettes. Matches, strangely enough, were in very short supply.

During the war there were so many incidents that a long story could be told. However, on one moonlight night when a German bomber jettisoned a large number of incendiary bombs along the whole length of the Foston by-pass, it was generally thought it was mistaken for a runway on Bottesford airfield. On another occasion, on a Sunday night we returned from visiting my mother and found Foston had been the target of a military exercise by the Parachute Regiment. Because we had the food and the facilities, the CO commanded us to supply food and drink to his men, which was quite a challenge – they were very hungry. The Commanding Officer signed a form which enabled us to get payment for the food we supplied and a permit for us to replace food which was rationed. We did not get paid for our labour, which we did not expect, it became part of our war effort.

There was a tremendous amount of voluntary work done during the war. The Home Guard, Police Specials, Fire Watching, Civil Defence covered so many activities. I was a member of the Food Decontamination Squad which was all about the threat of gas poisoning. Thankfully we didn't have to be called out, poison gas was never used, but it was as well to be prepared. Voluntary work was of vital importance at the hospitals and much unsung help was given, like Muriel who, because she had been educated in Belgium and could speak French and Flemish was on the police register as an interpreter. There were Free Frenchmen in the RAF, also some Polish airmen who could speak French. Muriel was called upon several times to help, especially when these airmen made forced landings away from their own station.

As it was impossible to blackout light from the churches, there were no evening services during the winter months. Blackout reminds me of the masked headlights on motor cars. This consisted of a metal cover with a one-inch slit to allow some light to come through. We didn't travel fast or very far at night!'

THAT'S WHERE THE GULLS WENT

'Evacuees came to Scawby from Hull, and a lot of children stayed at Manor Farm which was nicknamed "Hell Fire Corner". The schoolchildren collected waste paper for salvage, and the WI had a working party to knit comforts for the troops.

In the months before D-Day some Canadian soldiers were billeted in Twigmore woods and as they were on iron rations the gulls and their eggs were used to satisfy their hunger. This meant the famous gull ponds were without their gulls as they never successfully bred there anymore.'

LINKS WITH THE PAST

'A "comforts" fund was inaugurated at Stickford to provide scarves, gloves, socks, balaclavas and chocolate (a rare commodity needing coupons – as did the wool which was used) for the servicemen from the village. Money and coupons were regularly collected each week and put to good use in twice yearly parcels. The knitting was done by the ladies and girls of the village. There were National Savings collections too, sometimes highlighted with special weeks of savings with targets to reach. "Digging for Victory" was another occupation carried out on all available pieces of land and garden.

Sometimes eating apples from local orchards were given to visiting airmen from the nearby aerodrome and visits by the airmen to the homes of local people for a welcome meal were much appreciated. Many of these airmen who established links with the local people still visit them regularly and a reunion takes place every year of the Squadrons 57 and 630 based on the East Kirkby aerodrome where local people still recall, together with the airmen they knew and still know, the comradeship which then existed. Local dances, in the blackout, took place and either a well known band made up of blind men, or a band from the aerodrome, hastened tapping feet to the dance floor, usually in a local village hall.

On the nights – and latterly the days – when raids over Germany took place, many of the villagers would stand in their gardens or fields noting the aircraft going out and were always pleased to see them return, especially when they knew they contained particular airmen who were friends. It is from this association with the raids using the Lancaster bombers that a wave of emotion and recollection sweeps through the body and sends shivers down the spine when the present "City of Lincoln" Lancaster bomber now flies out from Coningsby on its weekly summer appearances around this country and abroad.'

PINEAPPLE SWEDES

'Cubed swede soaked in pineapple essence doubled as pineapple chunks – just one of the strange ideas we encountered during those years of rationing and shortages. Meatless stews were a frequent part of our diet, and recipes were issued by the Ministry of Food to educate people in the use of dried egg and dried milk. Their chocolate cake recipe, I remember, was particularly good!'

PRISONERS OF WAR

'When I was married with a small son, our family had a farm and during the war four German prisoners of war worked there, coming daily from their camp at Moorby for four years. One of them was only 18 years old. They would bring their own meat and this would be cooked at the farmhouse, and potatoes and vegetables and a rice milk pudding and fruit in season would be given to them for their midday meal. This was eaten in a barn, made comfortable by the prisoners – it even had a mirror. In return they made wooden push-along toys for our son with materials from the farmyard and bootbrushes for the family, with hair from the farm horses providing the bristles.'

A LONG COLD WAR

'As soon as war was declared all emergency services at Heckington were called together: the observer corps to monitor the aircraft, air raid wardens to patrol and to sound the alarm, firefighters to stand by. The Red Cross and St John Ambulance manned the first aid post whilst local defence volunteers formed themselves into the Home Guard with very few weapons or uniforms. Thank heavens we were never invaded!

We welcomed children who were evacuated from London, the Land Army girls and, eventually, the paratroopers. The local policeman greeted these with "You can do exactly as you like – but remember, not on my patch!"

The village soon became very alive. We carried our gas masks and accepted buying food on ration books and clothing on coupons. Petrol was rationed to two gallons a month, car head lamps were masked. All signposts were removed and windows were shuttered or blacked out with heavy black curtains. Shops soon became short of goods.

Luckily the radio came to our aid with people like Gert and Daisy and the Ministry of Food with their recipes and pamphlets. There was spam, dried eggs, soya and so on, which the Radio Doctor assured us was good for us. The Land Army girls formed a dance band, the WI entertained and performed plays in the Temperance Hall, so called since 1863 when it was first given to the village – the soldiers put an end to that tradition by placing a barrel of beer on the bar draped with the Union Jack, much to the dismay of the aged caretaker.

We became accustomed to the constant drone of the bombers setting out on their raids, almost hedge-hopping with their weight of bombs. Sad in the morning to see them limping home with parts missing. We hurried home to listen to Sir Winston Churchill who always gave us hope. When Vera Lynn sang *We'll meet again* we remembered all we knew who were far away in the thick of battle. We laughed with Tommy Handley and scared ourselves by listening to Lord Haw Haw. It was a long cold war; we lost our youth. Eventually the end came and we tried to celebrate. We danced on the village green – until some spoil-sport let off a tear gas bomb, and we all went home.'

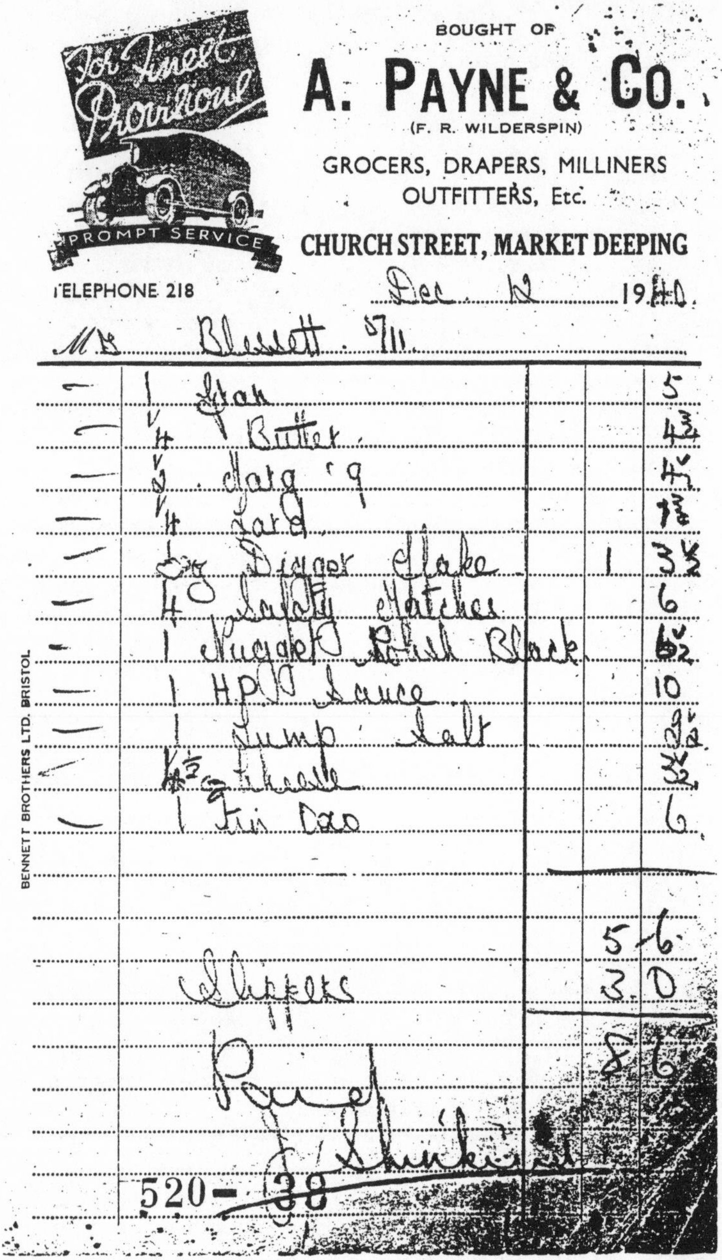
For Finest Provisions

PROMPT SERVICE

BOUGHT OF

A. PAYNE & CO.

(F. R. WILDERSPIN)

GROCERS, DRAPERS, MILLINERS

OUTFITTERS, Etc.

CHURCH STREET, MARKET DEEPING

TELEPHONE 218 Dec 12 1940

Mrs Blessett 5/11

1	Jam		5
1/4	Butter		4¾
1/2	Marg 9		4½
1/4	Lard		7½
1 pkg	Digger Flake	1	3½
4	Safety Matches		6
1	Nugget Polish Black		6½
1	H.P. Sauce		10
1	Lump Salt		3½
½ lb	Treacle		3½
1	Tin Cocoa		6
		5	6
	Slippers	3	0
		8	6

Paid

520—38

BENNETT BROTHERS LTD. BRISTOL

A grocer's bill from 1940 at Market Deeping.

'Stamford had evacuees from Camden in London and Nottingham. Householders were paid seven shillings a week to look after them. Local girls had their noses put out of joint when local boys went for the "Greenflys" (Camden girls who wore a green uniform). A few married locals and still live in Stamford.

Every Saturday morning people queued at Nelsons the butcher's in Stamford Square, there would be as many as 100 zigzagging across the Square. We didn't queue for anything in particular as we never knew what we were getting until it was our turn. After Nelsons we would go around the corner to Wrights and the same would happen. If we were lucky we would get out to play by eleven o'clock.

My mother would take the cream off the milk every day and put it into a Kilner jar. At the end of the week we would shake it until it separated and so we had butter for tea on Sunday!

We kept chickens on our allotment and I had to go up in my dinner hour to feed them. We were lucky when they laid as the ration was one fresh egg every six weeks. When they stopped laying they were soon in the pot. Sharing a pig was common in the country but living in the town we couldn't keep a pig; but we did have friends and there were ways and means – very cloak and dagger as it all went on at night and the meat was cut up on the kitchen table!

When the British Restaurant opened in Stamford you could get a three course meal for one shilling and sixpence.

Clothing coupons came into force but there were never enough especially when you are 16. We made dresses and skirts out of blackout material, which wasn't rationed, I also made a dress out of a wrap-around pinafore. Shoes could be made out of webbing and cork soles, they didn't last long but looked good for a while. When we went out we put Burdall's gravy salt on our legs and drew a line down the back with a pencil as stockings were scarce. We put pipe cleaners in our hair to curl it until "Dinkys" came in and everybody thought they were the tops.

When the war started, I started at the Fane School, Stamford. I cycled to school and if you could get home in three minutes you were allowed to go home when the siren sounded. We had a practice run, but no way could I do this and so it was down the shelters for me. One day we had cookery and we made junket. At 4.15 pm mine hadn't set and so I couldn't take it home on my bike. We hung about waiting for it to set, the siren went and we had to go down the shelter. This happened to be the only time a bomb was dropped on Stamford. It was October 1940, the bomb was six feet long, weighed a ton and landed on a house in St Leonards Street. It went through the door, across the living room and kitchen and landed unexploded in the coalhouse. The same plane machine-gunned Blackstone's works and followed the railway line up to Essendine.

Another girl and myself knitted a pair of sea-boot stockings – oh, what an awful smell when you knitted with that wool. We each had a letter from the sailor who wore them.

When I left school I worked in a shop in the High Street and enrolled for fire-watching. We trained in a wooden shed in West Street, where there was a door each end, a fire in the middle and we had to crawl on our stomachs through thick smoke wearing overalls and gas masks. If you made it you passed your test. We had to practise using the stirrup pump, one had to pump while the other squirted. Our instructor didn't think it funny when we answered him holding the squirter!

The bands at the dances were fabulous. The Squadron Airs played in Stamford and there was also a Polish dance band, all playing the Glenn Miller sound of course. American bands too came into Stamford, but they also picked up girls in their trucks and took them to dances at their bases – I was never allowed. Several Stamford girls married Americans and went to live in the States.

Some funny things happened in the blackout. One night as we were sitting around the fire listening to the radio, the door burst open and three American airmen and their girlfriends came in thinking it was the pub! Another time, a friend of mine was at the front of a party when she opened the first door she saw in a pub to discover to her horror that it was the men's toilet, and with everyone pushing she couldn't turn around to get out!'

DOING OUR BIT

From collecting for the Comforts Fund to serving in the Home Guard, we 'did our bit' in any way we could.

COMFORTS FUND

'During the war years a group of people met at the Duke's Head in Gedney Hill and formed a Comforts Fund. Many functions were held to raise money for our local men and women in the forces, including garden fetes, bowls matches and darts matches. One fundraising idea had people paying sixpence each to have their name embroidered on a tablecloth which was later auctioned. I can also remember selling raffle tickets at twopence each for the prize of half a stone of shallots and making £14, which was a lot of money in those days.

My father was a shepherd on a 250-acre fenland grass farm. It was ploughed up, dykes cut and some filled in to make bigger fields to grow food during the war. German and Italian prisoners of war worked in the fields and British soldiers stood guard over them with fixed bayonets.'

WE ALL HELPED

'Home life was very restricted during the war, with the blackout and rationing of food and clothes. At Navenby people raised money for food parcels to send to the troops and ladies knitted socks, pullovers and scarves for the servicemen. Gas masks were assembled at Boothby Hall in the next village by local people. Tea towels and bedding were made from used flour bags, and mothers sewed by candlelight to make clothes for their children, many being passed down.

Men who were exempt from service did Home Guard duties and women did fire-watching. After Dunkirk, troops were evacuated into large houses and halls, and entered village life.

When peace was declared, the church bells rang out, lights went on, bonfires were lit and parties were organised in the hall and the High Street.'

THE 'WAR AG'

'The War Agricultural Executive Committee issued cropping orders to all farmers, however small the acreage – shipping was needed for the war effort and Britain's farmers had to provide the food we might otherwise have got from overseas. Grants and subsidies were given to encourage people to make the best use of their land, including wheat and calf subsidies, potato acreage payments and grants for ploughing up grassland. Bird seed was grown on a permit – it was a paying crop and there were heavy penalties for those caught without a permit.

The "War Ag" brought Italian prisoners of war in to Kirton Holme from Horbling to work on the farms; they wore dark red uniforms and the lowest ranks worked while the others were "in charge". They were skilled craftsmen who could turn a silver shilling into a signet ring. Farm workers were supposed to be exempt from war service but still some were called up from the village. Even the roadman, in his forties, was called to war.

There was a small searchlight unit in the village but only one bomb fell here, doing no harm. It was thought that "Jerry" had probably dropped the bomb on his return to Germany.'

MORE FORTUNATE

'My father served in France during the First World War and he was a sergeant in the Osbournby Platoon Home Guard. I was allowed to peep inside the village hall to view the "disbandment dinner" of the Home Guard. Tables were set with best silver and white tablecloths; candelabra on the top table for the officers. The menu, despite rationing, was rabbit pie and apple pie.

Two WVS ladies brought meat pies (or substitute) to our house each week during the war, and these were sold on to farm workers – without the need to give up food ration coupons. A group in the village knitted garments for servicemen. Transport brought Land Army girls and also prisoners of war (German and Italian) to work locally each day. Forestry girls cut wood for pit props at Aisby Wood. Eventually some of these workers were billeted permanently on farms. There were no official evacuees in the village, but several children, relatives of parishioners, came from various cities to avoid the bombing raids and hopefully have a safer upbringing. We suffered isolated incidents of enemy action intended for the airfields near us but we were more fortunate than the town dwellers in every respect.'

HOME GUARD STORIES

'My Dad was a member of the Home Guard at Friskney. One evening as he prepared to go out to a Home Guard meeting my mum was not too happy. She was expecting a baby at any time and did not want him to go. He had to cycle two miles to the meeting and two miles home and she said it usually finished in the local pub so it was late when he returned home, so there was some tension in the atmosphere before he left. Mum went to bed and when he arrived home he had to get his own supper so he cut off a big chunk of bread and then chose a lovely, round onion and went to eat it in bed. Mum pretended to be asleep but when she passed some remark the next day about eating onions in bed he said, "I thought you already had one bee in your bonnet, so I'd better keep it buzzing."

Stickney Home Guard and the regular army held some joint manoeuvres during the war – the Home Guard defended the village against the "Regulars". To keep things looking authentic a light aircraft was used to drop flour bags representing bombs; the ones with flour inside were incendiary bombs and the ones containing soot were supposed to be proper bombs. One Sunday during these

LAYOUT OF A ROADBLOCK
— IN A TOWN —

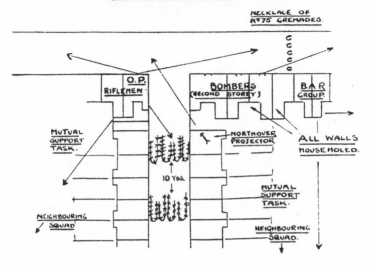

POINTS TO NOTE :—

1. THE BLOCK IS SITED TO PREVENT THE PASSAGE OF ENEMY A.F.V.s INTO THE DEFENDED LOCALITY. SIMILAR BLOCKS WILL BE SITED ON ALL OTHER ROADS LEADING INTO THE LOCALITY.

2. THE SQUAD IS SITED FOR ALL-ROUND DEFENCE.

3. THE POST IS CONCENTRATED.

4. THE BOMBERS HAVE MOBILITY.

A Home Guard instruction booklet issued in 1943 gave directions on everything from setting up road blocks to engaging the enemy.

manoeuvres a very prim and proper spinster was walking to church along the pavement in front of the railings outside the Methodist chapel and a soot bomb fell, right on the top of the spikes and covered her from head to foot. The local observers had a good laugh but she was most indignant and went home looking like a chimney sweep.'

'I served in the Home Guard at Stickford before joining the Navy. We used Stickford church tower as a lookout point. One watch would be at the top from dusk until dark, watching out for parachutists. If anything happened, you were to ring the church bell (then a national invasion signal). From our vantage point we could also watch the surrounding fields. One of our fears was of the loss of the harvest through the cornfields being set on fire. A similar watch was kept in the early mornings.'

THE WOMEN'S LAND ARMY

Women who were called up were given the choice between the services, munitions work or joining the Land Army. Those who became land girls entered a world of hard work, keeping vital food supplies going, but can look back now with satisfaction at a job well done.

I FANCIED THE UNIFORM

'I joined the Women's Land Army in 1943. It was the uniform I fancied – those jodhpurs, woolly socks, green jumper, the great-coat and the jaunty hat. I never really thought beyond that. I was a shorthand typist, living with parents on the outskirts of Nottingham. I had lived a very sheltered life, arriving rather late in my parents' life. All our pleasures were found within the chapel and I belonged to the chapel youth club. I decided the Land Army was the life for me, a complete change from the routine of office work. After filling in the enrolment form I was summoned for an interview in Nottingham where I was told that girls were urgently needed for milking and dairy work. I was much too shy to say that wasn't exactly what I'd had in mind – I would be given a month's training.

I had never been near a cow in my life, viewing them only from a railway carriage and occasionally seeing them in distant fields on a visit to the countryside. I was very dubious regarding the difference between a cow and a bull. Certainly I couldn't ask anyone – those sort of things just weren't discussed in those days.

About a couple of months later my uniform arrived – by post. When I went for my interview the woman produced a tape measure, flung it hither and thither, jotted down a few numbers, and hey presto, everything fitted. The instructions said I was to report to a farm near Torksey in Lincolnshire where I would receive my month's training.

There were several more Land Army recruits waiting on Nottingham station, but not one of them was a so called "urgently needed" milk girl. They were going to a hostel and would be sent out daily to work in the fields and when required by local farmers. They were full of high spirits and were aghast when I told them what I would be doing.

I arrived at my destination to find another Land Army girl, Christine, and we were both being billeted with a farm worker and his wife for the month. It was a large farm with two dairy herds, and each month they trained two girls, one to do hand milking, the other to do machine milking and we were asked to choose which one we would prefer to do. Before I could open my mouth my new found friend seized the opportunity to announce she would do the machine milking.

I felt she had a decided advantage over me, living in a Lincolnshire village not so far away. My first shock came upon my visit to the outside loo. I thought all houses had flush toilets. I was horrified to find an old earth closet way down at the bottom of the garden, nor was there a bathroom – only a sink and an old pump in the kitchen.

That evening a terrible homesickness swept over me. What had I done? My visions of tossing hay in the summer sun had faded, and I felt doomed and trapped. I was to report to the cow stable at 6.30 am, a time of day which had previously never existed for me. I carried my candle upstairs to bed as the cottage only had electricity downstairs. It was all there – the candle to light me to bed, the cold lino (it was February when I joined), the washstand with its marble top and flowery patterned bowl and jug, the matching pottie under the bed! I climbed into bed alongside Christine, clinging to the hope that in some miraculous way the war would be over in the morning. Peace would be declared, the armistice signed, and I could go running back to my nice, new modern home and comfortable life.

Six o'clock arrived – the war was still on and after a quick cup of tea, I walked along to the cow stable, a long building where about 20 cows were tied. It was lit by hurricane lamps and I found the smell revolting. Two men had already made a start on the milking and one of them introduced me to my "practice" cow. Apparently all the girls learned on that old cow. He sat down and gave me a hurried demonstration and left me to go back to his own milking, saying I would soon get the hang of it. He had shown me the art of holding the bucket between my legs, but my knees were shaking so much I couldn't keep it there. My mouth was parched and I felt sick with fear. My mind began to wander as I sat there. I thought of the number of times I had been taken by my parents to the pantomime in Nottingham – how everyone had laughed when Idle Jack, of Jack and the Beanstalk, had tried to milk the cow by pumping its tail up and down. I thought, sitting there, that it wasn't funny at all – it was just a jolly good idea. How I wished that was the way things were done!

I hadn't really taken in what the cowman had said. I'd rather expected to watch, just on that first morning. Had he said take the cow's back two "things" first? Or he could have said, take her front two "things" first. Would the cow know and object if I took her "things" in the wrong order? Perhaps it was one from the front and one from the back. The possibilities seemed endless. Was it rather like bell ringing? If you didn't get it right the first time round – everything fell apart! The cow was still munching away at her food and it seemed the most sensible thing to do was to get the job over before she realised what was happening at the other end. I leaned my head against the cow, stretched out my arm and felt around, I knew there were just four "things". The whole operation seemed positively disgusting to me. It just didn't seem the decent thing to be doing, groping around under that old cow. Had he said a squeeze and a pull, or a pull and a squeeze? I was just about to make a start when something nearly rocked me off my stool. No one had told me cows coughed! And thinking I was about to be attacked I fled with my bucket and stood shaking with fear with my back against the cow stable wall.

I could hear the milk swishing into the buckets at the other end of the cow stable and the two laughing and talking as they milked. There was no way out for me – I'd made my bed and I'd jolly well got to lie on it. I plucked up courage and went back, extracting about enough milk to make a cup of tea. The awful thing was, it wasn't just a one-off thing, it had got to be repeated every morning and afternoon for heaven knows how long. I had no appetite for breakfast and I wondered how on earth I was going to survive. My confidence increased and by the end of the month I was milking my practice cow and one more. The cowman wasn't at all impressed – it seemed the previous girl had been milking four times by the time she left.

My new posting instructions arrived at the end of the month. I was to go to North Somercotes on the Lincolnshire coast where I would be employed in milking and general farm work. I was to live in at the farmhouse with the elderly widowed lady farmer. On my arrival, the first thing I noticed, on the kitchen table, was an open copy of the *Christian Herald*, and one of the first questions she asked was: "Do you go to chapel?" Oh yes, I said – and we take the *Christian Herald* at home. Well, this seemed to clinch it, I was, it seemed, the answer to a widow's prayer. Over a cup of tea she told me that the farm

Cynthia Pearson and a friend in their Land Army uniforms.

worker and herself had not attempted to unpack the newly installed milking machine, but thought it advisable to await my arrival, seeing that I had been instructed in the art of machine milking and would, therefore, know all about it. It was when she began enquiring the make of the machine I had been using that I had to break the news to her – I had never handled a milking machine. It seemed the Land Army authorities had blundered, Christine had been sent to where they did hand milking, and I was where they did machine milking.

It was when I went to the toilet that I decided that at all costs I must master those milking machines – the toilet had a chain! I felt quite heady with relief. There was no toilet paper, after all there were shortages of most things in those days, but there, in a little wooden box at the side of the toilet was an old Methodist hymn book! I thought it was carrying things a bit too far – *Christian Herald* on the kitchen table, Methodist hymn book in the toilet. She was up to the section of the Christmas carols when I arrived – No 130, *It came upon the midnight clear*! I was quite sorry when we reached the index at the back of the book.

There was electricity both downstairs and upstairs, and a cold water tap at the kitchen sink – one of the most modern houses in the village, she told me. Between the three of us, we managed those milking machines and I was duly left in charge of the milking. My courage and expertise grew and a quiet confidence developed between me and the cows.

On my second morning I met Sam, an old bearded man who helped out at busy times. He was waiting for me in the yard, engrossed in lighting his pipe. Without looking up, he shouted at me in the broadest Lincolnshire dialect: "Fetch be-ast from cloo-as" I didn't understand a word of it, but I wasn't unduly worried, it wasn't unusual if you didn't get something the first time round so I said in a very polite voice "Pardon?" Without looking up, he said exactly the same thing all over again. I was just wondering what my next move should be and how I was going to get anything done at all if I didn't understand the language, when he looked up, glared at me and shouted: "Are ya dee-af – doo-ant ya spe-aak English?" The cloo-as, it seemed was a grass field. However, I thought what I lacked in knowledge, I would make up for in willingness, so I opened the gate, tore down the field and the cows scattered in all directions. It took a long time before Sam accepted me.

My lady farmer also kept pigs. The pighouse was a long, low building, a narrow passage down the side with five pig sties, and I was sent to clean them out. No one ever gave me any advice regarding the right way to tackle any job, it was a case of trial and error. The pigs were being fed kale – long, thick stalks. The pigs ate the leaves, gnawed the stalks, trampled them underfoot and then left them. They were lying in disarray in all that sloppy pig muck, I knew that somehow I had to get them out and on to the muck hill. I couldn't balance them on my shovel, but if I pierced them with my muck fork they wouldn't come off. I began to grow desperate. I still had a list of jobs to do, and it seemed the only way to deal with those stalks was to manhandle them, so I kept picking them up, one each hand, out of all that sloppy pig muck and carried them out and flung them one by one on to the muck hill. The mess I got into was unbelievable. The little pigs ran between my legs, my nice clean dungarees were absolutely lathered up. Every morning, I climbed into a pair of dungarees, stiff with a mixture of pig and cow muck and pig swill. I had pig potatoes to cook in a large steamer out in the yard, and I would sit on the meal bin and munch a couple, feeling rather like the prodigal son – "and he would fain fill his belly that the swine did eat". It wasn't that I wasn't well fed – there's just nothing tastier than a hot pig potato!

Next came the chickens. I had instructions to clean them out; no deep litter or battery hens in those days. My lady farmer had gone to Louth – quite a day's event in those times. It was my first attempt at mucking chickens. I flung the door open convinced I could manage those chicks better than I did the pigs. They were young chicks about six weeks old, and I think they must have heard about my inexperience, for as soon as I opened the door, out they started to fly. I really thought that when I opened that door, the chickens would just stand back and watch me. I slammed the door to keep the remaining ones in and went after the culprits. My only implement was a shovel, so I kept trying to pin them down with that, but I must have been rather heavy handed, because I laid them all out! I was absolutely horrified, I thought they were all dead. What could I tell my lady farmer? I could bury them in the muck hill, but I didn't know how long it would take them to disintegrate. Did she know how many chickens she had started out with in the first place? Would she miss the odd dozen or so? I decided I would clean the chicken hut out first and decide later, but after a few minutes the chickens started to come round, and whilst they were still staggering around and only half conscious, I grabbed them and flung them into the hut again, and no one was any the wiser.

Things gradually improved and I began to enjoy my new life. For some strange reason, my lady farmer wouldn't do my washing, nor would she allow me to do it, but in spite of this we got on wonderfully well together. I used to send my washing home to be done. In those days if you posted a parcel one day, it was delivered at the most two days later. My mother grew tomatoes, her part in the dig for victory campaign. She was absolutely delighted – she would soak my dungarees, and then water the tomato plants with the water! My three years in the Land Army were amongst the happiest years of my life, and I did, after all, become that tanned creature tossing hay in the summer sun.'

A CHILD'S WAR

Children soon came to accept war as a normal way of life, but many can recall their feelings of apprehension as their safe, everyday world changed around them. Particularly affected were the evacuees, facing a new life far from their families.

A FEELING OF APPREHENSION

'I was 13 years old when the war began, and I remember clearly on that Sunday morning sitting around our wireless and hearing Mr Chamberlain say, "We are at war with Germany." My father had been in the trenches during the First World War, and when I was young he told me quite a lot about it.

When evacuation from the big cities took place, Camden School for Girls was evacuated to Grantham, and the Girls High School shared their school with them. This meant that we only went to school in the mornings and the Camden girls in the afternoon. We had to share desks, lockers, cloakrooms and so on, and of course we had fewer lessons and more homework, and hardly any school activities. In the winter the buses were blacked out with blue painted windows. If there had been a bombing raid during the night and we had been in the shelters, at assembly the next day we were asked, "How many girls were up during the night?" If we had been we were allowed to sleep for one of the lessons.

I vividly remember coming on the bus through Ropsley village. The driver called at the shop to leave a bundle of newspapers. When he returned and climbed into the bus he said: "France has fallen." The whole bus load of people fell silent and a strong feeling of apprehension affected everyone.'

'I was living in Bourne when the war began, and I remember crying when I saw someone wearing a gas mask. My baby sister had a different type, one you put the baby inside, but luckily we never had to use any of them. We had to have blackout curtains and everything was rationed, even sweets. We didn't have any bad air raids in Bourne, but one night a German plane crashed on the public house, killing several people including the crew, who are buried in our cemetery.

Bourne had lots of evacuees from Hull. I remember seeing all these small children waiting for people to take them into their homes. They did look sad and forlorn. Our school classes doubled and we used the local chapel schoolrooms for lots of lessons like PT, singing and dancing.'

FLITTING IN 1940

'My childhood was spent in Leadenham, between Grantham and Lincoln. I remember walking down Leadenham High Street and seeing a big motor bike and Dad telling me that the rider was Lawrence of Arabia. He was then known as Aircraftsman Shaw and was stationed at RAF Cranwell. Apparently he used to come to one of the local pubs and talk to the village men on a Friday night.

On 6th April 1940 we flitted. This was the first time we had moved, though some people did it every year, but the farmer Dad worked for had retired and we had no option. The weeks before had been spent packing all our belongings. I had left school in December so I had to help. On moving day we were up early, for the beds had to be taken down and last minute packing done. At last a lorry arrived and loading began. The last to go on the lorry were various garden plants that my mother wanted, Dad's bike and the sofa. When all was finished, my mother, my sister and I were told to climb up and sit on the sofa, wrapped up with a blanket round our knees. It was a cold day, and we set off for our new home, which only Dad had seen, at Blyborough near Kirton Lindsey.

On our arrival at Blyborough we discovered we were no longer living in a village. In fact, it was so small it only had a cottage shop. Even more of a change was that we were living between two airfields, Hemswell, a bomber station, and Kirton Lindsey, a fighter station. Whichever way the wind was blowing for take-off, we had planes over us day and night.

I worked on the land and we grew a lot of potatoes so life was setting, picking or riddling potatoes. For a change we sometimes had to help when it was threshing time as Dad was in charge of all the threshing, including the steam engine. It didn't get me any special treatment though, and I was usually in the chaffhole, a very dusty job.

There were no evacuees in Blyborough but we once had a group of Jewish children from London. They occupied two cottages, with girls in one and boys in the other, and worked on the land. They were very surprised when they discovered where milk came from.

We also had boys from De Aston School, Market Rasen to help in the school holidays with the potato picking.

It was my job to weigh up the potatoes as they were picked and one of the masters who was looking after the lads saw me once rubbing a potato to eat and shouted at me not to eat raw potato as it was poison. The foreman who was passing at that moment said he had never heard anything so silly. "Down Boston way where I come from mothers give the little ones raw potatoes to chew while they pick them."'

RATS' TAILS

'I was five years old when the war started. I remember convoys of army lorries passing the house and Lancaster bombers droning overhead on raids, and taking my gas mask to school. Everyone had to do their bit for the war and the Ministry of Agriculture and Fisheries encouraged us to "Waste not, want not". It was important to keep the rat population down and being on a poultry farm, this was always a problem. My father caught numerous rats in traps and the dog also hunted them out. At school the headmaster paid us twopence for each rat's tail. I remember walking to school clutching my rats' tails in newspaper! I suppose the headmaster received money for them from the Ministry.

My father went to war when I was seven and the dog died so my little business came to an end.'

WELLINGTON BOOTS

'It was 1943 and wellington boots could not be bought for love nor money, as the war in the East meant that rubber was in short supply, and what was available went to the war effort.

So it was with great excitement that we heard an announcement at school – a consignment of boots had arrived from America and were for children who had to walk a long way to school. My brother and I qualified as we had to walk two and a half miles.

On the day the boots were to be given out we all assembled in the school hall. There were the boots – rows of ordinary black wellingtons and just one pair of shiny ones. Oh, how I longed for the shiny pair of boots but it was not to be. Names were called out in alphabetical order and as our surname began with "S" I was well down the list, and the shiny boots went to a girl whose name was Judson. I can still remember how disappointed I was, and really not a bit grateful that until I grew out of the new black boots I could walk dry shod, thanks to the generosity of our American allies.'

PLENTY OF ACTIVITY

'My earliest memories are of the war years when I was a little girl of six in 1940. My father died at 38 years old; he had a duodenal ulcer and peritonitis and there were no antibiotics to save him. My mother was left a widow with only ten shillings a week and five shillings for me. She took in lodgers to help pay the way, for as well as food and fuel to buy she was also buying our house.

Over the war years we had quite a variety of people staying with us including, we thought, two spies who were seen by the air raid warden signalling through the bedroom window during an air raid. The two men disappeared the next day, with the police wanting any mail that came for them. We also had an army deserter, only a 17 year old lad who had come asking for a bed. His mother was already staying with us. We were all woken by police banging on the door at 3 am and they took him away. I wonder what happened to him.

During an air raid a bomb dropped in the park near us. The teddy I was clutching bounced across the room. People who had been staying with us returned home with glass in their hair and blood on their faces when a bomb dropped on Lincoln where they had been visiting the cinema.

There was also plenty of activity going on with the Lancasters taking off from Waddington, trundling into the skies. Until the end of the war my mother and I slept in a Morrison shelter in our living room. It felt strange going upstairs to bed once the war was over.

At the end of the war, on VE Day, my mother and I went to the Grand Cinema for a treat. When we were coming out she fell down the steps and made her nose bleed. The manager sat her down and dropped a key down her back – a few minutes later he wanted it back to open the door!'

'Near to us was an old ironstone quarry with very rough terrain, where we used to go and play. Occasionally army cyclists and bren gun carriers came and drove round it, presumably practising. Great excitement for us kids.

A Lancaster crashed near Greetwell once and when we found out we went to look. Next day the police came round the school asking for the return of our "souvenirs", which included anti-radar foil and live ammunition taken from the aircraft!'

JUST ORDINARY MEN

'The ancient grammar school at Wragby was used to house local children when Wragby school had evacuees and their teacher moved into the school. Later all the children were integrated into Wragby school.

At this time there were numerous military units in the area who provided wonderful Christmas parties for local children. Many of the younger children had no memory of some of the foods provided. Prisoners of war who were working on local farms were also to be seen in Wragby and some of the children were afraid of them, until they realised they were just ordinary men far from home and loved ones.'

SALVAGE

'During the war years, as a school child, I used to help collect "the salvage" from all the houses in Uffington village. We worked in small groups and each had their own little patch to work in, and woe betide anyone who strayed over the boundary. The main items collected were used tins, jars, cardboard cartons, newspaper and paper.

Now to collect this, one had to have the latest mode of transport. In my young days any boy worth his salt had a home-made truck or cart. As a girl the nearest I ever came to having one was when my brother managed to obtain a couple of pram wheels, and I was allowed to help build this contraption by holding planks and generally making a nuisance of myself.

The ultimate pair of wheels would be those that could be steered by means of a rope attached to each one and the driver could sit in the box part. Having made up a good turn of speed with a sturdy pushing action by the feet, or a friendly push from behind given on the promise of "your go next", the driver would crouch in the box and fly down the road (no need to bother about any traffic on the roads in those days)!

Trundling our truck, we would visit the housewives on our patch to pick up what they had saved for us on a given day of the week after school. There were not many tins (all of which had to be rinsed clean) because of "rationing". Most houses in the village had their own gardens for growing vegetables, so just a few tins of peas or carrots might have been used. These days we have such a variety of tinned goods we cannot credit the meagre stock during the war. No cat or dog was ever fed from a tin, and a tin of fruit was a treat on a special occasion such as a birthday tea or at Christmas.

A jam jar was a rare commodity! Usually the housewife would save her jars to use when fruit came in abundance to the cottage gardens. If sugar had been scrounged, pounds of home-made jams lined the larder shelves. My mother's favourite was blackcurrant jam, and these few precious pots were stored on top of her wardrobe!

The newspapers in those days had very few pages and were thin compared with the size of today's, and were mainly broadsheets, (there was only one tabloid newspaper I think) but they were so necessary to everyday use. They were used for lining shelves and drawers, wrapping, and packing things put away for safety for the duration of the war years. Newspaper was even cut up into squares, a hole pierced in the corner with a skewer, and then threaded with a piece of string they were tied up in the outside loos as toilet paper. Incidentally, as there was no "night soil" collection the contents of the buckets were superb manure for the magnificent vegetables grown for family consumption.

Our collections would be carefully stacked in our cart, and we were very grateful for cartons to hold the tins and jars, also for the rare carrier bags for the papers. The carrier bags were made of strong brown paper with string handles, much superior to today's supermarket plastic ones. Everything was taken to a farmer's barn in the middle of the village where a team of WRVS ladies awaited us. They would seize our collection and the carton would be opened out and flattened, and the tins would be stamped upon before they were bundled into sacks (the brown hessian type).

Then, our labours over for that week we could wander off with our truck. In winter we hurried home, but during summer days the fields and river banks were our playgrounds. Then too we had the village pit to visit and plunder. This was a good half mile outside the village and was where people dumped unwanted items like old prams and bicycles with those coveted, super wheels!'

BY SCAMPTON AIRFIELD

'Scampton airfield was already built with its hangars and its quarters. During the war concrete runways were laid and much later the hallowed line of the Roman "Old Street" (A15) had a kink put in it to allow for the runways to be greatly lengthened for the newest generation of aircraft.

Actually the RAF made very little difference to us in the valley except for a few notable events. Early in the war many of the houses had aircrew billeted in their spare bedrooms. They were no trouble, and families became very fond of their big "sons" or "brothers". They lived with us to avoid being killed by enemy bombing of the aerodrome – only to lose their lives in missions over the Continent. One of the ladies in the village "lost" man after man and became very distressed. Our house was luckier, having only one man killed. I vividly remember that lovely summer evening riding round and round the big yard on my bike. Our own aircrew came out to enjoy the late sun, but one was missing. When I asked when would "Tonky" be back I was told never. I could not envisage this, it must be wrong. It was my first brush with death, and it left a hollow feeling – someone, above all the rest, had "failed to return". Of course, we were never told when they were going on a mission, but we always knew when they had been because, there on the sideboard, were left for us children a part of their in-flight rations – oranges, bananas and chocolate, the first two unseen by us for many months previously.

Funnily enough, unknowingly, we knew about the plans for the bombing of the dams by 617 Squadron (The Dam Busters). Evening after evening they did practice runs towards the cliff edge. After the famous raid, hindsight told us what they had been doing, and we felt very proud to have seen some of the preparations.

Other preparations we saw frequently. A favourite walk was towards Aisthorpe, up the hill, then back along the cliff edge towards Scampton. Bombers were dispersed quite close to the road, so that an evening walk would have the dubious entertainment of watching them being bombed-up for the night's raid. We didn't think of the deaths it meant, we were quite careless what happened to the enemy.

One night, after a line of bombers had had their deadly loads attached the fog came down and the raid was called off. I presume the bombs and ammunition were left on board for another day. By this date I was going to Lincoln to school, catching the 8.30 am bus each morning. As usual on a foggy morning, it was late, but there were to be some deadly events to enliven the waiting. We never heard the truth, of course, but it was fairly obvious that there had been an explosion or fire on one of the aeroplanes. Its ammunition went off rat-a-tat-tat. Then there were huge explosions, with shrapnel flying overhead and later found all over the local fields. The explosion of one aeroplane must have started the next one off, and so on down the line. It was most eerie in the fog. Today I would have been terrified, then I was just curious and interested.

In Scampton churchyard there is an Imperial War Graves section. Sadly the old graveyard was soon filled after hostilities began and a new one had to be consecrated by the bishop. An Air Force cortege was a frequent sight. I cannot hear "The Last Post" without a prickle on the back of my neck and an awful sadness inside me. In one corner is a small group of German graves, so far from home. Apart from this, village life had continued side by side with the pre-war growth of the airfield – largely oblivious of the preparations for war.'

'Germany had invaded Austria and Czechoslovakia in 1938 and when it appeared certain that Poland would be occupied, war seemed imminent and steps had to be taken to protect children and other vulnerable groups by evacuating them from the cities to other, safer areas. Thus it was that on Sunday 3rd September 1939, I found myself at Staniland school with colleagues from the Health Department, where we were to receive evacuees from some of the poorest parts of Hull.

They came in buses, which in those days had very hard seats and little springing, not at all like the comfortable travel coaches we know today. It was a hard, bumpy ride, very tiring and the evacuees arrived not knowing what to expect, from a busy crowded city to the quiet market town of Boston, having left behind other members of their families. They were weary and confused: pregnant women, mothers with babies and toddlers, and schoolchildren.

On arrival they were given food and drink, after which it was our job to inspect them for head lice. As they moved along the inspection line a black cross was put on the back of the hand of any who were verminous. Many were, but the crosses were soon rubbed off and the procedure had to be changed by marking the forehead instead. It all seemed degrading but as the evacuees were going to be taken into other people's homes, it was of course necessary for them to be clean. However, my heart went out to them.

Head lice were treated at the cleansing station (the old "casual wards" where tramps were able to spend the night), and this later became Wyberton West Hospital. Anyone thought to need medical attention was seen by a doctor and treatment was prescribed.

At 11 am everything stopped and there was complete silence as we listened to an important message on the wireless. Neville Chamberlain, the Prime Minister told the nation that we were at war with Germany. Even though the news was expected it was awful to actually hear the pronouncement and that moment lives in the memory. The business of the day continued.

During that evening we had an air raid warning. It was a false alarm, but that siren sounding the alarm, followed eventually by the "all clear" was to be heard many times after that first day of war.'

'We lived in a six-bedroomed house and Mum told me that we would be having two girl evacuees. The longed-for day came and two coachloads of children arrived at Sturton village school. My youngest sister, who was helping her Guide Captain, eventually arrived home with our two "new sisters", Dorothy and Brenda. They were treated exactly like family. My mother bottled extra pears and plums and

211

pickled eggs to give to the girls' families. I recall having to put my skipping rope with wooden handles away so that we could all share an old washline for skipping. We were each given a honey jar and taught to try and make our pennyworth of sweets last a week, after offering them round.

I shared my toys quite happily but quietly resented seeing my beloved books turned down at their corners, crayoned in and dropped noisily. We never fell out – but neither did I shed tears when they left.

There were quite a lot of evacuees in and around Sturton and we met up during and after school hours. If there was ever any friction I do not remember and my memories are happy regarding those years.'

'It was Friday afternoon, 1st September 1939, when buses came to a stop at Caistor modern school. Out tumbled travel-weary, apprehensive, homesick children, wearing luggage labels and carrying pillowcases containing garments and "iron rations" – I remember a block of chocolate and a tin of corned beef. We sat the children on the grass at the top of the drive, the entrance to the school. This was something of a shock, for we didn't sit on the grass in Hunslet, and we waited for prospective parents to choose the children they would take into their homes. The headmaster, the clerk to the RDC, the surveyor, and the local chemist registered particulars and we Leeds teachers in charge of the exodus from Hunslet stayed around to reassure everyone.

A fortnight before I had been on holiday in Switzerland, excited at the prospect of two glorious weeks climbing mountains, sailing on the lakes and crossing glaciers, until one night when we were advised to return to England, for there was no guarantee that we British would be able to travel home after the coming weekend. A few days later we were in Yorkshire, assembling our children from the Hunslet schools to board a train in a deserted siding bound for an unknown destination in Lincolnshire. Now, after a day of seemingly endless train journey we had arrived at Brigg and transferred to buses and here we were at this new school opened just a year before. It was built on one of the highest sites on the Lincolnshire Wolds, with breathtaking views of the countryside, in complete contrast to the situation we had left that morning where the outlook was grim to say the least and the view just dirty brick walls.

Much later that day when all the children had been collected, one other teacher and I were escorted to the home of a lady who had prepared for "six wee bairnies", and was most disconcerted to be confronted by two teachers. That night we bedded down on mattresses on the floor of an attic and crawled around with the aid

212

of torches. We were moved the next morning and found ourselves in yet another attic big enough to accommodate two complete suites of bedroom furniture. Yet another shock! At a quarter to nine that night we were handed two paraffin lamps and were told very kindly, "Goodnight, ladies. Bedtime." Imagine the horror of two town bred, unattached females accustomed to catching the last tram or train home from Leeds City Square! War had not been declared but this was certainly Evacuation. We spent the first two days visiting the adopted homes of our children and hearing the tales of woe and trying to sort out numerous problems. The main trouble seemed to be that they just wanted fish and chips and their mothers.

Monday morning saw us rounding up our youngsters and moving them like the Children of Israel across the Market Place, eventually to arrive at the church school where the headmistress was utterly bewildered and unprepared for such an influx of town children. There was insufficient furniture, so we sat on the floor; no spare equipment, so we divided into two groups and had half-time schooling. In later, happier days we looked back and laughed with that delightful headmistress blessed with a lively sense of humour.

War had been declared on the Sunday morning and the first air raid warning was sounded that night, which we spent in the huge cellar, very cold and all to no purpose, for it turned out to be a false alarm. I often wondered why I chose to return from the beautiful neutral country of Switzerland, to spend the next six years in what I then regarded as a most unattractive homeland. I wanted to be back in the Yorkshire Dales with the busy centre of Leeds offering concerts, hotels, theatres with the annual visit of the D'Oyley Carte. Well, you may wonder too, for I am still here after 55 years.'

'Evacuees came to Wrangle from Hull, and the village school could not cope so they used the Methodist chapel as a schoolroom. All the children went to the chapel for some of their lessons. The children came with their own teachers and it really broadened the outlook of the Wrangle children, and gave us a variety of lessons we would not otherwise have got, especially painting and activity lessons. One of the teachers, a Miss Warburton, was especially good. She had different ways of doing things, more adventurous. She taught us to paint large posters, and other things we had never done before.'

'Our tiny village school was reinforced with sandbags, and the windows were plastered with criss-crossed sticky tape to prevent them shattering in the event of a raid. We had regular gas mask drill – horrid, rubber-smelling masks that made our faces so hot. Our makeshift shelter was a large book cupboard in the porch. One day lessons were interrupted by the sound of air raid sirens. As we ran

VE Day celebrations sometimes got out of hand. Tea Pot Hall at Dalderby was burned down on VE night by jubilant revellers from Coningsby RAF station.

into our porch, we caught a glimpse of a single German plane flying low towards Newark. We heard later that it had machine gunned a Newark factory and several people had been killed. Odd stray bombs landed around us from time to time, but we were very fortunate to remain virtually untouched.

Strangely, we seemed unaware of the raids on Grantham, a mere ten miles away. It was years later when I worked in Grantham library that I came across a photographic record by the late Walter Lee, a well known local photographer, of the bombing of the town. The Germans were, of course, looking for the BMAR Company munitions factory, which thankfully they never managed to hit.

As the war progressed, several evacuees arrived to live with families in the village. They came from Gillingham in Kent. I remember with shame that we children were none too kind to these frightened little souls who had left their families and familiar town surroundings, and who spoke so differently from ourselves. We could not understand their fright at the sight of cows being driven along the lanes, and the huge but gentle farm horses filled them with terror.'

VE DAY

At last it was over and we could start to pick up our lives again. But first there were the celebrations to enjoy.

HAPPINESS AND SORROW

'In Europe the war was officially over. In Berlin, Field Marshall Keitel had signed Germany's final act of capitulation. In Boston the May Fair was back in town, the first time since war was declared on 3rd September 1939. It was 8th May 1945 – VE Day.

I remember Boston had an air of exuberancy that Tuesday. In the Market Place the steam yachts were operating outside the Scala New Theatre (now Marks & Spencer), amidst screams from the joyriders. The galloping horses outside Harlows butcher's shop, were ceaselessly turning round and round, up and down to the soulful sound of their organ music and people were queuing for rides on Lings Chaser.

There was an agricultural implement display in Wide Bargate and a bull fair in the Cattle Market. Mr C. L. Bembridge from Walcott won the Premier Award for best bullock for the ninth year running.

My cousins from Coningsby cycled to Boston that morning. They were hungry on arrival and went to Evans' fish shop for their lunches. Mr Evans did not have any fish that day and was only selling "battered scallops". The Lincolnshire potato crop had not let us down even if we could not obtain fish. Nourishing meals were served, however, at the British Restaurant (housed in the Guildhall), under the supervision of Miss Carter.

That night the Stump was floodlit. There were bonfires and dancing in the streets. Fireworks which had been purchased for the 1939 Guy Fawkes night and been carefully stored, were exploded instead of bombs.

But tragedy struck that May Fair evening in Boston. Private Robert Freesland of 1st Airborne Division, aged 26 years, an Arnhem man, was standing instead of sitting on the Lings Chaser ride. He collided with a Mrs West, was thrown off, and killed.

I, too, remember my own personal tragedy of VE Day. It was the day of my mother's funeral. The hearse and cars drove through the fair and Narrow Bargate to Centenary Church.'

SANDWICHES AND CAKES

'The VE Day tea at Pinchbeck will long be remembered by the 350 children from the village who assembled in the schoolyard. The event followed a bonfire the week before and was to be followed by a trip to Skegness the next week. In addition to the sandwiches provided for the children, a total of 1,800 cakes were eaten!'

HIGHDAYS & HOLIDAYS

WE MADE OUR OWN
ENTERTAINMENT

Even the smallest village created its own entertainment in days gone by, from weekly dances to local concerts. Sports were popular too, and many of us joined in, whether it was skating on the frozen fens or playing tennis, cricket or football. The early cinema was a firm favourite, and in the home the radio kept us enthralled for hours in the long winter evenings – soon to be superseded by that new gadget, the television.

VILLAGE CENTRED

'Entertainment at Freiston was largely home-made or village centred. Weekly whist drives and dances were held in the church hall, music provided by a pianist and a drummer, and occasionally a four piece band. There seems to have been no ending time, the dancing continuing until one or two in the morning, except if the workers were busy in the fields and had to be at work at 5 am. There was a well organised youth club, run by the vicar, and a garden fete was held each year in the Priory garden. In the 1960s local farmers jointly bought a field to be used as an amenity for the village and in the 1970s a community centre was built on this site.'

BY MOONLIGHT

'Little social life existed in Burgh le Marsh in the early days, but the highlight of the year was the Sunday school Anniversary, when people came from nearby villages to see the children perform. The poorest of families managed to really dress up for this occasion and great ingenuity by mothers was always praised. There was a tea for the scholars, with ladies in large, flower-decked hats and spotless white aprons pouring tea while the children enjoyed brown and white bread and butter, seed cake and plum cake. Games followed the tea, with children running races for the prize of a stick of rock.

The school treat was always a trip to the seaside. A farmer would make horses, waggons and men available for this major event. The waggon would be decorated with arches of willow, bunting and flags, and the horses groomed until their coats were glossy and decked with gleaming harness and brasses. Very early the children and anxious mothers would climb aboard and the slow journey begin to cheering and singing all the way. Each child on arrival would be given sixpence. Great care was taken to make this go a long way. All would meet at a pre-arranged venue for tea, then all aboard for the journey home, very tired but still cheering. A day to remember.

There was little entertainment during the winter, just the odd whist drive and the annual village concert. The latter was almost always a repeat of the previous year's programme and in spite of the elderly village spinster and bachelor performing *I will give you the keys of heaven* so many times, no wedding ensued. Any winter event was always planned to take place at the time of the full moon as there was no other lighting and people often walked quite a distance.'

CINEMAS AND CONCERTS

'The nearest cinema for us at Hibaldstow was three miles away in Brigg. The buses from the village were frequent and ten shillings would buy a bus ticket to Brigg and back, a cinema ticket, fish and chips and a packet of Woodbines.

Dances were held in the Memorial Hall or the church hall, starting at 10 pm and continuing until 2 am. Dancing classes were always well attended. Concerts were organised by the headmaster's wife, the entertainers going round local villages to perform.'

DANCES AND SPORTS

'For teenagers at Bardney in the 1930s entertainment took the form of a dance in the local church hall, where the floor was specially treated with flaked boracic to make it sufficiently slippery to dance on. The "orchestra" consisted of a violin, piano and drums.

The "pictures" were silent films shown by means of a hand-operated cine projector, the films being mainly Charlie Chaplin or cowboys. There was a local tennis club, which used the corner of a field, and rackets were loaned from the club and shared between members. The annual membership fee was five shillings. Croquet was played while waiting for a game or the boys would fish for newts in the nearby pond, using a stick out of the hedge with a worm tied on the end with cotton. The chapel had a sort of youth club where table tennis could be played in the evenings, in the lecture hall attached to the Methodist chapel.'

'In pre-war Mablethorpe entertainment was partly centred around the church and two chapels, especially at Christmas and Easter. There were also lots of dances through the winter and around New Year the Conservatives and Liberals held their own annual soirees in the Empire Garage in Wellington Road. The following evening the two dance committees gave the children a party, and these were great treats.

There was a golf course where Golden Sands caravan site was built at the north end of the town, and the old tennis courts also now have houses built on them. On the beach there were always the donkeys, pleasure boats and stalls. At the side of the Dunes Theatre of today there was a huge basin, built for drainage purposes to take water out to sea, and when the tide was high the water was held there and a one-legged diver gave exhibitions of swimming and diving. There was a summer concert party on the north beach and children paid a penny to go in the enclosure and sit on the sand.

In the 1920s there was a cinema in the Pie In Hand and Mrs Harper played the piano to accompany the films. Later came the Victoria, which was destroyed by a lone German bomber in the winter of 1942 when he dropped a string of bombs in daylight from Victoria Road to the Cafe Regent. One of our treats as children was the twopenny matinee at the Victoria with a special penny bag of sweets from Mrs Parrott. The Lyric came later and had live shows in the summer but eventually it turned into a cinema and is now a bingo hall.

Billy Butlin came to Mablethorpe in the late 1920s and opened his amusement empire on the corner of High Street and Admiralty Road. I remember he held a fancy dress competition for the children and Mrs Butlin presented the prizes.'

'In the early days people had to make their own entertainment. There was a cinema here in Crowle from the "silent" days, upstairs in the Market Hall. In 1936 a new cinema was built and upstairs at the Market Hall became a ballroom. The advent of television was the death knell for small local cinemas and it was turned into a bingo hall, the first of a long list of alternative uses.

Crowle had a local football club and cricket club, and there was a tennis club with three courts where regular tournaments were held. All these clubs, and other local organisations, had their annual dances, so in the winter there could be a dance almost every week. There was an Amateur Dramatic Society and various other groups put on concerts, all of which attracted full audiences. In the late 1930s a local girl began dancing classes and produced revue-style concerts and pantomimes. The Crowle Town Silver Band was also well supported and played at many functions and competitions, sometimes coming away with a prize. The Second World War seemed to put an end to that and it was never able to get going again.'

Competitors in the Louth to Grimsby Walking Match in 1910 drew large crowds of spectators.

A REGULAR DELIGHT

'I daresay not many pantomimes manage to have their Cinderella, Prince Charming and Buttons all in various stages of pregnancy. The bumps were known affectionately as Baron Hardup and the Ugly Sisters, but were later to be actually called Billy, Susan and Jillian. This was the situation in 1954 at the Hedon WI's Winter Entertainment. The pantos were a regular feature for years, and were written (all in rhyme) by a great stalwart of the WI, Mrs Kathleen Moody, in later years to become the first Lady Mayor of the ancient Borough of Hedon. The costumes for the concerts in those days were still suffering from the effects of clothes shortages during and after the war, and my own outfit, as Buttons, was actually rehashed and mutilated from an out-dated bus driver's uniform belonging to my father in law!

Was it because we were all much younger in those days that our memories bring back evenings of carefree meetings and get-togethers, with much laughter (muted of course) from the young mums on the back row, when a respected elder member "entertained" us with a rendering of *O My Papa*. She could not, however, remember how to reach that last line of the song and after several attempts gave up, accompanied by loud applause.

Does anyone else (or is it a figment of my imagination) remember

221

the ease of mind and safety when we were quite able to walk home alone from our meetings without a qualm? We seem to have lost a very precious commodity.

Our members in those days had a very healthy and happy troupe of folk dancers – apart from our rapped knuckles and ankles, the result of enthusiastic wooden stave wielders. We toured the county with our energetic cavorting. The teacher was a sweet and patient lady and her teenaged daughter accompanied us on her accordion. How I wish that cine-cameras had been available in those days!'

TO RADIO AND TELEVISION

'Mr Toplis from Middle Rasen hired Kirkby schoolroom and invited the public to hear his new wireless, a "cat's whisker". There was quite a crowd. I went with my mother and a neighbour, but all we heard were shrieks and squeaks. People said, "How does he expect to hear sounds over the air?" – little did we know. When we did get our own wireless, it was run on big batteries and a man from Market Rasen went round the villages collecting the flat batteries and returning them recharged.

We had the first television licence in Market Rasen, having obtained a secondhand Denco from a friend in the RAF. We had a room full of viewers on many occasions, but soon after this more televisions appeared in homes.'

'All our entertainment at Bardney was enjoyed within the home or the village environment. Families would enjoy the local sugar factories' sports day once a year, a whole day out with something for everyone, children's races, a cricket match and food eaten in the open air, during what always seemed to be wonderful weather. Another local event not to be missed was the local gymkhana, with Mum's picnic a wonderful memory.

Going to the pictures once a week in the village hall was very much looked forward to. George Formby and westerns were favourites, and everyone clapped when the cavalry came to the rescue. Mayhem ensued when the projector broke down, when orange peel and other missiles whizzed past your ears. Sometimes it could not be repaired so the next week's programme was free.

Saturday night dances in the villages with four-piece bands, everyone tripping the light fantastic, were enjoyed by both young and old. Graduating to the first "disco" with someone playing records, rock and roll was the new excitement and no self respecting girl would go without a full net petticoat under her dress, and not forgetting her beehive hairdo, the lads in drainpipe trousers and bootlace ties.

Television, a small square box, first came to our home in time for Queen Elizabeth's coronation in 1953. What excitement, the room was packed with friends and neighbours to watch this momentous event on the black and white screen. Programmes also remembered are Muffin the Mule, Andy Pandy, the Flower Pot Men, the Wooden Tops, Hopalong Cassidy, and the Lone Ranger. Even the interlude was an interesting part of this new invention. Little did we know that home entertainment would never be the same again.'

'After the war housing was scarce at Allington so my father built us a caravan and found a friendly farmer who was willing to let us park it on his land. Following this success my father must have thought he could build anything and his next project was a television set. He found a set of plans published in *Practical Wireless* magazine, obtained an old radar tube and sundry valves and set to work. It had a huge plywood box to house all the works and a tiny screen over which he fitted a magnifier.

There were very few television receivers then and only one transmitter at Alexandra Palace, Holme Moss had not been built. The reception was erratic as the transmitter was so far away and depended on atmospheric conditions. Sometimes we could get a good clear picture, sometimes a snow-storm covering the screen. Programmes were broadcast for only four hours a day beginning at four o'clock with Children's Hour followed by an Interlude until the News at 6 pm.

For the coronation in 1953 there were only two television sets in the village; one in the Manor House and the other in our caravan.'

RACING ON ICE

'There was a big area of land reaching from Burnham Common to Greenham Bank. Most of it was rough grazing and rushes. In May it became flooded and we were invaded with seagulls which nested in the rushes.

Another year it was flooded in the winter and we had a big freeze up. It was used for skating. The son of the landlady of the Duke William came over from Canada. He fancied himself skating and challenged the villagers to a race. The prize was a bottle of whisky. When the day of the race came there was a slight covering of snow but a track was swept around the five acre field. It created a lot of interest. The Canadian had proper skating boots with blades attached. The local had a pair of wooden skates in a sack. He took his working boots off, screwed the skates on and put the boots back on. He was ready for action. "Are you ready?" The Canadian went off like a rocket. The local took a while to get into his stroke. After the first lap he began to catch up. He soon took the lead and won the race quite easily.'

THE 'UT

'Where the village hall now stands at Sturton by Stow was The 'Ut, two huts really, dating back to the First World War. The two put together made one hall; it was raised off the ground and had two separated floors. Dances were held – and when we were going all out with the Gay Gordons, the dance floor used to move!

There was a kitchen, the main room with stage, and the men's and ladies' cloaks. The ladies had two bucket toilets, the men an outside urinal, at the back of the hall. Dances cost one shilling and sixpence, supper included.

It wasn't reckoned to be a proper dance without there being a fight outside, usually during the interval so as not to miss the dancing. Pass out tickets were issued, and there would be a rush to throw these down, to get outside to watch the fight! It was considered part of the fun.

Going to the pictures was the Tuesday evening treat – both adults and children could enjoy the programme. Sheriffs came from Gainsborough to set things up. I would listen to Dick Barton on the radio at 6.45 pm, get over to the fish and chip shop by the Plough for three penn'orth of chips, and be over at The 'Ut by 7.30. A shilling saw me through the evening – the pictures cost ninepence for children, one shilling and sixpence for adults. We used to take empty lemonade bottles back to Lucas to help pay for our treats.

But the Show Dance was *the* dance of the year – girls could take up to a fortnight to get ready for this. We made our own amusements, mostly in the village, or nearby villages – and we did have fun!'

GETTING AWAY

Holidays were few and far between, but those magical days by the sea are treasured memories. And for a real day away from it all, what about a trip to see Alpha, the amazing performing horse and surely one of Lincolnshire's wonders!

AT THE SEASIDE

'I was born in 1902 and I first went to Sutton on Sea in about 1903. I remember very little of this visit, only the donkeys, one of which, a very quiet one, I was able to ride. Its name was Bluebell.

The time I remember best must have been from 1908 or 1909 to 1913. We went every year and spent two weeks in a house owned by a fisherman and his wife, who had spent their savings on building a good brick house for summer visitors. They themselves still lived in a tarred cottage behind the house, and the wife cooked for her visitors while her daughter looked after them and the house.

The fisherman and his sons went out every evening when not at sea and set crab pots in the mudflats and trawled for shrimps with a horse and cart, the horse up to its knees in the water. They were also lifeboatmen. The lifeboat was kept in a little hut hard by the pullover; there was a mast standing on the beach from which a line could be fired to ships in distress. There was also a coastguard station in the sandhills manned by an old seaman, who could tell wonderful stories of shipwrecks and Chinese pirates to visiting children.

On one side of the pullover was the Beach Hotel, on the other the Parade, a raised promenade with iron railings and steps at intervals down to the beach. There were no gardens, only a grassy area behind the High Street shops where the pierrots had their stand and a tent for bad weather. These pierrots were a great attraction, mostly men, who wore black and white pierrot dress before the interval, and blazers, flannel trousers and straw hats later. The audience sat about on the grass or on the low wall bordering the parade. I seem to remember that the singers and pianist were pretty good for a small place; and one year, when they were in low ebb, there happened to be a London music hall producer staying in the hotel and he came to the rescue of the pierrots and got them together into a really good troupe.

There was a wonderful beach, sandy, and at low tide covered with shells and pebbles, sometimes water-worn fossils, "devil's toe-nails" and "thunderbolts". Small crabs scuttled about in the seaweed, and the groynes were covered with bladderwrack. Building sand castles was, as it still is, an absorbing occupation, though we put more hard work into it than the children of today. The castle had a moat, of course, and was turreted with bucketfuls of damp sand; and the culmination was to stand in it and try to prevent the rising tide washing it away.

The tools for all these building operations were bought at Sempers. As well as buckets and spades – wooden ones for small builders, metal ones for the older ones – the shop sold pretty nearly everything; water wings, rubber rings to float in, toy boats to sail in the low tide pools, and kites, lots of kites that flew well in the constant sea breezes.

My last visit was in 1913, the eve of war. Sutton was soon to change to a desert of barbed wire and look-out posts of ugly concrete, never again to be the children's paradise I remember. Children, there would always be, but children of a new generation, changed by the sad experiences of war.

I never visited Sutton again as a child. I still enjoy a walk – even a paddle – along the shore, but although the sea always charms and calls me, the magic is no longer there.'

THE AMAZING PERFORMING HORSE

'The following report appeared in a local newspaper in 1916.

THE END OF ALPHA
DEATH OF A WONDERFUL PERFORMING HORSE
WHO HAD BEEN PRAISED BY QUEEN VICTORIA

There has just died at Swineshead what was probably the most highly trained and wonderful horse, if not in the world, certainly in the British Isles. "Alpha", the property of Mr R. D. C. Shaw, who by his humane, careful, and unremitting training succeeded in producing such a marvellous example of equine and almost human sagacity. Alpha was known far and wide although for some years past he had lived in well earned retirement at the home of his master. Altogether Alpha was in every way an extraordinarily intelligent animal and won for himself the unstinted admiration of public and press alike. "Astonishing", "marvellous", "remarkably clever", "human sagacity", are but a few of the encomiums heaped upon him by the London Press, and a brief notice of his career will prove interesting.

Alpha was 25 years old, and was a powerful chestnut of very high breed, with a wild and resolute temper, bred by Mr R. D. Shaw at Swineshead. Alpha's education commenced when he was two years old, and extended over a number of years; the system employed being kind, quiet, and patient teaching – without a suspicion of brutality – with frequent rests so as not to tire his brain. The result was, although it was previously held that a horse could only be taught, or more correctly, forced through one or two feats which by long practice he would eventually learn to go through mechanically,

226

MR. SHAW'S. HORSE. ALPHA. PLAYING. GOD. SAVE. THE. KING
GREAT. HALE · 1911

Alpha performing at Great Hale in 1911. He is playing God Save the King!

that Alpha, assisted by his comrade, Beta, could give more than an hour's performance of high class, almost human feats that no other animal had been known to perform. Some of them were playing the National Anthem upon a harmonium; giving with his foot the answers to sums in simple arithmetic; playing a game of cards (nap); Alpha wheeling Beta in a perambulator; undressing him and putting him to bed in an ordinary bed, the two then kissing their trainer's hand; the climax being their playing upon eight musical bells "Home Sweet Home" with variations, this being the most wonderful feat ever performed by any animal.

When six years old Alpha appeared in London, and was quickly given the title of "The Human Horse" by the London Press, and was honoured by a special visit from Queen Alexandra, Princess Maud of Wales, Prince Nicholas of Greece and others. In 1897, at Queen Victoria's Diamond Jubilee Alpha played the National Anthem with the people around him singing it and received an official letter of thanks "by command" of the Queen. Ultimately, although offered a large sum of money to tour round the world, and also on the Moss-Stoll circuit in England, Mr Shaw, for various reasons, retired to his farm at Swineshead where Alpha roamed a pensioner until he was found dead with a fractured skull. Curiously enough he was probably shortly again to appear upon the stage. A brave, true and valuable friend, he had gained such confidence in his trainer that he would go with him into the most fearful places, and do his trainer's bidding without so much as a bit or strap upon him. Can it be wondered at that Mr Shaw grieves for him as for a brother?'

ROYAL OCCASIONS

Coronations and jubilees were celebrated with enthusiasm all over Lincolnshire, and Royal visits eagerly awaited. Memories go back as far as the postponed coronation of Edward VII in 1902, and embrace those cold June festivities for the coronation of our present Queen in 1953, when television was for the first time part of our lives.

THE CORONATION OF 1902

'On 26th June 1902 St Giles' church at Scartho was to celebrate the coronation of Edward VII with a service at 11 am, followed by games in the afternoon and a meat tea. It was hoped that 200 people would come to the tea, nearly the whole of the village. Then, on 24th June, news came of the King's sudden and serious illness and the postponement of the coronation ceremony. We had a meeting at Scartho to decide what to do, and the celebrations went ahead as planned to avoid disappointing so many people, though if news was received of a worsening in the King's condition it was agreed to call it off. The church service was held over until the actual day of the coronation, so that we were able to celebrate twice.'

A GREAT DAY IN 1911

'Great loyalty was outwardly demonstrated in Worlaby for the coronation of George V in June 1911, flags and bunting being displayed everywhere. In the afternoon a service was held in the parish church, which was packed to its utmost capacity; the special form of service being conducted by the Rev H. Lamb. Afterwards in Mr H. Robinson's field, a varied programme of sports took place, and then the children had tea in the school, which had been decorated by Mrs Lowe, the headmaster's wife, and a band of willing workers.

Children at Boston Day Nursery receiving coronation mugs in 1937 from Alderman Rysdale, Mayor of Boston.

In the evening, there was another lengthy programme of sports, notably the married men's race, married couples' race, obstacle race, slow bicycle race, and chain measuring, which event had 32 competitors. The tug of war teams comprised of men employed on Mr Bletcher's farm and the men engaged on the other farms in the village. After a severe tussle, victory rested with the men from the village farms. At the conclusion of the sports, again refreshments were served in the school and each child was presented with a packet of sweets. The great day closed by singing the National Anthem. A balance sheet of the Coronation shows that £31 7s 5d was spent on

Welton le Wold schoolchildren celebrating George VI's coronation in 1937.

hams, beef, bread and groceries for refreshments and money prizes for the sports. There was a balance on hand of £3 12s 1d which later in the autumn was spent on a copper beech tree, with rails and slabs round it, placed near Bond's shop, which was on the right-hand side as one enters Worlaby – the copper beech is still there.'

DOUBLE CELEBRATIONS IN THE 1930s

'My first visit to a cinema was during the Silver Jubilee celebrations of George V in 1935, followed by a tea party for the children of Skegness. To celebrate the coronation of George VI two years later, we were allowed three free rides on Butlin's amusements and were given a National Savings book with one shilling in (unfortunately mine stayed at that shilling). All the schoolchildren were given a book called *George VI, King and Emperor* by Skegness Urban District Council.

Another attraction that coronation year was Freddy Rye's lions on the beach. The infamous Rev Harold Davidson, the defrocked rector of Stiffkey in Norfolk who had become a familiar figure in the 1930s as the "Prostitutes' Padre", tried his luck at lion taming and was fatally mauled on 28th July. Many of us saw him there that summer.'

'Games and races were held at Grimoldby to celebrate George V's jubilee and my sister Emily won a ladies' race – for the lady who could keep a cigarette alight the longest during the race. She had never smoked a cigarette before, and never did again!'

CORONATION FESTIVITIES IN 1953

'One of my earliest memories is of the Queen's coronation in 1953; I remember it rained all day and my family went to Corringham to my elder sister's house to watch the ceremony on television. Afterwards we came back to the Reynard Hall at Willingham to a party and all the schoolchildren were presented with a coronation mug.'

'Coronation day at Hibaldstow was celebrated with tea in the Memorial Hall and everyone there received a coronation cup and saucer. Village football teams played for the honour of winning the Coronation Cup. In the next village the farmer John Day let his barn be used for the coronation party, with a cold ham tea being served. Many saw television for the first time that day and those with no access to a set went to the cinema in Brigg to see the ceremony.'

'A village party was held at Roxby, in a farmer's barn. A may tree was planted in the churchyard, with a bottle, containing the names of all the village people, buried beneath its roots.'

'The coronation took place in miserable weather, and I recall at Heydour having decorated bicycles pushed around inside the village hall to be judged. Food was provided there for most of the day for everyone, but some of us were invited by "the few" who possessed television sets to view (twelve inch screens with a magnifying glass fixed to the front). We were eager to see Major John Dymoke of Heydour, the Queen's Champion, walking in front of the Queen down the aisle of Westminster Abbey.'

'Weatherwise, 2nd June 1953 was not the best of days but a bit of rain was not going to dampen our spirits. We had been planning this day at Cranwell for months – money had been raised, the old pond (blamed for a polio outbreak in the village) had been filled in, a new oak gate had been purchased to replace a dilapidated one on the west side of the church, and the village hall had been booked to host a mammoth tea party. In the old school, a borrowed television set was showing the event live! It was the first time that a lot of people had seen television and the old people, in particular, could not get over such a marvel. The only problem was that they expected us "young 'uns" to know who everyone was. It was almost impossible to prise

231

the viewers away from the schoolroom and they were amongst the last to get their tea. It was a truly memorable day.'

A ROYAL VISIT IN 1958

'The Queen came to Lincoln in June 1958 for the official opening of Pelham Bridge.

First came all the demolition work to make way for the bridge. I recall the Durham Ox public house had to go and a bicycle shop called Gilberts which fascinated me as a child, due to the fact that a large penny farthing bike hung outside the shop for many years. My husband recalls a shop called Michael Roys situated between the Durham Ox and Robey's; this shop sold mainly theatrical costumes but was also handy for the apprentices from Robey's, an engineering works, to buy five Domino cigarettes for the princely sum of "one and a joey", 1s 3d, a joey being 3d. The Victoria Hotel went, along with numerous small shops and street after street of terraced houses in Lincoln's first major attempt to ease the traffic congestion in the city.

I lived in Washingborough at the time, but travelled into Lincoln daily to school and the excitement bubbled inside us as the day approached when the Queen and Prince Philip would visit our city. I was going to dance for the Royal couple at the Sincil Bank football ground.

Yes, I was one of the 11,000 or so schoolchildren from all the schools around who had been practising our dance routines for weeks, country dances in squares. The girls wore white sleeveless blouses and brightly coloured skirts; I remember mine was red. The boys were in charcoal grey trousers and white shirts. My sister five years younger was very envious.

The great day arrived and we all sat in our finery in the stands – in the rain. The pitch was sodden and there was no chance of dancing. The Queen drove round Lincoln fulfilling several engagements and the weather did not deter the people of Lincoln from turning out to catch a glimpse of our Royal visitors. Meanwhile, the children due to dance sat in the stands at the football ground clutching their song sheets and singing *John Brown's Body* and *Tulips from Amsterdam*. The dream crashed.

I remember the large black car driving very slowly round the field, so we just caught a glimpse of the Queen wearing a yellow coat and hat. We waved our Union Jacks and cheered for all we were worth, then it was over.

We did have our chance to dance when our families came along, and the irony of it was the sun shone. But somehow for me it wasn't the same – how could it live up to my schoolgirl dream?'

ALL THROUGH THE YEAR

Every year we greeted familiar dates with anticipation, from fairs and feast days to old favourites such as Oak Apple Day and May Day. Some have gone for ever, such as Empire Day, once looked forward to by every schoolchild because it promised a half day holiday but now gone the way of the Empire it celebrated. Others are with us still, and long may they continue.

PLOUGH MONDAY

'The second Monday in January was called Plough Monday. At Witham on the Hill, a group would visit each home in the village and if invited in would act their play, *The Plough Boy*. The characters were Headman, Tom Fool, Farming Man, Lady, Recruiting Sergeant, Bolden Tom, Doctor and Hopper Joe. Eventually, having gone round the whole village they would end up at the local pub – originally at the Black Dog but later at the present Six Bells. The play ceased to be performed in the 1930s.'

THE PANCAKE BELL

'On Shrove Tuesday we children who attended the school directly opposite to the church at Market Rasen watched eagerly for the arrival of the captain of our local bellringers. He would prop his bicycle by the porch and make his way to the belfry from where, promptly at noon, we heard the pancake bell. We had all been told why there were pancakes on Shrove Tuesday. In olden days all went to church on that day to confess their sins and to be shriven by the priest. There followed a big feast with pancakes fried in the fat from the meats. In Lent which began the following day there was fasting and no meat.

When the pancake bell was heard all over the village, all were reminded to get busy with their frying pans. As soon as we had been dismissed we children hurried home to enjoy the tossing and the tasting.'

MAY DAY

'On 1st May girls in twos or sometimes threes would make garlands of flowers at Crowland. These would be on hoops, trimmed with

Crowning the May Queen at Laceby in the 1950s.

flowers and carried on a broomstick. They would knock on doors and sing a Maytime song, and if you were lucky the occupant would give you a few coppers.'

'Some 70 years ago at Market Rasen 1st May was Garland Day. Flowers, preferably wild ones, had been collected, bunched together and fixed on top of a pole – often a broom handle, and then covered lightly with a cloth. A small chair would be decorated with flowers and on its seat would be placed the best doll, wearing a circlet of flowers. It was covered with a cloth after a pole had been fixed through the back of the chair, so that it could be carried by two proud children.

Early in the morning, we small girls and sometimes an odd boy, would set out on visits to the local homes. There, the cloths would be removed to display lovely flowers and the May Queen in her bower in return for a few small coins. What a challenge for the best display.'

'I can just remember decorating a clothes basket with many flowers and putting a best doll in the centre for May Day at Ropsley. My aunt talked about getting up early that day at the turn of the century to go to outlying farms carrying a decorated clothes basket between two, and singing a special song for a glass of milk ("I'm a merry little maiden in the merry month of May, come tripping o'er the meadows and sing this merry lay").'

'As a child I vividly remember Whit Sunday. It was a very special day to Christian families. My mother would buy my sister and I new white shoes and socks and make us new white dresses, and thus adorned we would go to our church to worship. At the end of the service we would all be given white narcissi. The scent of white narcissi always reminds me of Whitsuntide.

May Day was another great day to look forward to. My father would strip our garden of lilac and tulips and decorate large hoops with coloured ribbons and flowers. A pole was then put through the hoops and two children would carry the garlands door to door around the village singing this song:

> The first of May is garland day
> The bright time of the year
> And if you live to tarry this
> We'll call another year.
> The roads are very dusty
> Our shoes are very clean
> We've got a little money box
> To put the money in.
> So it is the garland day
> As we travel on our way
> May God bless you and give you
> A Happy May Day.

At the end of the day the garlands would be judged for the best one.'

'On May Day a May Queen would be chosen at Woolsthorpe by Belvoir, always a fair haired girl, and four attendants. They would be dressed in long white dresses, with coronets of fresh flowers, and the Queen had a long lace train. A garland was made with a wicker clothes basket with a hoop over and decorated with wallflowers and daffodils, and a big doll sat in it. Two people carried it. We would go all the way round the village and up around Belvoir including the castle, singing May songs. At the end of the day we had a tea party, and a trip to the seaside in the summer with the proceeds.'

'As a child before the Second World War, I would go out with a basket of flowers and a doll, covered over by a curtain. The garland on the basket was usually made from bluebells, wallflowers and daisy chains. We went from house to house in Old Somerby on May Day and sang this rhyme to the person opening the door:

> Good evening Lords and Ladies,
> It is the first of May,
> I hope you will view the garland,
> For it is so bright and gay.
>
> I love my little brothers,
> And sisters every day
> But I seem to love them better
> In the merry month of May.
>
> The nightingale she sings by night,
> And the cuckoo sings by day,
> So farewell, I must be gone,
> And I wish you a happy May.

When this was sung, hopefully, the person handed over a penny to view the garland. The money was then shared out at the last house in the village.'

MAYPOLE DANCING

'In the years up to the Second World War, our village school was the proud owner of a maypole with ribbons of red, blue, yellow and green. As the summer term commenced out came the pole to be erected in the middle of the headmaster's lawn, his wife being our trainer. Maypole practice was the highlight of the week as it meant being out of doors and out of a lesson. Colours were allocated and we were expected to remember which colour we were, as if one forgot the following week and thought they were red when it should have been blue a grand mix up occurred.

The school was always invited to perform at the Revesby Show on the last Thursday in July, one of the great events locally. As the show day approached it was time to choose the Queen and her two attendants. The dancers were all girls, but the crown bearer was a boy who was dressed in a satin suit and carried the crown on a velvet cushion in procession behind the Queen and her ladies. Dancers ranged from about six years to 13 years old. Dresses were pale coloured summery ones with artificial flowered headbands. The village shop sold these, which were also popular for Sunday school Anniversaries; with a bit of luck we all had a new dress for this and it was then worn at the maypole performances at shows. One year we had the great honour to be asked to take our pole to the Horncastle Gala which was then held on August Bank Holiday Monday. As the men were erecting the pole it snapped off, and then had to be held in place by someone whilst we skipped around twisting our ribbons into complicated patterns down the length of the pole, only to have to dance in reverse to unwind ready for the next design. The start of the Second World War brought an end to the school's maypole dancing.'

EMPIRE DAY AND WHIT MONDAY

'Where has Empire Day gone? Do you remember dancing round the flag-pole and saluting the flag, in the schoolyard, with pageants in national costume and the appropriate songs?

Another thing, Whit Monday – where has that gone, too? We all (elementary schools) had a day off but had been given tea tickets beforehand. We used to assemble on Bargate Green at Lincoln under our school banners and march to the Central Park, down into taped lanes to receive a stick of peppermint rock each, after which we watched the various heats for the schools' sports, or played with friends around the arena. Non-competitors also had races, when everybody got some sort of a prize, from the capacious bags of the judges.

The afternoon saw us at the football field where we all got a Union Jack, and again, processed by schools to the park. This time it was for the sports finals, and then the big event, in huge marquees, tea! The cakes, about three feet square, in pink and yellow, had been on display in the local baker's for at least two weeks, but woe betide anyone queueing for tea at the wrong "sitting", of which there were two.

Then came the fancy dress and decorated bicycles, again with a prize for everyone taking part. As it got later and small children grew tired, the older ones grew a bit bolder, trying to climb the greasy pole, with consequent results, until finally everyone was overcome and darkness and quiet overtook the park for another year.'

SPECIAL DAYS FOR THE FARMERS

'14th May was Pag-rag Day (pag, in Lincolnshire dialect, means to carry on the back), when maids and hired men went on their annual week's holiday from their employment. Some would be going back engaged for another year's service, others seeking new places. A bundle on their back carried their belongings, a tin trunk, wooden chest or straw rectangular clothes basket. Travel would be on foot, by carrier's cart or occasionally train. If anyone had been dismissed for some misdeed an employer might refuse to give them a "character" (reference) which would make it difficult to find a new situation. The village dressmaker was busy sewing new cotton summer dresses for the maids, to replace long, heavy winter ones.

6th April was Lady Day and for "flitting" from one home to another. Farms generally changed hands on that date, and married farm labourers moved to and from cottages. A waggon from a new master would arrive early in the morning and the family's worldly goods packed on. If the husband had one he would cycle. If there was room the wives and children rode on the waggon, or they walked. When my family moved from Anwick Fen to Blankney Fen in 1919, it was quite a procession. Mother was the leader, in a horse-drawn trap, and went on ahead; she carried sticks and coal for a fire and necessities for the first meal in the new home. Furniture was on the red-painted waggon, covered by a stack sheet; small farm tools and implements on the "moffery" (hermaphrodite), which was a cart with a front extension and "roves" (shelvings) at the sides. The pigs were in a wooden float, netted over, and another cart had crated poultry. Drovers walked behind the cattle. Mother's and Father's bicycles were suspended from the rear of the waggon. After the journey all the animals were fed and watered in their new quarters before the humans ate, prior to unloading household goods.

Lady Day and Michaelmas, 11th October, were rent days. Tenant farmers on the Tumby estate paid their half yearly rent at the Lea Gate Inn. Sir Michael Hawley of Tumby Lawn, owner of the estate, provided refreshments.'

OAK APPLE DAY

'On 29th May some 70 years ago we small girls living at Market Rasen made sure that we wore some oak leaves. We were reminded that Charles II sought refuge in an oak tree and for his safe deliverance and the return of the Monarchy after the austere days of Cromwellian rule, it had been the custom to show thankfulness by wearing leaves from the oak. Also at that time oak trees were providing timber for the ships of the Navy and so they were very special.

Failure to comply to the old custom brought stinging by nettles from the boys. I remember getting my grandfather to help me to find not only oak leaves but also an oak apple to make sure that I was doubly safe. For those who were stung there were frantic efforts to find dock leaves to ease the painful patches.

From old church records we learn that during the 18th century, a bell could be heard on special days during the year and Oak Apple Day was one of them.'

BEATING THE BOUNDS

'In Bennington, until the Second World War, every year four boys from the village were chosen to beat the bounds. The parish councillors chose the boys, probably for good behaviour. They would dig a cross at the boundary of the village and then upend one boy and beat him with the spade. This was done at several points round the boundary of the village, taking the whole day. In spite of the beating, to be chosen to take part was considered an honour.'

MAY FAIR DAY AT BRIGG

'Brigg Fair was always held the first Thursday after 16th May and was the day for young men and girls to be hired as farm workers and maids. If hired, they received a "fastening" penny. In the 1920s the hired girls were taken to Mr Patchett's or Varlows to get their uniforms and then they could enjoy the fair, which was held in Horse Fair Paddock. There were swings, cake-walks, roundabouts, flying chairs, fat ladies, boxing booths, coconut shies, shooting alleys and fortune tellers. There was always plenty to eat: rock, ice creams from Mr Peroni and fish and chips at Morris's for threepence.

Lots of lads got drunk by nightfall but they all had a good time, especially at the Grand Cinema which had two showings of the latest talking films! The Corn Exchange just showed silent films. Friends and relations crowded in for tea and it was always a lovely sunny day.

Brigg Horse Fair was held on 5th August when lots of gypsies invaded the town, the surrounding fields being full of caravans. The horses came in every type, shape and colour and were shown by running them up and down Wrawby Street and Queen Street. There were horse droppings everywhere and much bartering and arguing over the price, but once they had clapped hands, the sale was made. Very often a horse would be sold and re-sold four or five times in an hour by clapping hands. All the eating houses had a really good day, including the public houses. Sometimes traders got rather drunk and fighting occurred.'

HECKINGTON FEAST

'Heckington Feast has been held for hundreds of years in different forms. Feast Sunday was originally set by the nearest Sunday to 22nd July – the feast of St Mary Magdalene, patron saint of an earlier Heckington church. Feast Sunday between the wars was renowned for its afternoon musical service held in the church now dedicated to St Andrew. A peal of bells was rung by local ringers and early arrival was necessary to get a seat. The musical service included organ solos,

239

items by visiting professional solo singers and an anthem sung by the full church choir of at least 45 regular choristers. Heckington Town Band accompanied the hymn singing.

For many years an Agricultural Show has been associated with the Feast. The Tuesday following Feast Sunday was show day and the local children on holiday from school could participate. Everyone was up early – woken by a peal of bells. There was a free ticket to the show for the ringers. Everyone was on the move! Hundreds of visitors arrived by pony and trap, horse and cart, bicycle, special trains and buses – and many on foot. Homes were buzzing, setting out tables to entertain family and visitors. Food consisted of traditional stuffed chine, ham and pressed tongue, all of which had been cooked in the copper for hours. There were also pies, pastries and Lincolnshire plum loaf – made with flour from the Heckington miller – and of course trifle and then all washed down with copious cups of tea. Hard work for the housewife but an absolute field day for the visitors who greatly contributed to the success of the show. Strangely, I remember very few wet show days.

In 1992, the Show celebrated 125 years of being held on its present site in the grounds of Heckington Hall which for many years was the home of the Little family. An avenue of trees provided a lovely setting for the show and there were background views of the Hall and church.

There were two grandstands for the main ring – one was covered for "Members Only" – with additional seating on bales of straw and drays. Main events in the ring reflected the times – with judging and parades of heavy horses and hunters, mares and foals and ponies. Competitive horse jumping attracted many entries from far and wide but also included local celebrities such as "Darkie" who won many prizes, jumped at Olympia and qualified for the 1948 Olympics. Other events included pony trotting in harness, athletics and cycle racing – Lal White was a well known cycling competitor from Boston. All the prizes had been displayed in a village shop window prior to the show – a great attraction. Heckington schoolchildren were keen competitors and on show morning eagerly looked for the amount of "start" they had, depending on age and past performance. The children could also compete in a collection of local wild flowers, one of the many classes in the horticultural tent which was always popular with all ages.

In the evening there was dancing on the lawn in front of the Hall followed by the ever popular fireworks. As these finished, there was a rush to the village green for the last rides and attractions of the fair. The travelling fair had arrived the previous Saturday, causing much excitement among the young ones especially.

Feast Wednesday was the annual outing for the Sunday school

Heckington Fair in the 1920s, showing the children's slide and sideshows.

and church choir members with parents and friends, on a special train from Heckington to Skegness. That was a great occasion, and the only day out in the year for many. Something for everyone – but one of the highlights was gathering some friends together and enjoying singing all the popular songs of the day in the "Song Shop under the Pier".'

BASTON FEAST CHARTER

'In 1957 Baston celebrated the 700th anniversary of the granting of a Feast Charter by Henry III in 1257. Festivities spread over three days. On Friday a lorry and Land Rover, both carrying village ladies in crinolines, went round the surrounding villages; on the Land Rover was a barrel organ, and on the lorry a concert grand piano. On the Saturday there was a carnival procession to the playing field where a pageant crowning of the Festival Queen was performed by the village schoolchildren. The pageant was written and directed by Mr Norman Thwaite the head schoolmaster and the costumes designed and made by his wife.

A monster pork pie, weighing 250 lbs (six feet long by three feet wide, by four inches deep) was brought by lorry from Peterborough, and was ceremoniously cut by the Anniversary Queen. Tokens costing three shillings had been sold and these covered the cost of a portion of pie on a commemorative plate. A huge thunderstorm interrupted the proceedings and later portions of the pie were rather soggy! Special services were held in Baston church on Feast Sunday, one being a children's egg and flower service after which the offerings were sent to the Bourne Butterfield Hospital.'

CROWLE SHOW AND CARNIVAL

'There used to be two local fairs at Crowle, one in May and one in November. These were hiring fairs, where farm workers were hired for the following year. This died out between the wars, but the fairs kept on for a while.

Another annual event was the Crowle Show, dating from 1895. Between the wars this was a two-evening event and coincided with the fair held in May. On the Monday evening it consisted of athletics and cycling and other events, and on the Tuesday it was the turn of shire horses and showjumping events. The evening ended with a horse race round the outside of the ring with the spectators in the middle. This show eventually evolved into a one-day affair on the last Saturday in May. The cycling events disappeared, and the serious athletics, but other attractions were brought in, including a very popular dog show.

An annual event of my childhood days was the Hospital Carnival, held on August Bank Holiday Monday (then the first Monday in August) to raise money for Scunthorpe Hospital. A parade of decorated floats would be headed by the Carnival Queen and her retinue, and ended in a field where there were all sorts of games and activities. The first one took place in 1933 and it carried on until 1939. It started again after the war, but slowly faded into oblivion. Most of these events ended with a Grand Dance in the Market Hall.'

FEAST WEEK AT WOOLSTHORPE

'Feast Week was the second week in August, when all the locals who worked away from home had their holiday and came home for a week. There was always a funfair in Welbourns field, and in later years in the Chequers field. There were dances in the village hall, to which two or three bus loads of people would come. Thursday was Flower Show day with a big marquee in the Chequers field, with a gymkhana or sports in the afternoon and a dance at night. Tennis tournaments were held between the village hall tennis club and the Chequers Club.

Tuesday was children's day, with the Ancient Order of Foresters (members of the sick paying-in club). The children assembled at the Ring Tree in the morning to parade behind the village brass band and officers of the club with their red sashes and rosettes and big banner. They paraded up to the rectory to fetch the rector, then back to church for a service, and then to the Chequers where they were dismissed – the children to go home and the band and officers to go into the Chequers for a dinner. The children went to the village hall at 4.30 pm for a tea and a social evening.'

STURTON SHOW

'Sturton's annual show (now the Agricultural and Horticultural Show), which celebrated its centenary in 1987, had its beginnings in the yard of the White Hart, as a competition to see who grew the best potatoes. It proved popular and was soon promoted to a more prominent position – The Pond Bank. A field up Stow Park Road was the next venue, then it moved to the centre of the village, to Mr Staniland's field, at what is now the corner of The Close and High Street. I well remember my first year as show secretary – 1927; the show included horse racing that year and a lot of strangers came, bookies too. Two stewards in a marquee took the money and placed it in a bag at the side of the tent. It disappeared – the police found the empty bag on Saxilby Road, in the Fossdyke, and the money was never recovered. Not a good start for me as secretary!

In a way, Stow Fair was a forerunner to Sturton Show; it was a much older fair, granted by Act of Parliament in the reign of George III. It dealt in young horses and foals and was a popular event, certainly from the turn of the century, although in 1915 I believe only two foals were on show. In the 1880s Sturton's show was held on the afternoon of Stow's fair, people attending both.

In 1931 a Ploughing and Plashing Society was formed – many thought this would affect the attendance at Sturton Show, instead it increased the gate. People came to the ploughing match in the morning, and the show in the afternoon. I was brought up with horses, they were very much part of my life and I regularly entered. The competition took place at different places, depending where suitable land was available at the time. Each competitor had to plough one-third of an acre – the plot was drawn for in the morning. The judges made allowances if your plot was sandy or difficult to plough well. When the match was held too far away from your home to use your own horses, you had to hire ones you'd never worked with before, horses that might even come from different farms and not be used to working together. So you had to be a good horseman as well as being skilled at ploughing. In 1936 I won the Sturton, Stow & District Ploughing Society Cup – the competition was open to All England.'

DEEPING FEAST

'The highlight of the year for Deeping St James was the visit of the fair, which was sited in the field adjoining Broadgate Lane Dairy. It was the field where the cows were herded after milking so, yes, you have guessed the cows pats had to be covered with straw before things could begin. It was a travelling fair that arrived in August for two weeks, and it was known as the "Deeping Feast". Villagers and people came from miles around, it was a chance to meet up with one another again and to swap stories and local news. It was also a time for the children to spend their pocket money on the rides, a pot shot with a gun or the coconut shy for men, whilst the ladies would show off next week's washing in the swingboats!'

OWSTON FERRY WATERSPORTS – AND A TRAGEDY

'During the month of August the village had a fair or "feast" as we call it. It had no connection with the church patronal festival which was in November. In a field in the centre of the village steam roundabouts, hand-turned roundabouts for small children, coconut shies, rifle ranges and stalls were all set up. On the river a regatta, or to be more precise, watersports were held.

A semi-retired fishing smack, owned by one of the several keel proprietors who lived in the village and who made their living by water transport in a similar way to today's road haulage contractors, acted as a Committee Boat and was anchored out in the river, and various sports were arranged. There was a yacht race over a short course, which to the uninitiated was a rather boring affair, as it was done on timing. Owing to state of wind and tide the course had to be set in such a way as not to cause the competitors to sail directly to windward against the current as the flow is so strong. A sailing boat can go against the tide by tacking across it at an angle if the tide flowing against it is not too strong, otherwise the wind must be either abeam, that is on the side of the yacht, or astern directly behind. The race would be several hours' duration, and as they only sailed round two moored boats acting as marker buoys placed about half a mile apart, unless one saw the start and watched the race, it was difficult to pick out the winner.

The more popular events were the greasy pole which was put out over the river and lashed down to the Committee Boat, the pole being liberally spread with soft soap. The competitor had to walk to the end of the pole and grab a flag fastened to the end. Very few reached it and there was no question of a return journey. Most of the competitors fell off at about the halfway mark. I should perhaps say here that the competitors in all the events, with the exception of the yachtsmen, were locals, chiefly from the village with a few from the surrounding area.

There were races for cob boats. These were the tenders that the keel and sloops towed astern for various purposes such as travelling to and from the parent vessel home and back again when working near to the village, or for standing in when painting the ship's sides. These cob boats were about ten or eleven feet long. To give them strength they were made of much heavier timber than, say, a yachtsman's dinghy. They were not rowed in the usual way by the use of a pair of oars, but sculled by a single oar placed in a half-round cut-out in the stern. The oar was placed in this scull hole and by moving the loom of the oar from side to side and twisting at the same time, the boat was propelled forward.

In 1917 one such regatta ended in a tragedy which cast a gloom upon the village for a long time. The ferry boat would go off to meet the eagre (bore). Sometimes the ferryman would take the odd passenger with him for the thrill of the experience. On this particular evening the duck hunt had held the crowd together until it was quite dusk and the eagre was almost due. The ferry boat was just setting out to meet it when one or two people asked to go for a ride. The ferryman agreed, but instead of a couple of passengers as he expected, suddenly out of the crowd on the landing a dozen people jumped in. He remonstrated with them and asked some to get off, but as no one made any move and time was passing he set off. The passengers, with the ferryman, ironically made the number 13. All sat at the stern of the boat to give him room to row.

They met the first wave but with the weight being in the stern the boat didn't rise and shipped a lot of water, then simply ploughed into the second wave, and the third wave followed by the "whelps" turned the craft over. Some of the rescued people said later that when the situation appeared hopeless, just before she turned over, the ferryman put his oars down and dived his hands into his trouser pockets. Whether he was about to try and throw out some of the copper coins, of which he would be carrying a good quantity having been plying backwards and forwards all day, or whether he did what for him was an instinctive action, no one knows. He was usually found with his hands in his pockets when not actually using them.

My parents and I were standing about a quarter of a mile upstream from where this happened. We could tell from the cries of the crowd that something had gone wrong. Presently the upturned boat, with the passengers clinging to it, was swept past. Fortunately, being the regatta all the sloops and keels were at home and manned to fend them off the bank when the eagre came. As soon as the accident happened, some of the crews jumped into the cob boats and dashed to the rescue. Mother took me home while Father went along the bank to give whatever help he could.

The ferry belonged to the public house situated on the bank above the landing and five people connected with the house were aboard – the ferryman of course, two barmaids, and the landlord's daughter and youngest son. Whether a cob boat picked these two up and put them ashore on the mud, or whether the girl who would be about 17 at the time, swam bringing her brother with her I can't remember, but Father scrambled down the warp and helped them up and carried the boy who was only about five years old, home. Consequently when he arrived home he was as wet as though he himself had been in the river.

When a count was made it was found the ferryman and the two barmaids were missing. The younger barmaid was a popular village girl, the elder being from away. The ferryman was married with a large family and when he was eventually found, by dragging the river, he still had his hands in his pockets.'

SWINDERBY FEAST

'We always had a feast the first weekend in November. A fair came from Collingham, as they had theirs the week before. It used to be marvellous, that feast. They had roundabouts and horses and all these stalls – coconut shies and skittles and all that – it was a big thing, the feast was. Us kids used to go and raid mother's rag-bag to take some rags for them to clean the brasses – you got a ticket for a ride if you did that. It used to be Warreners came with the roundabouts. It was thought a lot of. All the family used to come home for the feast and you had a big stuffed chine.'

BILLINGHAY FEAST

'Billinghay church is dedicated to St Michael, so the patronal feast is always on the first Sunday after 11th October, old Michaelmas in the Gregorian Calendar. Before electricity and cars were commonplace, the feast was a highlight of the country year, second only to Christmas in importance. Many visitors, particularly those born in the village gathered there that weekend.

Scents of harvest filled the church, with a whiff of paraffin from the oil lamps. A bunch of black grapes adorned the altar, with the harvest loaf, sheaves of corn, potatoes, red and green cabbages, giant marrows, onions, beetroot, honey, jam, raspberry vinegar and other local products as thanksgiving gifts. No exotic flowers or out of season fruits were flown around the world then. Later these offerings would be distributed to widows and poor families around the village. One year, a sharp frost blackened all the dahlias and chrysanthemums, but the resourceful flower ladies made a display with bulrushes, reeds, pampas grass, trails of ivy and rosy apples. On Feast Sunday afternoon there was a christening service; some parents had been married in the church or maybe had first met at some past feast.

The funfair was located in the Coach and Horses field and operated Saturday, Monday and Tuesday. Smith and Warren's steam roundabouts, towed by a traction engine, had a central position. The Gallopers, horses and cockerels, rose and fell as they circled to the strains of the built-in organ. For young children there was a small man-powered carousel.

Around the perimeter of the field were stalls and sideshows, all illuminated by unguarded naphtha flares. Swinging boats were not for the weak stomached. A Try your Strength game was shaped like a large thermometer, the contestant struck a metal button with a mallet, with a marker which if it reached the top rang a bell to secure a prize. There were coconut shies (what bliss for a child to be given a nut so won), rifle shooting, darts, and an array of trophies for the winners, from tawdry tin brooches often worn for months afterwards on ploughboys' caps, to befeathered celluloid dolls, lustre-ware dishes and garish jugs and vases. Water pistols were on sale, and sawdust-filled paper balls, attached to elastic; wooden rattles, paper flowers and doo-dahs, a coiled up paper tube attached to a mouth-piece. As air was blown into the mouthpiece, a feather on the end of the coil tickled the target's face. As the air left, the mouthpiece whistled.

A prize-fighter challenged onlookers to box bare-fisted. If the challengers were the victors there was a money prize, but not many succeeded. The sweet stall displayed a wonderful variety of rock, in many colours and flavours, mint humbugs, brandy snap, pontefract cakes, whipped cream bon-bons, nougat coconut ice, and Packers wafers. Love hearts (Cupid's kisses) were pastel coloured heart-shaped tablets overprinted in red with "I love You", "Kiss me", "Sweetheart" etc. There were also violet cachous to perfume the breath. The stall was strategically near the field entrance.

Bystanders watched fascinated as the man at the crockery stall deftly cascaded plates from one hand to another, or displayed the fine transparency of china by holding items before the light. His assistant served customers and threw loose change into a chamber pot. Some unfortunate clients, unwrapping half tea services at home, discovered that only half the goods were china and the rest earthenware.

Visitors called on friends and relatives in Billinghay, when it was "open house" and anyone was welcome to a cold meal from a table spread with stuffed chine, roast beef, pork pie, haslet, home-made butter, bread, pickled samphire, pickled walnuts, trifle, mousses and cream. A variety of cakes including Lincolnshire plum loaf and cheese, were followed by tea or coffee. On Sunday the family meal was roast duckling and green peas, followed by Christmas pudding. Everyone wore their new winter outfits at the feast, relatives and friends gave children "fairings", money to spend at the feast, pennies, threepenny joeys or, great treasure, "tanners" (6d).

Some feast events are part of the village's folklore. Bands of youths from neighbouring villages went to challenge the "Billinger Roughs" to fight. It is reputed that an ear was bitten off in one skirmish. A Coningsby family had a fine row of parsley ready to stuff their feast chine. One morning, the parsley was all gone, cut to the ground. Although the thief was never found, he was always thought to be a Billinger Rough.

When it was time to return home after all the excitement, the horse was harnessed to the trap, the candle lamps on the vehicle lit. Parents and children wrapped themselves in rugs, huddled together for warmth. Sometimes a child, cocooned in a blanket, slept in the back of the trap on sweet smelling, clean oat straw. It was unlikely that any other traffic would be encountered on the twelve mile journey.

It is doubtful if today's village feast makes as much impression on the wider-travelled modern children, who have light and sound at the flick of a switch. To the 1920s children who lived in isolated places with no amenities, socialising, sound and illuminations were a wonderland. Billinghay Feast was a part of a secure and happy childhood remembered with pleasure and gratitude.'

MAKING THE CHRISTMAS PUDDINGS

'At the beginning of November the butcher delivered a lump of beef suet. It was trimmed and chopped into pieces the size of breadcrumbs on a board by a special knife that could be held by a handle above the sharp blade. A few Bramley apples were peeled and cored and also chopped into small pieces.

Currants, sultanas and raisins were washed and dried and the stones were removed from the raisins. Carrot was grated and breadcrumbs were prepared. Everyone had a few secret ingredients to add before the mixture was stirred. All the family had a hand in this and made their wishes before it was put into well greased basins. Usually two or three puddings were made – one for Christmas and the others for special days during the year.

Greaseproof paper was placed over the mixture and then a square of linen, usually from an old sheet or pillowcase, was laid over the top of the basin and tied down with string. The opposite corners of the square were tied together and the basin could be lifted.

The copper in the outside kitchen where the clothes were boiled, was filled with water and the fire below lit. The puddings were suspended on a broom handle which was placed across the copper top so that they were well above the water level. The heavy wooden copper lid was put in place resting on the projecting broom. Soon there were clouds of steam and the puddings were gently cooked. When removed the damp cloths were taken off to be replaced by dry ones. All were then hung on hooks from the pantry ceiling.

Often small silver threepenny pieces were wrapped in greaseproof paper and hidden in the pudding mixture for Christmas Day and there was great rejoicing when one was found. Older members of the family were pleased to see some of the pudding left after the meal and they enjoyed cold slices with lumps of cheese.

The housewife was very proud when her pudding with a small sprig of holly was placed on the table for all to enjoy. What a lot of work went into the production of the pudding, but what a lot of satisfaction from the family when it was served!'

BYGONE CHRISTMAS

'In my early childhood at Osbournby the very mention of Christmas gave rise to much excitement. Of course it was not possible then to buy so many seasonal items in the shops as it is now, but still preparations began very early. On sunny days in the autumn women were busy cleaning and washing the pounds of dried fruit needed to make the Christmas cake, puddings and mincemeat, and these were put on flat baskets on kitchen window sills to dry.

As December approached we children crossed each day off on the calendar and time seemed to drag by. While Mother was busy with all the extra cooking in preparation for the expected guests my sister and I made as many of our presents as we could. We embroidered designs on handkerchiefs, or made spills from old newspapers to be used to light the oil lamps, candles and men's pipes. We put the spills into bags made of French knitting. We also made lavender bags, spectacle cases, kettle holders, tea cosies and other useful items.

On Christmas Eve Father placed a branch of an old fir tree which grew in the garden into a bucket which was then covered with red crepe paper tied on with red ribbon; there was no sellotape in those days! We decorated the tree with special baubles saved from year to year, and we always made paper chains from coloured crepe paper and hung them round the room. All the pictures had sprigs of holly over them, and mistletoe was hung in the hall. We were sent to bed very early on Christmas Eve, but sleep did not come, we were

249

far too excited! We never did see Father Christmas arrive, despite trying so hard to stay awake, but none the less our stockings were always filled when we awoke. How excited we were to find out what presents we had! All the gifts were from our parents, grandparents, uncles and aunts. I liked the books best, but we had many other games and toys. We always had a Christmas stocking made from net material which contained small toys, sugar mice and sugar pigs, and nuts and oranges. There were also sugar mice and pigs on the Christmas tree as well as chocolate shapes covered in silver paper.

We always had a special breakfast on Christmas Day. Instead of the usual porridge we had home-made pork pie and home-cured ham. After that we went to church and then played with our toys until it was time for dinner.

Our grandparents also lived in Osbournby and always invited the whole family. This included all the relatives who lived near enough to visit for the day. Grandma cooked a splendid meal of goose with seasonal stuffing and sauces, including onion and apple sauce, and this was followed by Christmas pudding and mince pies. The pudding had silver threepenny bits hidden inside it and there was great excitement if you found one.

Christmas night was spent roasting chestnuts and relaxing around a big fire on which a huge yule log was burning, and playing games. We played Postman's Knock, Consequences and Charades. The dressing up clothes for this were kept in a special drawer. Of course we had another meal, and the grown ups had a few glasses of sherry or port wine. I remember one year when my sister was very small, one of our uncles dressed up as Father Christmas and knocked on the front door. When Grandma opened the door and brought him into the sitting room my sister screamed and screamed! Santa had to make a very quick exit! We all had such fun together and I shall never forget the happy times of long ago.'

A SPLENDID CUSTOM

'Most of the ships from Grimsby tried to be in dock for Christmas as the fish market was very poor at this time of the year, and there was no fish market on Christmas Day. On Christmas Eve there was a special market on Freeman Street. The market place was open to the elements and the stallholders wrapped up well and stamped about to keep warm. The place was lit by naphtha flares which blew about wildly in the wind. There was a great deal of competitive shouting: "Oranges five for a tanner, twelve for a bob!" The market sold everything for Christmas and most people did their shopping then, from turkeys to gifts.

On New Year's Eve there was a splendid custom, as church bells rung out and ships' sirens sounded. They made a tremendous noise, almost indescribable. The house doors opened and everyone came out into the streets to let in the New Year. There was much shouting of greetings and we looked for a young man who was "tall, dark and handsome" to come round the houses with sticks and pieces of coal. These were left and in return he received a glass of wine and a mince pie.'

Index

List of Contributing WIs

Contributions were received from the following Lincolnshire Women's Institutes:

Aby, Alford Afternoon, Alkborough, Allington, Appleby, Alvingham, Bardney, Barrowby, Barton, Baston, Belchford, Blyton, Bourne Centre, Branston, Brigg, Brigg Morning, Burgh-le-Marsh, Burton Corner, Burton-upon-Stather, Carlton le Moorland, Cherry Willingham, Colsterworth, Conningsby & Tattershall, Cowbridge, Corby Glen, Cranwell, Crowland, Crowle, Deeping St James, Denton, Dunholme, Dyke, Eagle, East & West Keal, Faldingworth, Fenside, Foston, Fotherby, Frampton, Freiston, Friskney, Fulney, Fulstow, Gate Burton, Goxhill, Hagworthingham, Hainton, Harlaxton, Haxey, Healing, Heckington, Heighington, Heydour & District, Hibaldstow, Holton le Moor, Hougham & Marston, Hundleby, Hykeham Forum, Hykeham Moor, Keddington & Louth Park, Kirton Holme, Kirton-in-Lindsey, Laceby, Langworth, Lea, Leasingham, Legbourne & Little Cawthorpe, Mablethorpe, Maltby le Marsh, Manby & Grimoldby, Mareham le Fen, Market Deeping, Market Rasen, Marton, Middle Rasen, Morton, Moulton, Navenby, Nettleham, New Waltham, North Hykeham, North Kelsey, North Scarle, Osbournby, Owersby & Osgodby, Owston Ferry, Pinchbeck, Quarrington, Reepham, Revesby, Rippingale, Ropsley, Roxby, Scamblesby, Scartho, Scawby, Scotten, Scotter, Skellingthorpe, Sleaford Centre, South Elkington, South Holland, Springthorpe & Heapham, Stewton & District, Stickford & Keal Cotes, Stickney, Stubton & District, Sturton by Stow, Sutton on Sea, Swaby, Swinderby, Swineshead, Tathwell, Tealby, Tetney, Thornton Curtis, Thurlby, Uffington, Utterby, Wainfleet, Waltham, Washingborough, Welton le Wold, West Ashby, Whaplode, Willerby, Willingham by Stow, Willoughby, Witham on the Hill, Wold Newton, Woodhall Spa, Woolsthorpe by Belvoir, Worlaby, Wragby, Wyberton Church End.